T0036771

OPEN EMBRACE

India–US Ties in a Divided World

VARGHESE K. GEORGE

FOREWORD BY AMITABH MATTOO

VINTAGE

An imprint of Penguin Random House

VINTAGE

USA | Canada | UK | Ireland | Australia
New Zealand | India | South Africa | China

Vintage is part of the Penguin Random House group of companies
whose addresses can be found at global.penguinrandomhouse.com

Published by Penguin Random House India Pvt. Ltd
7th Floor, Infinity Tower C, DLF Cyber City,
Gurgaon 122 002, Haryana, India

First published in Viking by Penguin Random House India 2018
This edition published in Vintage by Penguin Random House India 2021

ISBN 9780143453055

Typeset in Bembo Std by Manipal Technologies Limited, Manipal
Printed at Replika Press Pvt. Ltd, India

www.penguin.co.in

VINTAGE
OPEN EMBRACE

Varghese K. George is the associate editor of *The Hindu* based in New Delhi. He has previously worked as the newspaper's US correspondent, based in Washington, DC, and political editor, based in New Delhi. He has written extensively on politics, political economy, society and the foreign policy of India and the US, particularly the rise of nationalism in both countries in recent years and its impact on their ties with the world.

Prior to joining *The Hindu*, he was chief of bureau at *Hindustan Times*. He has also worked for the *Indian Express* in various roles. His reports have won several awards, including the Ramnath Goenka Journalist of the Year, the Prem Bhatia Memorial Award for Excellence in Political Reporting, the Transparency International Award for fighting corruption and the International Press Institute Award for Excellence in Journalism.

PRAISE FOR THE BOOK

'This is an engaging study of the India–United States relationship, one of the most consequential for the twenty-first century, that locates diplomatic imperatives in the evolution of domestic society in both countries. While there may be different views on the author's interpretations, his recognition that local politics and foreign and trade policy increasingly form a continuum is well taken, and worthy of granular analysis'—Ashok Malik, policy adviser, Ministry of External Affairs, Government of India

'Varghese travels an unusual path in *Open Embrace* to connect the ongoing internal transformation in both the United States and India to find the logic behind stronger ties. His deep knowledge of the BJP and its ideological mentor, the RSS, helps to clarify the underpinnings of India's foreign policy under Prime Minister Narendra Modi, something that readers of all persuasions will appreciate'—Seema Sirohi, columnist

'*Open Embrace* is an outstanding work—a superb analysis of the state of Indo–US relations, with a lucid explication of the Hindutva Strategic Doctrine and detailed discussions of Indian and US policy differences on China, Pakistan and Afghanistan. Marked by meticulous research, conscientious reporting and lucid commentary, this is a highly readable book that should be required reading for anyone who seeks to go beyond the headlines to the substance of policy. A triumph!'—Shashi Tharoor, member of Parliament

'*Open Embrace* is very different from most other studies on the subject. It uses an analytical perspective that draws on both political sociology and international relations. It addresses the impact of a growing nationalism in India and the US on their conduct of diplomacy . . . Readers may differ, but he asks the right questions and his analysis is always riveting'—Walter Andersen, senior adjunct professor of South Asia studies, Johns Hopkins University

Contents

Contents

Foreword

Robert Blackwill, former ambassador of the United States and Harvard academic, used to often recount at his dinner roundtables in New Delhi's Roosevelt House an intriguing story about how he was persuaded to take up the job. In 2001, President George W. Bush called him to his ranch in Texas and said: 'Bob, imagine: India, a billion people, a democracy, 150 million Muslims and no Al Qaeda. Wow!' In 2008, Prime Minister Manmohan Singh—uncharacteristic for him—reciprocated; he effusively praised President Bush and told him that the people of India deeply loved him. Two decades after President Bush's first exclamation, India–US relations have moved much beyond their 'wow' moment. Indeed, even Namaste Trump and Howdy Modi seem passé as we move to confronting unprecedented new challenges in a world that seems even more uncertain than it was a year ago.

We are, of course, at a moment of profound transition in the US as the new Democratic administration of Joe Biden and Kamala Harris confronts the troubled legacy of President Donald Trump's four years of almost unbridled power.

The policies they formulate will have a wide-ranging and long-term impact on the world, including and especially India. *Open Embrace* is thus not just perfectly timed, but it is also a deeply thoughtful commentary on the past, present and future of the relationship between the world's two greatest democracies.

In a strategic sense, not since India signed the treaty of peace, friendship and cooperation with the Soviet Union in 1971 has New Delhi aligned itself so closely with a great power. More important, outside the Left, both within India and in the US, the consensus across the mainstream of political opinion favours stronger relations between the two countries. Anti-Americanism, once the conventional wisdom of the Indian elite, seems almost antediluvian today, even while some may question the wisdom of aligning so closely with President Trump's personal political agenda.

But will the new Democratic administration be less sensitive to India's concerns? Are the Republicans traditionally more India-friendly? Other than anecdotal evidence and flaky intuition, there are few hard facts to support this contention. True, Republican regimes are often associated with the surgical pursuit of American interests and can be less woolly headed on issues like democracy, nuclear non-proliferation and human rights; but we have had Presidents across the partisan divide who have engaged India with passion and vigour.

Take the two Presidents often viewed as being the most affectionate towards India since World War II: John F. Kennedy in the 1960s, and George W. Bush in the 2000s. The former was a dyed-in-the-wool Democrat and the latter a neoconservative Republican. Both reached out to India and engaged New Delhi with uncharacteristic zeal, in two very different times. But on both occasions the China threat acted as a catalyst to ensure that the bonding extended beyond just personal chemistry.

Recently declassified sources have revealed the extent to which Kennedy was willing to support India in positioning it as a democratic counterweight to a totalitarian China in Asia in the 1960s. The President sent one of his most trusted aides, the Harvard Professor John Kenneth ('Ken') Galbraith, as ambassador; Ken had unfettered access to Prime Minister Nehru and a hotline to the White House.

Later, the first lady, Jacqueline ('Jackie') Bouvier Kennedy's goodwill visit to India in March 1962 was not just a spectacular success but built a deep bond between an ageing Nehru and the Camelot of brilliant minds that Kennedy had assembled (the previous 1961 Nehru visit to the US was surprisingly disappointing).

Jackie was put up in the 'Edwina Mountbatten' suite at Teen Murti House while in New Delhi, and according to former CIA analyst Bruce Reidel, Panditji was so smitten by Jackie that for the rest of his life, he had a picture of her on his bed stand. (Reidel's study *JFK's Forgotten Crisis: Tibet, the CIA, and the Sino-Indian War*[1] is easily the best account of those years.)

Earlier in 1959, Kennedy (as senator) had given a major foreign policy speech (drafted by Galbraith, which one reads today with a sense of déjà vu). He said: '[n]o struggle in the world today deserves more of our time and attention than that which grips the attention of all Asia. That is the struggle between India and China for leadership of the East, and the respect of all of Asia.'[2] A battle between a democratic India that supports 'human dignity and individual freedom' against Red China which ruthlessly denies human rights. To help India win the race against China, Kennedy had proposed that there be an equivalent of a 'Marshall Plan' for India funded by NATO allies and Japan, as it was the duty of the free world to ensure that democratic India prevailed over Red China.

During the Kennedy years, India received unprecedented economic assistance, and in the 1962 war almost a carte blanche in terms of military aid (specifically requested by Nehru). Kennedy also played a role, according to Reidel, in restraining Ayub Khan of Pakistan from opening a second front against India during the Sino–Indian war. More exceptionally, there were senior figures within the Kennedy administration who wanted India to be helped to test and develop nuclear weapons, before China did so, to give a psychological fillip to its standing in Asia.

Had Kennedy not been assassinated in 1963, and Nehru not died in 1964, the history of the US–India relationship may have taken a different course during the difficult 1960s and 1970s.

And then take the case of George W. Bush, whose simplicity many compared to that of the fictional character Chancy Gardner—a simple-minded gardener thrust into the presidency (played by Peter Sellers in the Hollywood movie, *Being There)*. But his passion for India and his desire to arrive at a modus vivendi with New Delhi was driven by a zeal uncharacteristic of US Presidents. It even provoked the staid Prime Minister Manmohan Singh, as we noted earlier, to become emotional in his final meeting with President Bush in September 2008.

It was the personal weight that Bush put into it that ensured the success of the nuclear deal between India and the US, despite the naysayers within the state department. The agreement mainstreamed India's nuclear programme. The deal was designed in a manner not to box India and its nuclear programme into a corner, but to welcome a rising power on to the high table of the management of the international system.

Similarly, the worst phase of India's relations with the US was during the Republican Richard Nixon administration and the early years of the Democratic Bill Clinton administration. The pro-Pakistan tilt of the Nixon Presidency in the 1970s is well known (especially since Islamabad was acting a conduit to China in the new opening of US towards Beijing.) But as the Princeton academic Garry Bass has recently unearthed, Nixon held deep prejudice against India and Indians.

During the early Clinton years of the 1990s, we had a dip in bilateral relations, with pressure on India to 'freeze, rollback and eliminate' its nuclear programme and to settle Kashmir. The presence of the impetuous Robin Raphael (a FOB—Friend of Bill) as assistant secretary aggravated the situation.

The reason for the new drastic change in India's geostrategic outlook in New Delhi can be summarized quickly. The 1971 treaty was a response to the continuing US tilt towards Pakistan and the beginnings of a Washington–Beijing entente (President Richard Nixon's then national security adviser, Henry Kissinger, went secretly to Beijing via Islamabad a month before India signed the treaty with the Soviet Union). In contrast, in 2021, it is the prospect of a powerful, belligerent and potentially hegemonic China in the Indo-Pacific region that has helped to cement the relationship. While this may seem like a parsimonious explanation, it is rooted in an understanding of the manner in which great powers, rising powers and emerging powers have responded to changes in the balance of power in the international system since the Peace of Westphalia in 1648.

Asymmetrical partnerships, as we know from history, are rarely easy. Partnerships with superpowers are even more difficult; in international politics, as in life, even the best of unequal relationships results in a loss of some dignity as well as considerable autonomy. It took all of Churchill's weight, foresight, wisdom and the frightening imagery of communism invading Europe to convince the US of the need of a special relationship across the Atlantic, after the end of World War II; and even then the British had to accept that London would be just another city in Europe, and Washington would consult Whitehall only when deemed necessary. But as Churchill had realized, on that fateful day in March 1946 in Fulton Missouri, when he delivered his Iron Curtain speech, the consequences of not arriving at a modus vivendi with the US would be disastrous.

It has been clear for some months now that the Indo-Pacific has arrived at an Iron Curtain moment in its history. Without the US, the region could become willy-nilly part of a new Chinese tributary system; with a fully engaged US, the region has at least the chance of creating a more organic rules-based order. Will there be a difference of nuance or direction during the Biden–Harris years? Will this mean compromising further on India's long strategic culture rooted in strategic autonomy?

Open Embrace is a masterly study of the relationship; perhaps one of the most insightful since Dennis Kux's 1994 classic, *Estranged Democracies, 1941-1991* (with an introduction by Daniel Patrick Moynihan), especially given the focus on the domestic politics of the two countries. There are few books on foreign policy and international relations that are scholarly as well as readable, accessible but rigorous, and profoundly wise in their analysis and judgements. Each one of the chapters in this book provides deep insight into the key issues that will have an impact on the India–US relationship: America first; Hindutva; China; and Islam and terrorism.

Much of my initial understanding of the US, its relationship with the world and especially India, and the narrative of American exceptionalism was born in unlikely surroundings, in a different time and during a period of profound personal transitions. I spent several summers, over several years, as visiting professor, at the University of Notre Dame located at South Bend, Indiana, in the early 1990s. Today, however, just reading *Open Embrace* is what I would recommend to anyone seeking to engage with the mystique of contemporary India–US relations.

Melbourne
January 2021

Amitabh Mattoo,
Professor,
School of International Studies,
Jawaharlal Nehru University, New Delhi

Introduction

Populism and the Pandemic

Populist politics in the last decade had already reopened several questions that were considered resolved by the end of the last century. The COVID-19 pandemic fanned the trend and upended our familiar world further in 2020. Since the first edition of this book was published in 2018, the questions raised in it have become more salient and pertinent through the reelection of Prime Minister Narendra Modi in India in 2019, and despite the defeat of President Donald Trump in 2020.

In at least ten significant ways, the pandemic has added new context and momentum to the rethinking of the prevailing organizing principles of humankind that was initiated by populism and nationalism. New equilibriums will have to be found on these issues. Cultural nationalism in the US, India, China and the Islamic world engage with these questions.

First, the virus has resurrected the classic utilitarian question in an immediate life-and-death situation: whether or not, how many, and whose deaths will be acceptable for a greater common good. 'I'm sorry, some people will die [. . .]

that's life,' declared Brazilian President Jair Bolsonaro. 'You can't stop a car factory because of traffic deaths,' he said. That an ageing population is an economic burden on society had long become the common sense in development debates. There is indeed an incentive in their dying—Social Darwinism, the survival of the fittest principle, has never been tested this close to the bone. The relative net utility of different responses to the virus will be debated for several years. What is the balance between economic and social goals?

Second, what is national power? 'We need to have more "germ games" like we have war games,' Bill Gates said some years ago.[1] The US is the pre-eminent military and economic power. The diminishing potency of military hardware has been constantly demonstrated since 9/11, but that has not reduced the global appetite for weaponry. Strategies for expanding national power involve extracting public wealth for national projects and military planning. While global corporations are big beneficiaries of this approach to national power, there is an accompanying politics that drums up a sense of power, real or not, among the public. The paradox of power is global. India is in a particularly vexed situation. Will there be a new understanding of power and security?

Third, the globalization debate has to account for the unprecedented pandemic. All countries have tried to enforce border controls to stop the virus, which ironically also demonstrated their futility. Global cooperation and multinational governance can be jettisoned only at the world's peril, as we know now. A more serious threat to humanity, climate change, has always appeared distant, but this one is urgent. Hence, the question is not whether we have more or less globalization, but is about its character. It is now a profiteering expedition of soulless greed. Can there be a new globalization where humanity and environment take precedence? Is there a new life for multilateralism? What is the new balance between nationalism and self-reliance on the one hand, and global cooperation and exchanges on the other? We have witnessed the US's hurried exit from the World Health Organization (WHO) under Trump and return after the election of Biden. Vaccine nationalism has added a new question of equity in global development debates and a new reference point for national pride.

Fourth, how much more power will the state accumulate vis-à-vis the citizen? The 9/11 security horror, followed by the 2008 economic crisis, had ushered in the steady comeback of the state, as neoliberal arguments progressively weakened. The pandemic ascribed divine powers to the state. Their dread now hysterical, the citizenry seeks benevolence and control from the state. Those who consider the human body as an inviolable space now support a mask mandate; those who are generally supportive of free movement of people across borders now want laws that force people to lock up in their homes. We see ingenious uses of technology for surveillance. State, private firms, particularly technology firms, and society are caught in a negotiation with regard to their respective boundaries and new terms of engagement. This is going to be a protracted one.

Fifth, will this expanding state be increasingly democratic or progressively authoritarian? China and Singapore showed that authoritarian measures work; Germany showed that democratic and inclusive methods work too. But Italy and the US showed that individualism and markets can impede collective goals. India, which deployed a hybrid of democratic measures and force to combat the pandemic, withstood the challenge with considerable aplomb. The government cited the pandemic to restrict assembly of people in India, while in the US, a new wave of protest against racial violence by the police lashed the country in the midst of it. The US that has prided itself on being the leader of the free world is caught in a paradox of having to exercise more control over speech and freedoms to maintain its liberalism.

Sixth, the neoliberal wisdom that unbridled competition of all against all improves efficiency and brings progress—questioned by the likes of President Trump and Prime Minister Modi who mobilized the dispossessed—has been further delegitimized by the pandemic. 'This is not the way to do it. I'm competing with other states, I'm bidding up prices,' New York Governor Andrew Cuomo lamented, about the desperation to procure more ventilators. Cuba, considered inefficient, sent healthcare professionals to many countries. The virus told us that competition is risky; cooperation could be redeeming. What is the alternative? Chinese President Xi Jinping, in his speech at the 19th Communist Party Congress in 2017, and Prime Minister Narendra Modi, in his speech to capitalist moguls in Davos in 2018, outlined alternatives to liberal orthodoxies. Collectivization has a new life. Italy nationalized Alitalia, hospitals. Trump doubled down on his economic nationalism; Biden announced his own 'Make in America' programme; Modi announced a new thrust on self-reliance, 'Atmanirbhar Bharat'. History may not have ended.

Seventh, populism has not merely survived the pandemic, but flourished due to it. Populists have shown remarkable resilience in the face of crises, partly through their gift of rhetoric, and by reiterating the national purpose, but also by blaming other countries, communities and political opponents. Trump lost the US presidential election in 2020, but gathered 10 million more votes than in 2016, and the underlying resentments that built his politics have become more intense.

Modi's popularity remained intact, and his party, the BJP, won elections in Bihar, a state whose people took a heavy hit due to the pandemic. Brutal inequalities within communities and between communities grew as a result of the pandemic; a K-shaped economic recovery continues to propel some sections further up and doom the rest downwards.

Eighth, the inhuman exploitation of labour under globalization, labelled 'efficiency' and 'competitiveness', that had been concealed by the glitz of globalization and consumerist seduction, came out in the open. Reports on sweatshops in the developing world have occasionally explored the exploitation of labour, but the virus brought the lives of labourers out into the spotlight, in a parade of shame—working 16-hour days, but unable to get paid leave or healthcare in the US; migrant labourers in India walking several days to go home; and the wretched labour camps in West Asia. If the rise of Trump had brought working class agonies upfront since 2016, the virus of 2020 and the shutdown of the economy exposed the global scale of the crisis in the relationship between labour and capital. But the economic measures that democracies took in the aftermath of the pandemic had little focus on their welfare.

The ninth question is related to travel, a critical component of globalization. At the end of 2019, when the virus was just about launching its global tour, some were travelling for no better reason than keeping their frequent flier status. In October 2019, a report commissioned by the UK's Committee on Climate Change had called for 'a ban on air miles and frequent flier loyalty schemes that incentivize excessive flying'. The travel of the privileged has a parallel parody too: the large-scale forced relocation of people. The massive flow of refugees into democratic societies has triggered political forces, the effects of which will stay with us for decades.

The tenth is how our idea of community and boundaries has changed. The COVID-19 crisis has let loose contradictory forces. On the one hand, everyone is confined within the tiniest spaces, but on the other, the crisis has also urged us to community action. Neoliberalism had made all human interactions transactional, and each transaction, standalone. Such short-termism delinked the current quarter from the next; the current generation from the future—the prevailing approach to climate change being instructive. A sustainable organizing principle of humanity will require a conception of self-interest that is not immediate in terms of time or geography. The risks and rewards need to be spread over a longer period of time and larger expanse of space. And that is the most consequential challenge thrown up by the pandemic.

All these questions regarding a post-COVID world order are being negotiated globally. India has an exceptional opportunity to be a 'leading power' in the emerging new world order. And an unprecedented opportunity to script the most consequential phase in India–US ties. But there are severe challenges to be overcome too.

Nationalist politicians proffer soft power attributes of their nations, but their emphasis on hard power is unprecedented. India, strongly influenced by a Hindutva Strategic Doctrine, is showing new resoluteness in its ambitions and power. The emergence of this grand strategy can be argued to have come at a price to its minorities in the social and geographical periphery of the country. The social core of Hindutva is understood as upper caste Hindus, a core group with strong loyalty to the BJP, more than any other section across the country and worldwide; the geographical core of this is central and western India, where the party gets its votes and the majority from. This is bound to trigger protest in a democratic society as has been happening in Kashmir, and across the country on the new citizenship law that introduced a religious test in fast-tracking the route to citizenship for refugees from some neighbouring countries. The US strategy had long ignored its own population on the margins—the workers who lost out in the trade deals, the African–Americans who face systemic racism in the country and the soldiers who die and are crippled in foreign wars. The pandemic pushed them to further extremes of precarity. Those who feel disempowered lose trust in the system, take to violence and assault institutions. That leads to more repression by the state.

It is the consolidation of a new national resolve that is opening and widening social rifts in India; in the US, the inability of its liberal capitalism to sustain the material promises it has made to its citizenry and the increasing diversity of its society are the sources of popular resentment. The country's traditional political system is struggling to negotiate it all.

As S. Jaishankar says about American nationalism under Trump, it 'is better to analyse than just demonize the phenomenon,' which is the attempt of this book. This is not a thesis on the strategic interests and calculations of the two countries, or on the technical questions related to military equipment and tactics, minutiae of trade deals and disputes, nor geopolitics. There is no dearth of literature on these. The scope of this discussion is to explore how a new wave of ethno-religious nationalism is reshaping the respective countries and the impact of that process on their external ties. *Open Embrace* also attempts to offer an unconventional approach to understanding strategy.

1

'America First': From Trump to Biden

'I didn't come along and divide this country. This country was seriously divided before I got here.'

—President Donald Trump, White House press conference, 16 February 2017[1]

'What is on the ballot here is the character of this country.'

—Joe Biden, in the last presidential debate before his election as President of the US[2]

'We can make America great again [. . .] National security begins at home, for the Soviet empire did not ever lose to us on the field of battle, it rotted from the inside out. It rotted from economic and political and ultimately from spiritual failure.'

—Bill Clinton, lamenting the challenges faced by the American middle class while announcing his candidacy for US presidency, 3 October 1991[3]

'Russia is our friend.'

—White nationalist slogan in Charlottesville, Virginia,
13 May 2017[4]

'Since 2010 we have seen the return of Great Power
competition. To varying degrees, Russia and China have
made clear they seek to substantially revise the post-Cold
War international order and norms of behavior.'

—US Nuclear Posture Review Report, 2018[5]

America is the world's foremost military superpower by miles.
It has 6800 nuclear warheads, and 430 ships and submarines.
The US spends more than $600 billion on military every year,
and the next seven biggest spenders—China, Saudi Arabia,
Russia, United Kingdom, India, France and Japan—combined
spend less than that. America has 800 military bases in more
than seventy countries. In contrast, the only place outside of
the former Soviet republics that Russia has a military base in is
Syria. Russia, Britain and France together don't exceed thirty
military bases abroad. China has one foreign military base, in
Djibouti. It may be planning more.[6]

Traditionally, the US has sought to deal with the rest of the
world, including India, with the self-assurance of such military
power, along with its ability to control the course of the global
economy. The then US ambassador to India, Harry Barnes,
had 'threatened Indian Prime Minister Indira Gandhi saying,
"We will make a horrible example of you," when he heard that
there might be another nuclear test in the early 1980s.'[7] 'We
are going to come down on those guys like a ton of bricks,'
President Bill Clinton said as he opened a meeting at the White
House to plan the American response to Pokhran-II in 1998.[8]

The US's ability to sway world events according to its interests is now restricted by multiple factors. This is frustrating for America's ruling elite. The rot from within that Clinton warned about in 1991 is showing up in America in multiple ways. For a country that started the post-Cold War era with a decisive world leadership role and was able to meet its military and strategic objectives in forty-two days in early 1991 to expel Saddam Hussein's invading Iraqi army from Kuwait, this is a large shift. When George H.W. Bush decided to use military force against Hussein, the United Nations Security Council voted overwhelmingly for it, and the US Congress supported it with a bipartisan majority.

The years that followed saw a decline of the US's global leadership position, and the COVID-19 pandemic brought this in sharp focus, as the US left the WHO and struggled to design a national response to the pandemic. The change in the US attitude towards the world is best captured in the wide variance between two slogans, three decades apart—the first heralding globalization and the second calling for drawing a curtain on it. 'Mr Gorbachev, open this gate! Mr Gorbachev, tear down this wall!,'[9] President Ronald Reagan said, speaking in what was then West Berlin on 12 June 1987, in front of the Berlin Wall that had symbolized the division of the world into Communist and Capitalist blocs. Three decades later, 'Build that wall'[10] became the war cry of the 2016 Trump presidential campaign, echoing his promise to build a wall along America's southern border with Mexico, if elected. The wall came to represent an America yearning to separate and secure itself from the rest of the world. Trump did erect walls around the US—metaphorically and literally.

'America is back,' Joe Biden told world leaders after being elected President, and promised to erase Trump's imprint on the country's foreign policy. Under Biden, the US would rejoin the Paris Climate Agreement, the WHO and other UN bodies, and try to resurrect the Iran nuclear deal, concluded by the Obama administration and wrecked by Trump. But a complete reset of the US strategy to pre-Trump era—'it's not going to happen,' according to long-time Biden adviser and now Secretary of State Antony J. Blinken.[11] A more forceful, and perhaps provocative, view is that 'Biden is getting ready to bury neoliberalism.'[12]

The COVID-19 pandemic has had the paradoxical effects of reinforcing Trump's politics on the one hand and contributing to his electoral defeat on the other. Trump had everything going for him until the novel coronavirus arrived. It disrupted his campaign for a second term, but ironically, reinforced a wide spectrum of his politics—travel restrictions, national manufacturing and a new sanctity of borders, economic nationalism, and, most significantly, belligerence towards China. Biden put Trump on the mat for his COVID-19 response, but he also appropriated his 'America First' agenda in manufacturing and anti-China rhetoric, though the same slogan may not have been used. Biden got the highest number of votes in the history of US presidential elections; Trump got the second highest number of votes—in his defeat he got 10 million votes more than what he got in 2016.

The strategic culture of a community is a framework that defines its idea of the self, the enemy and the allies. The ongoing American crisis arises from the confusion over these questions—who we are, who are our enemies, and who are our allies. Samuel P. Huntington raised these questions in his 2004 book, *Who Are We? The Challenges to America's National Identity*. As early as 1981, in *American Politics: The Promise of Disharmony*, he identified the fundamental tension of American life as the gap between the values of the American creed—liberty, equality, individualism, democracy and constitutionalism—and the government's efforts to live up to those values. He even predicted the schedule of the Trump revolution.[13]

'America First', Trump's nationalist slogan, might at first sound definitive, but it is an expression of that confusion, in theory and practice. It marked the end of strategy, as the country's grand designs over the previous decades lie in ruins. In the 2020 election, these questions were debated yet again and Biden framed it as an occasion to define 'who we are as a country'. He promised to restore American grand strategy for the world. But his victory did not bring a closure to the many contentious questions that gridlock the US's policy making and its societal dysfunction. Left or Right? Revolution or Reform? Democratic Socialism or Capitalism? Globalization or Nationalism? The collective confusion over these questions is spread across both the Democratic Party and the Republican Party. The fragmentation of public opinion is such that the bi-party system in the US has become redundant and unable to process it. The 2020 election has not resolved anything. In fact, the fractious bugle for the 2022 midterm elections, and then for the 2024 presidential election, has already been blown. And Trump is trying to be at the front and centre of it all.

The current crisis in the US began from an obsessive conviction that its political and economic model was ideal for the rest of the world—an idea that it unabashedly promoted following the collapse of the Soviet Union and the end of the Cold War. The political model was that of representative democracy and the economic model was unbridled market capitalism driven by global trade. The overdrive of the market and its success created social fissures that played out rather starkly in an open society. The promotion of market economy as a world system also opened up opportunities for other countries, particularly China, to grow to threaten the global primacy of the US. The aggressive promotion of its own models unleashed violent forces in many other parts of the world, particularly the Middle East. The current American crisis is actually a result of the successes of neoliberalism—wherein the capacity of the state is curtailed, that of the private sector expanded and the notion of national sovereignty weakened. America, its homeland, is what neoliberalism threatens the most. The American response to the COVID-19 pandemic was widely noted as a failure of the Trump administration. But the underlying morbidities of the US economic and political model are not Trump's creation—he is, in fact, a creation of them. Or a symptom.

A Challenged Supremacy

Challenges to US supremacy began almost immediately after what many Americans still consider the country's greatest success—the collapse of the Soviet Union and communism. Exactly at that moment of victory, it was faced with a new challenge. America, collaborating with Pakistan's Inter-Services Intelligence (ISI), had propped up jihadis in Afghanistan to counter communism. Soon after the withdrawal of the Soviets, America left Afghanistan, but the jihadis did not go back to celebrate the success of free market and liberal democracy. More than three decades later, the US is staring at a black hole in Afghanistan that is sucking its spirit, resources and will. The old adage that Afghanistan is the nemesis of empires has come to haunt it. Global jihadism, as an ideology, shows no signs of waning. And the war in Afghanistan, for America, is turning out to be what it was for the Soviets—an impossible place to stay on or exit, with significant costs in terms of money and prestige. The country is today fighting the monsters it created to fight the Soviets. On the wars in Iraq, Afghanistan, Pakistan and Syria and on Homeland Security, from 2001 to 2020, the US has committed $6.4 trillion in expenses, which includes a minimum of $1 trillion to care for veterans in the coming decades, according to a study by the Watson Institute of International and Public Affairs at Brown University. 'Since 2001, the wars have expanded from the fighting in Afghanistan, to wars and smaller operations elsewhere, in more than 80 countries—becoming a truly "global war on terror".' The study estimates that by the end of 2019, nearly eight lakh people died from direct causes of these wars.[14] It is a war in which victory is indefinable. Trump promised to end the 'endless wars' and accused Biden of having championed them in the past. But by the end of his tenure, Trump could not bring American troops back from Afghanistan, as he had promised. Biden has that burden to deal with.

Afghanistan starkly demonstrates the dilemma of American power. It represents a debate America cannot easily conclude—what is it fighting for in Afghanistan? Or more broadly, who or what is its enemy and who are its friends? These questions have been tailing the country since the end of the Cold War, but the overwhelming military and economic power that it commanded throughout this period helped it to deflect them. America acted as a Noah's ark in world politics, where all kinds of seemingly incompatible species could cohabit. Israel and Saudi Arabia, South Korea and Japan, India and Pakistan, Saudi Arabia and Qatar, Germany and Turkey— all these nations that have varying degrees of mutual animosity jostled for space under an American umbrella, complaining to it about each other. America's perceived neutrality and its ability to control the actions of their adversaries held these countries close to it for the three decades since the collapse of the Soviet Union.

President Obama sought to expand the ark even further, reaching out to Iran and Cuba, for instance. Presidents starting with George W. Bush tried to bring about an understanding with Russia, with varying degrees of success. Whether or not America offered justice to all, it led the world order that followed in the wake of the end of the Soviet era.

In the first decade after the end of the Cold War, America used post-Second World War institutions such as the United Nations (UN), the World Bank, the International Monetary Fund (IMF) and the World Trade Organization (WTO) to reinforce the primacy of its world view. Bush Senior and Bill Clinton worked hard to keep international and domestic opinion on their side through global institutions and domestic social alliances. In the immediate aftermath of the September 11 terror attacks, the world appeared to stand solidly behind the US, but that unravelled soon enough. When George W. Bush made what now bears out as one of the most catastrophic of American moves since then—the invasion of Iraq in 2003—it was a unilateral move without complete endorsement from the UN.

Following Bush, and inheriting the worst economic collapse in US history—which was structurally different from the cyclical capitalist dips—Obama had little option but to accept the relative decline of American power. His very presence at the White House awakened the hidden racist bones in many Americans. His attempts to reboot America's terms of engagement with the world by a calibrated accommodation of rising powers and seeking to turn over a new leaf in relations with countries considered 'enemies' angered those with entrenched notions of American foreign policy. Most notable among these was his outreach to Iran and Cuba. His appreciation of the limits of American power and the need for building broader and newer coalitions caused some degree of backlash domestically and internationally.

Harsher views on this were represented most effectively by Trump himself, who accused his predecessor of surrendering American self-respect. But even officials working for Obama found his reticence 'degrading'. For instance, Andrew Exum, who was the US deputy assistant secretary of defence for Middle East policy and one of the negotiators with Russia between 2015 and 2016 on the crisis in Syria, wrote:

> We initially offered up carrots—such as increased military and intelligence cooperation with the Russians against Islamist extremists—if they would help us remove Bashar al-Assad from power, but by the end, we were practically begging the Russians to just let humanitarian aid shipments into East Aleppo. As one of the US negotiators, I found the whole experience degrading.[15]

Exum welcomed Trump's decision to bomb Syria in response to the alleged use of chemical weapons by Syrian President Bashar al-Assad—a measure that won Trump bipartisan applause in the early days of his presidency in April 2017.

The notion of an irreconcilable enemy figure, in a binary world of good and evil, has been the hallmark of American foreign policy for most of the last century. First, it was Nazism and then, communism, which gave moral clarity to American self-perception. Communism's end made such a distinction difficult to sustain, and American thinkers began to reflect on this question: 'Since the 1940s, the central purpose of the foreign policy of the US has been the global containment of communism. If the Cold War is ending, or even changing its character in radical ways, the question arises: What should America's purpose be in the conditions likely to prevail during the rest of this century?' said the *National Interest*, an American conservative magazine, as an introduction to a debate on the issue in 1989, when the Soviet Union was still around.[16]

The fundamental question that faced America was whether it should retreat into a cocoon of blissful isolation or whether there was anything else that it needed to be present for and continue to fight for. 'What purpose have we in such a world?' asked American political commentator Charles Krauthammer.[17] He argued that the US had won the battle against communism and Nazism and made the world safe for democracy. But the expansion of democracy required continued American engagement, for which he proposed the model of 'Universal Dominion', in which America would work 'for a super-sovereign West; economically, culturally and politically hegemonic in the world'.

'This would require the conscious depreciation not only of American sovereignty, but the notion of sovereignty in general,' which would need to be replaced with 'super-sovereignty mechanisms such as G-7 and G-5, which are beginning to act as a finance committee for the West'. How would the new order function internationally? The America-led West would remain at the centre of the world, and around it 'will radiate in concentric circles, first the Second World, the decommunising states, dependent on the West for technology and finance [. . .] As they liberalized economically and politically, they would become individually eligible for status as associate members of the unipolar center.'

Krauthammer was a conservative thinker, but it is safe to argue that there had been a general consensus among the US policy elite that the path he outlined was the one to pursue. But world events and America's own evolution would not let that vision progress in the manner envisaged by Krauthammer. For one, it is noteworthy that his essay made no mention of the jihadis in Afghanistan, who also thought they had brought communism down and now wanted to bring capitalism and its culture down. Secondly, it did not mention China even once! China attached itself to the outer circle first, quickly moved inwards, and now threatens the US. As per President Xi Jinping's vision, unveiled at the 19th Congress of the Chinese Communist Party in October 2017, China now wants to be at the centre of the world's political and economic system.

In 1989, American calculations about maintaining its presence in Asia revolved around concerns about Japan. 'In the absence of Pax Americana, there would be enough nervousness about ultimate Japanese intentions and capabilities to spark a local arms race and create instability and tension,' Krauthammer argued. The rise of China had not overshadowed American concerns about Japanese militarism, as recently as during the Obama presidency. 'How can I stop Japan starting a war with China?' John Kerry would wonder soon after taking over as secretary of state in 2013.[18]

What could be called an age of innocence ended for America on 11 September 2001. The US lost its patience to lead a world order where countries would join it in concentric circles. 'You're either with us or against us,'[19] President Bush declared in 2001, resuscitating a dead Cold War logic in the new context of terrorism that would soon invalidate most existing strategic theories and reimpose a fresh moral clarity and certitude to America's raison d'être.

This would not last long, as Islamism and the jihad it inspired were no longer the sole threats to America or the world. As global complexities grew, friends and enemies mutated and fused to form a galaxy of 'frenemies'. Islamism, its rise aided by Bush's policies, was not territorially confined as the earlier enemy ideologies, Nazism and communism, had been. For a country used to partners swaying at its will and being able to force enemies to fall in line, the US was suddenly faced with an unfamiliar world.

The notion of 'enemy' is often defined by the notion of self and vice versa. Both are fraught questions in today's America. The internal debate on these issues has become so polarized that the country is unable to arrive at answers. America's strength—its democracy that it used to proudly present to the world—seems to be smothering it in the absence of a common set of values and objectives that its increasingly diverse citizenry can share and cherish. Various interest groups, communities, corporations and other countries, using lobbyists and election financing, are pulling the country in different directions.

The dismantling of American strategy by Trump cannot be undone merely because of his exit from the White House. His argument that faulty policies and 'stupid leaders' made America less safe, less powerful and less prosperous today has many takers in the country. His 'America First' politics is based on this argument. The country's strategic culture has not made it any safer, prosperous or powerful. At the same time, state power has been eroded also because of the growth of corporations that began to influence policy, domestic and strategic, to their own advantage. Whether Trump's own policies offered relief to middle-class Americans or reinstated America's power over the world remained an open question at the end of his term, but his supporters—that is half of

America—view all his foreign policy initiatives as efforts in this direction.

Even when the era of neoliberalism was being inaugurated, Trump was a sceptic, though it took three decades for his arguments to find widespread support in America. Three months after Reagan made his Berlin speech, on 2 September 1987, Donald Trump—then a forty-one-year-old real-estate businessman—made his first move that could be called political. He took out an advertisement in the New York papers on the 'stupidity' of American politicians and spoke to CNN's Larry King in an interview. He had a world view.

> 'Looking at our own stupidity, other countries are laughing at us. [. . .] This is a great country. But we have stupid leaders [. . .] The country is losing $200 billion a year [in trade deficit] [. . .] Japan, Saudi Arabia [. . .] these are countries that would be wiped off the face of the earth if it were not for the USA. This country will go bust in a couple of years. Japan and all these countries must pay for protection.'[20]

He was asked whether America should protect its trade through protectionist policies or by making its businesses more competitive. 'There is no free trade in the world; it is virtually impossible for an American company to go and do business in Japan or Saudi Arabia. In the meantime, Japan is coming to this country and buying up all of Manhattan,' he said. 'Our farmers are dying, the homeless are all over the streets of our cities [. . .] We give so much money to the wealthiest countries of the world, but we can't take care of our own people—the poor, the sick, homeless, the farmers; those people we are not helping.'

'Every country takes advantage of us, almost, I may be able to find a couple that don't. But for the most part, that would be a very tough job for me to do,'[21] Trump said, explaining the 'America First' policy in February 2017. His opponents, the traditional US foreign policy pundits, often insist that American interventions, wars, military sales and trade pacts are done in the interest of humanity. This is a contested claim, but is part of the country's perception of its own goodness. This exaggerated American sense of its own goodness apart, it is true that many countries allied with the US and linked to its market have benefited from the world order that America has promoted based on the twin principles of market economy and liberal democracy. Access to its market was the big incentive the US offered to its partners. American leadership, or dominance if seen from a different perspective, came from a compact of international institutions and alliances controlled by the US, all of which accepted market economy, though not necessarily democratic politics, as their fundamental creed. The rest of the world might think that the world order has been designed to America's advantage, but Trump went about dismantling it. He was convinced that global institutions, pacts and trade deals were all working to America's disadvantage, and he sought to undo them. A large part of that legacy will remain intact under the Biden presidency and beyond.

The US, as a country, and its thought leaders are obsessed with primacy.[22] As we discuss throughout this chapter, America's primacy has relatively declined due to what Fareed Zakaria calls the 'rise of the rest' and not due to any absolute decline of the country per se.[23] Obama was, arguably, the first American President to appreciate the rise of the rest, though he made it a point to dismiss fears of an American decline. He sought to charter a new course in the new world, configuring his country's position in a web of criss-crossing global linkages, and in the face of emerging new challenges such as climate change. On the other hand, the National Security Strategy (NSS) of the Trump administration, released on 18 December 2017, did not mention climate change even once. Trump's rhetoric outlined the world in stark, inescapable binary choices. Biden has committed to work with allies and bring climate back to the heart of US foreign policy—it could be one point where there will be a discernible break from Trump.

It could be argued that this reordering of American priorities triggered by Trump worked in India's favour. There is a view among pro-India strategic thinkers that due to Obama's considerations of the complexities of global power equations and the resultant strategic restraint, he took a more accommodating stand towards China and Pakistan. Trump's rigid views on jihadi danger and Chinese assertion did work to India's advantage. Far from worrying over the disturbances that his actions may cause to the world order, Trump was happy to be the disrupter. India, being a rising power, could draw some benefit from the shake-up. As Biden seeks to restore order, India hopes to gain from that too.

The American Decline

While Obama contested the theory of American declinism— numerous books have been written on the subject—Trump accepted it and attributed it to trade deals and military interventions around the world in the last three decades. The alternation between notions of greatness and lamentations of decline is an essential character of nationalism. The factors that destabilize US politics are many, and include the changes in world politics due to the rise of other powers, and the changing nature of capitalism that has led to an undermining of state power by American corporations. Steve Bannon, an ally of Trump, has explained the tensions in America as the result of the stranglehold of American corporations over its policy and the deviation of its capitalism from Judeo-Christian roots.

In general, the mainstream of American politics has a propensity to decontextualize and ahistoricize problems and solutions. Trump is a disorganized, undisciplined and often toxic champion of American discontent. His electoral defeat does not obliterate the discontent. He could well remain its champion and continue to influence the country's politics in the coming years. Alternatively, the discontent might find a sharper champion. Or Biden could take measures to address the disenchantment and alleviate it. Whichever way, a more stable polity in the US requires a fresh national consensus and a new framework for US engagement with the world.

Today, Islamism, China and Russia certainly challenge American power, but it is also undermined by Apple, Google and Facebook—companies that have business models that thrive on negating the notion of rigid national boundaries and sovereign powers. The idea of depreciating the sovereignty of America—Krauthammer's idea for the new century—has been effectively adapted by multinational companies. Democrats try to tinker with American capitalism and refine its social compact to deal with public discontent occasionally, like Obama's partially successful effort to overhaul the country's healthcare. His attempts to address the country's economic and social stresses, however, remained superfluous. Trump tried to force American companies to return manufacturing to the US, and rein in pharma companies that he said were 'getting away with murder'. But devoid of a comprehensive understanding of the working of capitalism, his measures may have had the opposite effect in many cases.[24]

A Democrat template to maintain America's pre-eminence in the world is to sharply bring the focus to a challenge that humanity faces together—climate change. Biden's attempt to reclaim US leadership of the world will certainly have climate politics at its heart, but there is also the new component of pandemics. On both questions, Trump had surrendered leadership. These threats are not only America's to handle, but the responsibility of other rising powers as well. A Democrat approach evolved during the Obama presidency on such global challenges involves maintaining the US's place at the centre and at the top, while at the same time allowing other countries and rising powers to feel important and play their role. The place of China in the US approach in a post-pandemic world remains an open question.

Succeeding Bush, who set out to change the world according to his vision, Obama started in 2009 with an appreciation of the way the world is and the need 'for the tempering qualities of humility and restraint' in America's conduct of its foreign policy. While he said he considered the senior Bush and his team great practitioners of reasonable strategic policy, he considered the junior Bush's decision to invade Iraq stupid. 'Don't do stupid stuff'[25] became a motto of the Obama White House. This approach came in for sharp attacks from Republicans and a section of Democrats led by Hillary Clinton. Clinton pushed Obama to topple the Libyan government while she was secretary of state; and after she left that office, she held him responsible for the mess in Syria. 'Great nations need organizing principles, and "Don't do stupid stuff" is not an organizing principle,' she said.[26]

Among Republicans, before Trump, senators such as Ted Cruz and Marco Rubio accused Obama of going on an apology tour for America's success around the world[27] and deliberately setting the country up for failure. The insinuation, in both Trump's and Rubio's repeated statements about Obama's 'deliberate' attempts to undermine America, was that he was a closet Muslim.

Obama classified the thinking that guided American foreign policy over decades into four streams—isolationism, realism, liberal interventionism and internationalism. He considered himself a hybrid of realism and internationalism. 'You could call me a realist in believing we can't, at any given moment, receive all the world's misery,'[28] Obama thought. He said he was also an internationalist as he sought to empower global institutions and enter into multilateral agreements for solutions to the problems faced by the world.

Trump's 'America First' was not about non-interventionism, but about unilateral interventions, outside of multilateral organizations. This approach is writ large on all decisions he took as President. The America before Trump had been mindful of defining its role in the world as hegemony rather than domination. Trump was intellectually incapable and temperamentally disabled to make that distinction.

Trump's politics was based on the argument that all countries were taking advantage of America. The Paris Agreement, the Trans-Pacific Partnership (TPP), the North American Free Trade Agreement (NAFTA) and the North Atlantic Treaty Organization (NATO) were all instruments through which other countries duped America and took advantage of its goodness or stupidity; they are certainly not the means to American hegemony. Trump argued that everything significant that Presidents George H.W. Bush, Bill

Clinton, George W. Bush and Barack Obama did in the last thirty years had gone against the interests of the American people. 'Foreign nations got rich at America's expense—and many special interests profited from this great global theft of American wealth . . . Every other nation on earth protects its own interests. America is finally going to do the same,'[29] he said after taking over as President.

Trump could not offer any coherent alternative strategy; in fact, several of his actions contradict his own stated position on many fronts. He championed a new era of military build-up while terming military interventions abroad in recent decades 'stupid'. He represents a dominant view among the American public, though the establishmentarian elite of the country tries to ignore this as uneducated opinion.

Critics of globalization, particularly those of a Leftist persuasion, largely looked upon the World Bank and IMF as instruments of America's pursuit of global hegemony after the fall of communism. Commentaries on Indian reforms in the 1990s never failed to discuss the Washington Consensus, a version of market doctrine that the two organizations have promoted with an alleged hidden agenda to facilitate American primacy. But Trump politics see these organizations as wasteful distractions for American money and power, rather than instruments of authority. The US is the biggest owner of these institutions. Trump's first budget draft proposed to cut US support for multilateral development banks over the next three years by $650 million. The American ability and willingness to support development funding around the world has diminished in recent years. The US's development assistance through the World Bank had already shrunk to its lowest before Trump took over. Can Biden restore the US's leadership role in this? Unlikely.

The UN, the World Bank and the IMF have been viewed as instruments of American hegemony for decades. The collapse of the Soviet Union was validation for the US of the power of market economy and liberal democracy. The globalizing world required a gradual depreciation of the concept of national sovereignty, including the US's own, its liberals and conservatives agreed, though not from entirely overlapping perspectives. Promotion of market economy and democracy, defence of human rights and environment, and so on were assumed to be part of the American global hegemony. Bankrolled by the US and its followers, institutions like the World Bank and the IMF, through aggressive advancement of neoliberal economics, and the UN through non-proliferation, climate protection and the Responsibility to Protect doctrine, helped chip away at the concept of national sovereignty. Moreover, it was assumed that the US's own example of prosperity—'the shining city upon a hill,' according to Ronald Reagan—would lead the rest of the world to accept its model of democracy and market economy.[30]

Trump politics questioned this. 'The United States is one out of 193 countries in the United Nations, and yet we pay 22 per cent of the entire budget and more. In fact, we pay far more than anybody realizes,' he told the UN General Assembly (UNGA) in 2017. It is national sovereignty—he mentioned ten times—that will safeguard the world and not globalism, upending the US gospel that guided the order. 'For too long, the American people were told that mammoth multinational trade deals, unaccountable international tribunals, and powerful global bureaucracies were the best way to promote their success [. . .] Now we are calling for a great reawakening of nations.'[31] Biden swears by multilateralism, but yet again, it is certain that a revival of US leadership and commitment in the new context will be in an entirely new format, to the extent that it is possible. Optimists believe Biden will stick to the traditional US style of using development funding as a tool of its diplomacy. This is also salient, considering the enlarging footprint of China in this field.

Meanwhile, the World Bank and the IMF have rolled back their trickle-down economic doctrine, though they remain pro-trade. While the Trump administration was hostile in its policy towards multilateral institutions, the World Bank firmed up its collaboration with the Chinese-led Asian Infrastructure Investment Bank (AIIB), signing a memorandum of understanding instituting an overall framework for cooperation between the two bodies for development financing, staff exchanges and analytical and sector work. In early 2018, partly as an attempt to push back against Chinese influence in global developmental financing, the Trump administration agreed to support a significant capital enhancement of the World Bank. The move surprised many observers as it went against the rhetoric of the Trump administration.[32]

The Trump administration cut down US aid to the UN. On 13 October 2017, Trump destabilized an international agreement that the US, four other UN Security Council members and Germany had reached with Iran on its nuclear programme. Biden wants to restore it, but it will be a task. On 12 October 2017, the US quit the United Nations Educational, Scientific and Cultural Organization (UNESCO), and in 2020, the WHO. Biden wants to rejoin them.

The US quit the Paris Agreement—Biden would take America back to it. Trump renegotiated the NAFTA—Biden will live with it as he will with the new trade deal with South Korea. Biden's biggest challenge will be in finding the rightful place for the US in Asia-Pacific trade, after Trump took it out of the TPP. Through the Regional Comprehensive Economic Partnership (RCEP), China has expanded its influence in Asian trade.

American Self, America's Enemy

America's notion of self-identity is complex and ever-evolving. George H.W. Bush, who followed Reagan, opened the American borders to greater immigration, even as the digital economy was taking shape. This also marked the origins of the H-1B visa programme, which brought young Indian technology experts to the US in large numbers in the years that followed. Through the three decades of neoliberal globalization, a broad consensus emerged among the political and economic elite of the US that immigration is fundamental to the greatness of America. 'Immigrants aren't somehow changing the American character; immigrants are the American character,'[33] President Obama said during the 2016 campaign when Trump began assailing the country's immigration policy. Trump himself is not opposed to immigration per se—he opposes the influx of cheap labour and helpless refugees. The tweaks that he made to the US immigration policy as President also reflected this approach.

That immigrants are the American character is not just a romantic notion; it also made economic sense as the economy expanded in a regulated manner, absorbing cheaper and brighter talent from other countries over decades. What held them together was the 'American dream', the promise of prosperity. Those who spoke different languages, looked different and even carried their cultural baggage to their new land were united in their pursuit of wealth in a way that was only possible in America. Over several decades, the notion of a closet alien community threatening the nation continued, though it kept changing according to circumstances. Italians, Japanese and suspected or actual communists were targeted during different periods. But overall, argument that immigrants contributed to the prosperity and the forward march of the US was widely accepted in the initial decades of globalization.

The promise of globalization was interrupted by two events at the turn of the century—the meltdown on Wall Street and the 9/11 terror attacks. Just as the country was recovering from them, in 2008, two disruptive forces struck again—a second economic crisis and the election of the first African-American president.

'An African-American whose last name was one consonant removed from the world's most infamous terrorist becoming President,'[34] as Samantha Power, US ambassador to the UN, put it, marked a new era in US democracy and diversity. But Obama's election also created grounds for a white backlash. The number of white supremacist 'patriot' groups in the US jumped soon after he became the President—from 149 in 2008 to 512 in 2009, 824 in 2010, 1274 in 2011 and 1360 in 2012. It dipped a bit after his second election, but in 2017, the number shot up again to 998.[35] Obama has himself pointed out that the Republican obstructionism that brought his administration to a standstill, through a Congressional logjam in his second term, was driven by a racial element. Forty-three per cent of Republican voters and 15 per cent of Democratic voters believed he was a Muslim.[36] The White House website did not use his middle name 'Hussein' at all—coincidentally also the surname of the slain Muslim leader of Iraq.

Obama symbolized change and promised change. How much of the change that he promised has been realized remains open to interpretation, but it is clear that his tenure coincided with changes in the global order and the country's internal dynamics, creating and spreading resentment among a large section of the people. The average American is more stressed, financially and socially, today than he or she was in 2008. Trump's 'Make America Great Again' slogan—which has been used by Presidents and candidates for decades, from Jimmy Carter to Bill Clinton—had a new resonance in this context. When Trump entered the Republican primary in 2015, pundits dismissed him as a 'protest candidate', a moniker they put on those who question entrenched notions of US liberalism. Unlike earlier 'protest candidates', Trump would go on to win the presidency, and would so change the direction of the country's politics and strategy that they would outlive his tenure in office.

The distress, disenchantment and divisions that spurred his growth have continued. The class divisions in the country reflect even in marriages. US marriage rates are falling consistently and the pandemic has further reduced it. 'For every 1,000 unmarried adults in 2019, only 33 got married. This number was 35 a decade ago in 2010 and 86 in 1970.' Marriage and family life are increasingly a privilege of the economically better off, and the 'poor and working-class Americans increasingly disconnected from the institution of marriage'.[37] Scholars have even suggested a link between marriage instability and China trade in some places, which we discuss in the fourth chapter.

Meanwhile, suicide rates are consistently rising—there was a 35 per cent rise between 1999 through 2018. 'The rate increased on average approximately 1% per year from 1999 to 2006 and by 2% per year from 2006 through 2018 . . .' In 2018, suicide rates were higher in the most rural counties compared with the most urban counties.[38] Such underlying factors are rarely discussed in the context of the rise of Trump nationalism.

As Edward Said theorized, the best way, and often the only way, to define yourself is to define your other. Trump continues to frame these questions through his politics— 'Who are we?' and 'Who is our enemy?' As President of the US, he expanded on the same thesis of American identity and its enemies in a civilizational context, much like Indian greatness is articulated in terms of Hindu civilizational ethos by Hindutva. The idea of 'One nation under one God and one flag' became the cornerstone of Trump politics. He accuses the Democrats of undermining the Christian heritage of the country. The resonance of this theme is evident in the fact that Biden's 'speeches were woven with references to God, biblical language or the Pope'[39] in 2020.

'We write symphonies. We pursue innovation. We celebrate our ancient heroes, embrace our timeless traditions and customs, and always seek to explore and discover brand-new frontiers. We reward brilliance. We strive for excellence, and cherish inspiring works of art that honour God. We treasure the rule of law and protect the right to free speech and free expression,'[40] Trump said about Western, rather Christian, civilization.

Using the slogan of nation 'under one God', Trump also sought to make a crucial change to the racial politics of America, somewhat like what Modi has done to caste politics in India. Those who oppose Trump can easily locate white supremacist and anti-Semitic undertones in his politics.[41] It might be safe to assume that xenophobes, racists, misogynists and homophobes support him, but it will be erroneous to assume that they are the only ones who do so. A nation 'under one god' that has an enemy in 'radical Islamic terrorism' conveys a totally different and unprecedented meaning to a lot of Americans. The whistle of Christian nationalism might subsume white nationalism, but is not restricted to it. The rise in support for Trump among Hispanics, African-Americans and Asians in 2020 suggests that his base is not only white. This potent population mix will await a more organized leader and another opportune time.

Obama's global outreach had entailed a fresh elucidation of enemies and friends. He challenged actions of some 'friends' such as Israel and Saudi Arabia, and began to look at new openings with 'foes' such as Iran and Cuba. The pushback was stormy, as the Saudis and Israelis began to play with US domestic divisions to undermine Obama's presidency. Prime Minister Benjamin Netanyahu of Israel expanded Jewish settlements, closing the door on a two-state solution that America has been pushing for decades. He addressed the American Congress on a Republican invitation in 2015, and questioned Obama's foreign policy and his negotiations with Iran. Obama's pent-up frustration with the Israeli leader found expression in a dramatic refusal to veto a UN resolution that rebuked Israel over settlements, weeks before he left office in December 2016. He challenged Saudi domination of West Asia and believed that the Saudis and other American allies needed to learn to live in 'cold peace' with Iran. The traditional Sunni allies in the region, Saudi Arabia and the UAE, which wield tremendous influence in Washington, would not accept this. Trump turned Obama's policy upside down in the Middle East by shifting the US embassy in Israel to Jerusalem, and undermining the US position in support of a two-state solution. In tandem, the Netanyahu government expanded settlements further. There is little that Biden can or try to undo in these areas. Trump brokered regular diplomatic ties between Arab countries, the UAE, Bahrain and Sudan, and Israel. This environment also paved the way for initiating massive US arms sales to the UAE, even reducing the qualitative edge of Israel's defence. By pushing Iran to the periphery of international community, and throwing his weight behind an Arab-Israel friendship, Trump triggered a new polarization in the Middle East, while erasing the Palestinian question from the US diplomacy handbook. At one level, it has aggravated the Sunni–Shia polarization; at another, it has led to complete abdication of Palestinians by the US and its allies. These moves have restricted the leeway for Biden, if at all he wants to explore a different course. At any rate, Biden inherits a Middle East crisis vastly different from what it was when he was vice president.

Obama was 'willing to question why America's enemies are its enemies or why some of its friends are its friends'.[42] Trump tried to shuffle the pack of friends and foes as per his own understanding. He confronted America's closest friends—Australia, Germany, Japan, South Korea and even Canada did not escape his wrath. What makes foes of some of his cultural allies is the second component of 'America First'—economic nationalism. 'The Germans are bad, very bad,' Trump had told European Union leaders.[43] 'See the millions of cars they sell in the US, terrible. We will stop this.' Germany has the third-largest trade surplus with the US, after China and Japan. Trump was not the first President who told his European partners that they were not spending enough to keep the NATO alliance in shape. Obama had complained that they were 'free-riding' for defence. The tensions between the EU and the US continued to rise even after the election of Biden in 2020.

Trump raised the rhetoric to a different level altogether. In 2006, NATO members pledged to spend at least 2 per cent of the GDP on defence, and reiterated the pledge in 2014 after Obama pushed for it. Only five members of the alliance met that threshold in 2016. The US is particularly peeved at Germany, which spends only 1.2 per cent of its GDP on defence despite being a robust economy, while the US spends 3.6 per cent. Trump turned up the heat, forcing most countries to increase their spending.[44] Biden is happy about that.

Russian Roulette

The US's struggle to reconcile with a post–Cold War world is singularly pronounced in its wobbly relations with Russia. During Obama's presidency, at one end of the spectrum of the US–Russia engagement was the Iranian nuclear deal that both agreed had capped the Shia regime's nuclear capabilities. At the other end was Syria's descent into the abyss, a bloody and grim reminder of the limits to their cooperation. Russia managed to prevent the fall of Bashar al-Assad, against the wishes of the Obama administration. And by the beginning of 2018, there was a complete breakdown of even elementary diplomatic interactions between the two countries. Trump defied America's security establishment and conventional politicians from both parties to meet Russian President Vladimir Putin in July 2018, in Helsinki. But far from improving ties between the two nuclear powers, the summit only showed how internally divided America is over the question of Russia. The Russia pitch had been queered for Trump even before he took over the presidency.

The charge that the President of the US owed his victory to Russia not only undermined his authority, but also vitiated the bilateral ties between the two P-5 members. It all started in July 2016, as US newspaper reports citing anonymous intelligence sources accused Russia of trying to influence the outcome of the US presidential election. The reports said hackers working for the Russian government obtained the emails of Democratic Party functionaries, which were published by WikiLeaks. Subsequently, emails of John Podesta, chief of Democratic presidential candidate Hillary Clinton's campaign, were hacked and appeared in the public domain. These revealed details about the internal functioning of the party, and exposed some facts—for instance, a few paragraphs from one of the several paid speeches that Clinton made to Wall Street firms—that her campaign had tried to conceal. A special counsel, Robert Mueller, led an investigation into allegations of Russian meddling in the 2016 presidential election. The report spoke about 'numerous links between the Russian government and the Trump Campaign' and found that 'a Russian entity carried out a social media campaign that favored presidential candidate Donald J. Trump and disparaged presidential candidate Hillary Clinton'. The investigation was unable to establish a conspiracy between members of the Trump campaign and the Russians involved in this activity.[45] The issue continues to roil US politics. Biden has vowed to 'make Russia pay'.

At the core of the US security establishment's discomfort with Russia is the fact that the NATO alliance is based on Cold War logic—or a pre-Islamism logic, if you will—according to which the US military-industrial complex developed. Technologies and weapons more suitable for combating non-state actors are now developing at a fast pace, but not at the cost of more advanced fighters and missile systems. The hard threat from the erstwhile Soviet Union continues to haunt US strategists even after the menacing rise of China.

In July 2016, the last NATO summit during the Obama regime in Warsaw resolved that the alliance had to deal with two distinct threats—on the east from Russia, and on the south and south-east from Islamist groups. On Russia, there is a remarkable convergence between the Republican and Democrat security establishments. By the end of his tenure, Obama had more or less come around to his 2012 opponent Mitt Romney's view—which he had earlier contested—that Russia is the US's 'number one geopolitical foe'.[46]

While Obama was packing off Russian diplomats from Washington in late 2016, Russian President Vladimir Putin sent Trump a year-end greeting card hoping to 'take their interaction in the international arena to a whole new level' in 'a constructive and pragmatic manner'.[47] Putin sent roughly the same message on the new year of 2018, even as the rivalry between the two countries reached the level of a new Cold War during the first year of the Trump presidency. On Syria, however, Trump made a significant reversal in the American position that predated him by no longer insisting on the exit of the Assad regime. But he could not make any breakthrough in ties with Russia as the hysteria over Moscow's interference in the US elections gripped the country.

Addressing the UN in September 2015, Putin had called for a 'genuinely broad alliance against terrorism, just like the one against Hitler'.[48] A segment of the US establishment, for instance, Henry Kissinger, appreciated this position. Trump was in complete agreement with this position, but he was forced to walk the opposite path. On 2 August 2017, he signed the legislation voted for by almost all Republican and Democratic lawmakers, imposing stricter sanctions against Russia. On 16 March 2018, the US imposed sanctions against nineteen Russian individuals and five entities for interfering in the 2016 election and for other cyber intrusions. Earlier, the special counsel investigating the Russian interference in the election had indicted thirteen Russian individuals and entities. On 26 March 2018, America expelled sixty Russian officials and ordered the closure of the Russian consulate in Seattle. The downslide in bilateral ties continues.

An equally important reason, along with global terrorism, that led Trump to seek a partnership with Russia was China. Obama's presidency witnessed an increasing closeness between Russia and China. Trump had declared that 'China is our enemy',[49] contradicting the prevailing wisdom until the end of the Obama presidency. Trump's overtures to China gave conflicting signals on his approach towards it, and he sought Beijing's help to resolve the North Korean nuclear crisis. But, by the end of 2020, it was clear that Trump had pushed the mainstream American position to acknowledge that China had become the most consequential threat to the US.

Seeking support for improving ties with Russia has been a component of populist revolts across Europe.[50] Giuseppe Conte, the prime minister of Italy, is an advocate of better ties between Russia and Europe.[51] Trump called for reinstating Russia in the group of major economies at the G7 Summit in Canada in June 2018. The G7 was G8 until 2014, when Russia was expelled. 'Why are we having a meeting without Russia being in the meeting?' he wondered.[52] America and its allies are confused about the attitude towards Russia among them and within their societies.

The domestic diatribe in America over Russia has affected India's relations with the United States too. America's anti-Russia politicians, both Republicans and Democrats, primarily in their enthusiasm to tie Trump's hands on relations with the country, have also introduced a sweeping law called Countering America's Adversaries Through Sanctions Act (CAATSA). The sanctions target any country trading with Russia's defence and intelligence sectors. India is potentially a target of US sanctions under this law. In July 2018, under pressure from American arms manufacturers worried over roadblocks to sales to India, the US Congress passed a law that allows for exemptions for countries such as India. The question of exemptions from sanctions for India will surface when India takes delivery of the Russian-made S-400 missile defence system, probably in 2021.

Trump and his supporters believe that the allegations of Russian collusion with his campaign in 2016 was a conspiracy of the American Deep State, that is, its intelligence and security apparatus, to undermine and dethrone him using Russia as a smokescreen. Democrats and other Trump opponents appear to be convinced that Trump won the election in 2016 only because of a Russian conspiracy that helped him.

The debate on the Russian influence operation in the US following the 2016 election brought to the forefront another crucial challenge to American power—the conflict between the interests of American global corporations and the interests of the US political establishment. The tussle between American technology giants, icons of the globalized world such as Apple, Google, Facebook and Twitter, and the American state over security questions have surfaced periodically. The use of these social media platforms for amplifying social divisions within the US raised a whole range of questions about the obligations of these companies to be national, and not global.

Terrorism investigations had already been battlegrounds for state agencies and tech companies that argued that their primary obligations were towards the consumer and not to the state or society at large. In a widely noticed case of public and security interest, the Federal Bureau of Investigation (FBI) asked Apple to create a tool to break the encryption of an iPhone used by Islamist Syed Rizwan Farook who was killed, along with his wife, by the police after he shot fourteen of his co-workers dead in San Bernardino, California, in December 2015. Apple refused to oblige.

Apple, Facebook and Google were first off the block to publicly denounce Trump's move to restrict immigration and impose a temporary travel ban on citizens of seven Muslim-majority countries, making the argument about global markets and universal talent pools. But the Russian investigation, in which the roles of Facebook and Twitter came into sharp focus, put these companies in an awkward position, and raised new questions about how American a global company must be. American lawmakers and law enforcement agencies accuse social media platforms of falling prey to a Russian conspiracy to spread information to aggravate social divisions in the country. On the one hand, Facebook and Twitter epitomize the success of an unregulated and globalized economy, while on the other, they represent the risks that America as a society and country face. These companies that operate on a global scale cannot make themselves tools of American strategy without surrendering their claims to be global citizens. What could be a sound logic in support of barring a Russian user—or an Indian for that matter—of Facebook or Twitter from commenting on a political issue in America?

It is notable that the rise of American corporate giants that dominate the world today was underwritten by American public funds.

It is from the US government's attempts to 'expand human knowledge that powerful new businesses grew, with technology titans such as Apple and Google building world-class companies on the backs of technologies emerging from federal investments in research'.[53] The US government has been the world's biggest supporter of basic science, which makes America the holder of the highest share of knowledge in the world. Some of the most commercially profitable and life-changing technologies today—such as the GPS, MRI scanner and the Internet—were created on the basis of knowledge produced by federally funded research decades before these became marketable products and services. Between 2008 and 2014, US R&D grew just over 1 per cent annually, and there was a sharp decline, by nearly 20 per cent, in federal funding between 2009 and 2015.

While the US was shrinking its funding for R&D, between 2008 and 2013, China and South Korea increased theirs by 17 per cent and 9 per cent, respectively. In 2013, Beijing's Tsinghua University leapt ahead of Stanford, for the first time in history, in the number of patents filed in a year.

While Trump was high on rhetoric in confronting China on emerging technologies, his focus on the issue was patchy and haphazard. His administration sought cuts in several sectors, but the US Congress voted for significant rises for scientific research since 2016. The National Institutes of Health (NIH) funding rose by 39 per cent since 2015; the National Science Foundation (NSF) funding went up by 17 per cent since 2017, 'rising more than twice as fast as it did under . . . Obama'. The Trump administration was more generous in the funding of research in artificial intelligence (AI) and in quantum information science.[54] 'He poured money into quantum computing and artificial intelligence, and invested heavily in space exploration, promising a return to the Moon this decade.'[55] Overall, Trump promoted an anti-science attitude, but the nationalist flames that he fanned laid the foundations for a new era of US focus on science and research. The vulnerabilities of the country exposed by the COVID-19 pandemic have added a new urgency to this question. Biden will continue the course. A tenacious focus on developing and controlling new technology keeps the US ahead of other countries. This aspect has become a field of combat between the US and China now.

President vs Washington

Unlikely as it may sound, there is one thing common between Obama and Trump—both questioned the foreign policy orthodoxy in Washington. Trump and Obama may have questioned different sets of assumptions, but both did question it. Public repudiation of the American defence and foreign policy establishment was critical to Trump's politics, whereas Obama was more tactical about confronting it. This led to serious conflict within the administration and the President's ability to push his agenda in the sphere of international relations. Of his struggles with the Washington establishment, Obama said that there was a playbook that Presidents were expected to follow unquestioningly: 'It's a playbook that comes out of the foreign-policy establishment. And the playbook prescribes responses to different events, and these responses tend to be militarized responses.'[56]

American media assumes that the President has to automatically follow the instructions of the playbook. See one report on the controversy over Trump 'congratulating' Putin. 'Trump was instructed in briefing materials "DO NOT CONGRATULATE" before his call with the recently re-elected Putin, but congratulated him anyway', according to the *Washington Post*'s report.[57]

Obama was a tactful politician who breached the playbook selectively. Trump's entire politics is built on his chest-thumping confrontation with what he describes as the 'Washington establishment', the custodians of the playbook. His confrontation with the intelligence agencies and the media that began during his 2016 campaign continued through his presidency and will possibly continue in the coming years, now that he is out of the White House, even more ferociously. Biden is expected to be conventional, scripted and a strict follower of the playbook. He will face furious attacks from Trump on this count.

The American media's courage in taking on the political executive is often remarkable, but it can be unquestioning in its propagation of the security apparatus' world view, as in the reporting on Russia. This is a structural challenge of the information environment everywhere. In autocracies, the control of the media is absolute and stringent; in democracies, it takes a more refined shape. Indian media is comparable to the US media on this count. There is little questioning that it does of the narrative that is set by the state apparatus of what constitutes national interest and how it is to be pursued. But social divisions, and reduced dependence of the public on legacy media for information, have led to alternative notions of what comprise national interest and their easy propagation. Trump continuously questioned the security and foreign policy establishment's wisdom and ability, part of which has gained wider acceptance, even among his critics. He has said that everything that the US did in the last three decades has been disastrous, that American policies built up China into a challenge and that Russia is not an enemy, but a potential friend, confronting prevailing wisdom.

He never tires of reminding that the 2003 invasion of Iraq was based on forged intelligence collected by the Central Intelligence Agency (CIA) about Saddam Hussein's weapons of mass destruction. Trump has even said publicly that American agencies also carry out assassinations, when it was pointed out to him that the Putin regime in Russia does so.

The conflicts between Trump and the foreign policy establishment were symptomatic of a wider conflict within America. It is one thing for the foreign policy establishment to tutor an incoming President on the playbook and quite another for there to be different and often conflicting versions of it within the establishment and the public. Interdepartmental and inter-agency rivalries in the government are nothing new, but what is new are Presidents who carry limited political authority. Obama and Trump were undermined by their political opponents, often through control over the US Congress. Biden begins with an advantage because the cultural and economic elites in the US are generally fatigued by too much disruption. Biden's singular quality is the reassurance that he brings to them. But there are other destabilizing factors in the Democrat tent that he has pitched in 2020.

A President with overwhelming political authority, clarity and perseverance could assert his opinion over rival views within the government, but Trump had none. Advancing age is Biden's challenge in this regard. The attempt to create a common agenda with Russia in Syria during the Obama years collapsed due to a divergence between the Pentagon and the state department. There is constant bickering between them on questions related to India as well—the Pentagon sees bilateral relations from a military planning perspective, while the state department places it within a broader strategic calculation. Consequently, the defence department has been a champion of enhancing cooperation with India, and its initiatives often get challenged by the state.

Far from clearing the confusion and galvanizing a divided country, Trump's 'America First' added to the chaos, which did not end with his election loss in 2020. The election itself was a display of divisions and acrimony, and by refusing to concede the election, Trump has kept the resentment boiling for the next opportunity, which will be the 2022 midterm election. Trump had offered to bring clarity to America's self-image and its place in the world. While his civilizational interpretations of both are popular among his core support base, in a country that is ethnically diverse, its economic powerhouses—its corporations—are unwilling to play ball in the interest of the state. Its multitude of internal actors—the courts, the media, the states and cities—are all marching to different tunes.

The crisis of American power runs deep. The Trump era gutted the US's soft power attributes and openly declared a hard-power strategic policy. The state department's international aid programmes were cut, while defence spending grew. US diplomats deeply resented this policy, and feared a grievous reduction in America's global influence. In practice, this means a shift away from trying to nudge the rest of the world via global institutions and through the lure of the American market and its offer of technology, propped up by the implicit threat of American military power, to a sole reliance on military force and trade wars without any enticements.

Militarist Response to Everything

When America's ability to sharply define itself and its enemy increasingly got limited by internal and external factors, one easy response was to use force randomly. *How Everything Became War and the Military Became Everything*, an account by Rosa Brooks[58] who was an adviser in the Pentagon during Obama's presidency, captures this expanding role of the military in American policy. Often, military strength is used as a substitute for diplomacy. *War on Peace: The End of Diplomacy and the Decline of American Influence* by Ronan Farrow explains how the dismantling of American diplomacy started much before Trump became President.[59] Trump's public commitments to 'hard power, not soft power' aggravated both trends that predated his rise. His budgetary allocations and choice of personnel leaned toward reinforcing and furthering American militarism. But he was the first President since Jimmy Carter to not start a new war. There is little public support in the US for wars in distant lands for distant reasons, though the military establishment and the country's military industrial complex have a different take. Biden will have a difficult challenge in managing this contradiction. Besides the economic factors at play, war is also about a community searching for moral clarity—about itself and the enemy that needs to be fought and overcome.

During Obama's presidency, Republican states and the Congress stalled a multitude of his initiatives as well as his appointment of a Supreme Court Justice. Trump was impeached by the Democrat-controlled House of Representatives, and a range of actors arraigned against him until he was evicted from office. The same cycle is bound to repeat for Biden. It would seem as if America is at war with itself. When Obama was

President, the government system was brought to a standstill because Republicans were determined that a half-black man with a Muslim middle name had no legitimacy to govern, forget the fact that he had won two elections decisively. The other half built a 'resistance' to Trump's presidency. The roles were swapped in 2020, but the show has not stopped.

The US has had to deal with questions of its own identity earlier too, but having a clear notion of the 'enemy' helped it through most of the twentieth century. Indian commentators who identify themselves as realists have over the years admired the US for its single-minded pursuit of strategic culture, its ability to foresee the future and its willingness to use military power to shape it. But the Trump movement was based on public repudiation of the American strategic culture of the last three decades. A Biden victory has not restored trust in US institutions; if anything, the 2020 election has only aggravated this crisis of credibility.

The National Security Strategy (NSS) announced by the Trump administration in December 2017 named China, Russia and Islamism as threats, and marked a wide array of goals and objectives, but with little clarity of strategy. Trump's politics was to prioritize Islamism and China as threats to American power and security. Between the NSS, the Nuclear Posture Review and the National Defense Strategy during the Trump presidency, American military planners sought to make sense of the current era as a reincarnation of the great power rivalry in which Russia counts as the primary rival, China following it. This is, at one level, forcing an argument to seek elusive clarity about the self and the enemy.

A less charitable view could be that American planners are itching for war, as Micah Zenko, Whitehead Senior Fellow at Chatham House, wrote in *Foreign Policy* in March 2018:

> As one anonymous senior Defense Department official told
> [. . .] 'Real men fight real wars. We like the clarity of big
> wars.' If you have spent time in the Pentagon or a service
> school recently, you have heard versions of this sentiment,
> or worse.[60]

Most of the analyses on the lack of strategic culture in India have juxtaposed so-called Indian timidity with the apparent long-range view adopted by the US. It seems ironical, then, that the Americans elected a President in 2016 who had campaigned on the single-point agenda that all that the country had done in the last several decades were strategic blunders; his successor won the presidency in 2020 by considerably disowning his own legacy of shaping American policy for over four decades.

From Syria to Afghanistan, from China to Jerusalem, events have been shaped by the US pursuit of national interest. Against the backdrop of war, strife and agony across continents, including within the US, it is natural that certitudes of the past are being called into question.

> The United States has found itself in a seemingly endless
> series of wars over the past two decades. Despite frequent
> opposition by the party not controlling the presidency and
> often that of the American public, the foreign policy elite
> operates on a consensus that routinely leads to the use of
> military power to solve international crises.[61]

Biden's NSA, Jake Sullivan, was among the experts who studied middle-class perceptions of US foreign policy, after it had become a source of popular resentment. The study concluded, 'it becomes clear that foreign policy professionals need to reexamine how they are defining the national economic interests intended to be advanced through U.S. foreign policy.'

Trump's anti-war rhetoric did not mean that he observed military restraint or eschewed unilateral interventions. It actually meant that the US could act without much consideration of consequences or long-term planning. If American interests are at risk, or to show the world who is the boss, the US would attack any country it deems necessary. Beyond that, it would have no patience or appetite for supporting nation-building efforts in that country. The killing of Iranian military leader Qasem Soleimani in Iraq in July 2020 was a case in point.

The one and only time Trump got approving nods in Washington from across the political spectrum was when he bombed Syria and Afghanistan. Military action unites the strategic community. 'Where am I controversial? When it comes to the use of military power [. . .] That is the source of the controversy,' Obama had said, explaining how he faced criticism for his decision to not bomb Syria.[62]

India has been a beneficiary of Obama's strategic patience, George W. Bush's strategic adventurism, Trump's strategic disruption and now it hopes to ally with Biden's strategic stability. At one level, the India–America friendship is a result of American weakness; a stronger America had a different approach to India.

I would like to close this discussion on America's relative loss of influence in a changing world with one topic of great importance to India—its association with the Nuclear Suppliers Group (NSG). In 2006, President Bush placed a direct call to Chinese Premier Hu Jintao. According to a US official who related that story, Bush told the Chinese leader: 'If you oppose the NSG waiver for India, that will have serious consequences for our relations with you.'[63] The message was unambiguous and definitive. And the Chinese were the last to receive that call from Bush. America's friends, countries which had been holding back from supporting India, had already received the same message directly from the President of the US—that you oppose the waiver for India at the cost of your friendship with the US. No country in the world, including China, could risk that confrontation with the White House in 2006.

Despite that level of assertive display, the power of America was disintegrating from within. When Bush was making such calls to world leaders on India's behalf, America's economic edifice was shaky from the inside. Within two years, the economic collapse occurred, after which the country has never been the same again, its notional recovery and the macro statistics that support the claim of a revival notwithstanding.

Obama's policy of working with rising powers and accepting a multipolar world translated in India's favour. This was seemingly at variance from the Bush-era thinking in which India was seen as an ally against China. Obama genuinely believed that since America could not go around the world policing the bad spots, other Asian powers could be supported in their rise. By then, more and more people in the US administration had become appreciative of the fact that India could not be pushed to be a treaty ally of the US.

Despite his rhetoric, Obama did not fundamentally change the nature of American foreign policy and its strategic behaviour. A key point in support of this argument is the widespread use of drones during his presidency to target Islamist militants as also the raid that killed Osama bin Laden, where Obama acted unilaterally to sustain American interests.

Henry Kissinger has compared the Richard Nixon administration's bombing of Cambodia between 1969 and 1973—kept secret from the American public—to Obama's drone strikes against Islamist militants. Kissinger was the key interlocutor for Nixon who opened diplomatic ties with China. 'I think the principle is essentially the same [. . .] You attack locations where you believe people operate who are killing you,'[64] he said. The Obama administration carried out 473[65] drone bombings around the world, which many see as a flagrant violation of international norms and having great civilian costs. The fact that Kissinger was one of the key advisers to Trump completes the circuit of continuity in America's strategic behaviour at a fundamental level.

The assertion of American power has become increasingly difficult in a changing world, and that is the reality that the country's strategic community and politicians are unable to make complete sense of or come to terms with. Obama noted that even the consequences of invading Iraq had not tempered the interventionist enthusiasm of what he calls the 'foreign policy establishment'. America's Cuba policy is a classic example of this. As Obama sought a new opening with the Caribbean nation, Republican politicians warned against returning Guantánamo Bay, a 45-square-mile piece of coastline in Cuba that the US has been using as its territory for decades. America has been imprisoning its captives from jihadi badlands at a high-security facility at Guantánamo, which Obama had promised to shut down. Republican politicians were riled by this suggestion and accused him of trying to return the land to Cuba. Each year, America sends a cheque of $4095 to Cuba as lease charges for Guantánamo, which Cuba stopped cashing in 1959.

What is American Interest?

Arguments for a resetting of the US's ties with the world predate the rise of Trump and outlive his presidency. Obama warned against hubris. He wanted other countries to share the burden of global challenges. He also wanted America to take a step back in order to account for the overreach of its power and the pain it had caused to the rest of the world, and accommodate rising powers in an orderly fashion, while reshuffling America's own definitions of the self and the enemy. Trump wanted America to retrench because he believes that the country has been a loser in the world order. He thought that the US leadership only meant an unnecessary drain of its resources in meaningless pursuits.

Different constituencies within the American political system have different notions of what constitutes the country's interests. In the last three decades, as the notion of common interest fragmented, the American state increasingly acted in favour of the interests of the corporations, consumers and investors at the cost of the labour. 'America First' upended this equation. Trump sees global ties from the perspective of American labour, which got a bad deal in globalization and trade treaties. Roughly the same social group also bears a disproportionate share of the cost of America's unending wars abroad, as soldiers. The common sense of the last three decades included a correlation between economic interests and security interests. This correlation saw America's global ties largely from the perspective of its corporations. Trade deficits, which helped companies, were often overlooked in instances of strategic arguments in favour of a country, for example, South Korea or even India. In China's case, this logic allowed expanding trade with the country, while continuing military build-up against it. Trump also correlated security and economic interests, but in a manner that has shocked the country's professional strategists. He invoked national security provisions in trade laws to impose tariffs against America's closest allies such as Canada and Germany. Trump's Commerce Secretary Wilbur Ross explained the rationale such: 'National security is broadly defined to include the economy, to include the impact on employment, to include a very big variety of things [. . .] Economic security is military security. And without economic security, you can't have military security.'[66] This change in the US approach is not going to vanish under a Biden presidency. Biden would be calmer and traditional in rhetoric, but he would be under pressure to follow a nationalist agenda at home and abroad.

Narendra Modi's rise is a result of both the division and consolidation of Indian society. The consolidation of large parts of Hindu society and the papering over of the differences of caste hierarchy and Modi's rise have been two mutually reinforcing phenomena. This consolidation comes at the cost of alienation of India's religious minorities, but, broadly, the Hindutva Strategic Doctrine has wide acceptance in India—among its judiciary, media and most importantly, its state agencies. That is not the case with Trump's 'America First' agenda or a Biden presidency. While Trumpians are against trade and global institutions, Democrats who are opposed to Trump also have a nationalist agenda. In their demand that US-based companies such as Facebook and Twitter work in the national interest and not as global corporations, is the liberal call for the pull-back of globalization.

Parallel to the confusion in global liberal order is the Chinese offer of its own model as a global alternative. Such a prospect is of concern for India, but then, it has its own model to offer to the world—the notion of India as Vishwa Guru, an idea that drives Hindutva thinkers.

Though Indian leaders repeatedly say that a strong US and American leadership of the world are in India's interest, the history of that dynamic is more layered and nuanced. While American leadership and ability to arm-twist other countries, including China and Pakistan, have benefited India on occasions, the space for New Delhi's global ambitions can become available only with America's retreat. It was the US that forced China to accede to the NSG waiver for nuclear commerce for India and forced Pakistan to resolve the Kargil conflict. But it was a relatively weakened US that took a friendlier view of India to begin with.

The flashiest advertisement for free market globalization has been the apparent freedom, competence and prosperity of the US. 'A shining city upon a hill,' as President Ronald Reagan said. '. . . a beacon, still a magnet for all who must have freedom,' he said, after noting that 'countries across the globe are turning to free markets and free speech and turning away from the ideologies of the past.'[67] That was in 1989. 'Be like us,' was the basic argument that the US made to the rest of the world. The use of force by America, at home or abroad, was only for the protection of liberty, it claimed. There was merit in that argument, as it expanded freedom for its own people through the twentieth century. In 1963, when Alabama's Democrat governor, George Wallace—who had vowed 'segregation forever'—resisted desegregation orders of the Supreme Court, President John F. Kennedy deployed the National Guards to enforce it. President Donald Trump's threat to use the US military to 'dominate' people who erupted in protest after the death of an unarmed African-American by the police was history taking a reverse turn. The use of force against dissenters of a certain kind contrasts with the reticence of law enforcement in the face of white, gun-wielding protestors against the lockdown in 2020 and those who stormed the US Capitol in January 2021.

The video footage of a police officer pinning down George Floyd by his neck until he died could not have come at a worse time for the US whose reputation was already undermined by the fatal failures of its free market in the wake of the pandemic. Still, there was a moral defence that the US was a free society that does not coerce its members. There was also a convenient contrast to make—with China, which under Xi Jinping has offered its model of development as an alternative to liberalism. The Trump administration, and a section of the commentators, focused on whistleblower doctor Li Wenliang in Wuhan who noticed the novel coronavirus first. He was silenced by the local government, though posthumously declared a martyr by Beijing. Two US senators wanted to rename the street in Washington, DC where the Chinese embassy is located after him. Because of the Chinese fetters on freedom of expression, information regarding the pandemic was suppressed and it went out of control, the mainstream American argument went. Meanwhile, Washington confronted China on a range of questions from technology trade to the Hong Kong uprising. Then came the brutal images from Minnesota. 'Send in the troops,' senator Tom Cotton, who was clamouring for democracy in China, wrote in a *New York Times* editorial piece in June 2020, to crush American protests.[68]

It is not that holes in the American story were not visible earlier. Edward Snowden, who was born two years after Reagan became President, is today living in Russia in asylum, accused of espionage and theft in the US. Many American liberals argue that he crossed a line by revealing national security secrets; and no mainstream American politician hails him as a martyr for free speech. How much force is legitimate in law enforcement might depend on the context and place, but the US ranks number one in the world in terms of incarceration—there are

2.2 million people in its prisons, a five-fold increase in the last four decades.[69] The US has 655 per lakh of population in prisons—the highest in the world.[70] African–Americans are disproportionately represented in the US prison population, but that is no reason to overlook the whites. The police in the US targeted reporters and photographers in several cities during the 2020 protests.

There used to be an argument that globalization would gradually turn China democratic. China imbibed American-style consumerism, but as for democracy and freedom, a reverse osmosis appears to have taken place. As Democrat Senator Bernie Sanders repeatedly points out, the police in the US resembles invading armies in local communities. But it will be disingenuous and dishonest to blame the police, or individual officers who behave violently. It is not a coincidence that the degradation of democracy in the US corresponds with its economic entanglement with China over the last forty years.

Houston Police Chief Art Acevedo told CNN in an interview that had gone viral for him asking Trump to keep his 'mouth shut': 'Let's be honest . . . This is not about policing, it's about the society, the disproportionality of things going on in our country from education, to health, to food, to everything that we as human beings, hold near and dear.' He noted that rioters were those who had stopped voting.[71] US ranks twenty-sixth among OECD countries in voter turnout, at 55.7 per cent in 2016. In India, 67 per cent voted in 2019. The poorer whites had the option of voting a demagogue to victory; the blacks were battling it out on the streets. The 2008 victory of Barack Obama, the first African–American, was a democratic surge which was soon overcome by the reaction. In 2020, yet another surge in voter participation catapulted Biden to victory, with a historic high in popular votes.

If the US manages to sustain its leadership in technology that began by the 1890s and gets its demographic strategy right, the twenty-first century also will belong to it. The battle for technology leadership has several dimensions. It is between the US state and the country's global corporations first; it is between political factions within the US as there is no consensus on how to retain control over the runaway explosion of innovation; and it is between the US and other countries, particularly China.

Changes in global demographic patterns indicate advantages for the US. 'But in 2018, for the first time ever, there were more people over the age of 64 than under six. The United States will soon be the only country with a large, growing market. Among the world's 20 largest economies, only Australia, Canada, and the United States will have growing populations of adults aged 20 to 49 throughout the next 50 years, while China will lose 225 million young workers and consumers aged 20 to 49, 36 percent of its current total.'[72] The US could also claim even more demographic advantage by welcoming more immigrants, but that is a very contested topic. And the intake of more and more people into the country from diverse backgrounds could further aggravate the question of American identity.

It was global trade that disrupted American social and political organization in the early decades of the twenty-first century and dislocations will continue and may even aggravate in the coming days even after trade is scaled back, due to technological changes. On the one hand, technology will eliminate more jobs than trade could; on the other, it will also enable the state to enforce discipline and order in society, and undermine and manage dissent more effectively than ever before. The manner in which Twitter and Facebook banned

Trump, and the decision of Apple, Google and Amazon to bar free speech platform Parler on grounds of security has set a new precedence in the free world.[73] Is there a qualitative difference between the Chinese Communist Party restricting speech and US corporations doing so?

The US could continue to dominate the world for many decades, but its character could be changing. 'The halcyon days of the post–Cold War era, when American presidents organized their foreign policies around the principles of liberal internationalism, are unlikely to return anytime soon,' according to Walter Russel Mead.[74] Another scholar argues: 'The era of liberal U.S. hegemony is an artifact of the Cold War's immediate afterglow. Trump's transactional approach to foreign policy, by contrast, has been the norm for most of U.S. history. As a result, Trump's imprint could endure long after Trump himself is gone . . . Like the twentieth century, the twenty-first century will be dominated by the United States. But whereas the previous "American century" was built on a liberal vision of the U.S. role in the world, what we might be witnessing today is the dawn of an illiberal American century.'[75] Both at home and abroad, the US could be heading towards an illiberal iteration of itself, beyond Trump.

The universal liberal euphoria over Trump's electoral defeat is based on flawed reasoning as was the desolation over his victory in 2016. Ahead of the 2016 presidential election, there were two types of challenges to the neoliberal political and economic order. Bernie Sanders, a self-declared democratic socialist, offered a more structured critique of the American neoliberal order than Trump's scattergun approach. Trump's cocktail of cultural and economic nationalism inebriated the nation but it turned victorious also because the establishment would rather deal with it than the Sanders model. Trump convinced the poor that they had shared interests with America's wealthiest and their enemies were other poor people of different colour or religion.

Trump's savage cultural politics, ego and bluster became the focus of the opposition to him and the underlying reasons of his appeal were overlooked by design or debility. Trumpian cultural politics was countered with liberal cultural politics—of sexual, ethnic and religious minorities, of gender rights, topped up with environmentalism. The argument that cultural anxieties, not economic dispossession, are the driver of nationalism has been a diversion. Cultural anxieties are real for sure, but they work in conjunction with other factors. Surveys in 2020 asked respondents to assign an order of priority to a bunch of issues—say COVID-19, immigration, economy, race relations—on the baseless assumption that these are isolated factors. The reality is that someone can be opposed to migration because the economy is battered due to COVID-19 or they were infected.

It bears repeating that material conditions and situations shape political behaviour. Those who consider the human body as an inviolable space supported a mask mandate; those who are generally supportive of free movement of people across borders, now argued for laws that force people to lock up in their homes. To tell the working class that they must lose their jobs today to avoid an environmental apocalypse fifty years later is bad enough; to assume that those who are incapable of caring about the environment are actually agitated over their grandchildren living in a more diverse country is logical fallacy.

Another mainstream response to Trump's 2016 victory was to question the legitimacy of his election itself by linking it to Russian influence operation and calling into question the utility of the US Electoral College mechanism itself. A key purpose of inserting intermediaries between the voters and the chief executive in a representative democracy is to stall mobocracy and make the process more thoughtful. This creates anomalies, such as Trump winning the presidency without winning the popular vote, and the Indian prime minister, Narendra Modi, winning 55 per cent Lok Sabha seats with 37 per cent popular votes concentrated in a limited area. In India, if a party can win 272 Lok Sabha seats each with a margin of one vote, it can rule the whole country regardless of what happened in the other 271 seats. But dismantling of the intermediaries in a representative democracy is a dream, not of the pluralist, but of the demagogue. Representations are anyway also linked to the size of the population—the distribution of the electoral college (EC) votes shifts according to the changes in population distribution. If it was the Democrats who continuously questioned the legitimacy of Trump victory in 2016, there was a role reversal in 2020. The optics of the mob violence at the Capitol in January 2021 when Biden's election was being confirmed by the US Congress was dramatic; but the underlying divides are intense and enduring. Texas led seventeen other states, and was joined by 126 Republican members of the US House of Representatives, in moving the SC to overturn the election results in Georgia, Michigan, Pennsylvania and Wisconsin—four key states that secured the victory of Biden. After the SC refused to entertain their plea, the Republican Texas chair Allen West said the SC decision meant that 'a state can take unconstitutional actions and violate its own election law resulting in damaging effects on other states that abide by the law, while the guilty state suffers no consequences'. 'Perhaps law-abiding states should bond together and form a Union of states that will abide by the constitution.'[76]

The American media's response to the rise of Trump has been equally curious. While one segment became his unabashed promoters, the self-styled mainstream media, with isolated exceptions, took it upon itself to bring him down. The American media's unquestioning deference to the country's security establishment is historical, but under the Trump presidency, that became even more intense. It is good that the President gets questioned, but it is certainly not good that his opponent does not get questioned. Long-held principles of journalism were thrown out of the window. In its willingness to fall for numerous unsubstantiated stories about the President and in the refusal to truthfully examine Biden's track record, the US media thought nothing mattered more than saving democracy from Trump. It is a case of illiberalism for the protection of liberalism.

This double standard lends credibility to the view that a cartel of vested interests controls the US. The presence of Trump in the White House should have spurred a more honest national self-reflection, but the elites who could have led this, pivoted to do the exact opposite. Once all the crises were pinned on Trump, there was no other end to pursue, other than his defeat. He became the excuse to avoid any relook of the neoliberal order. All that burden is now on Biden, who has made a good start by reaching out to the white working class during his campaigning. The liberal ecosystem of the US had gone into a cytokine storm—immune overreaction that causes more harm than the affliction itself such as in COVID-19—in response to Trump. Biden benefited from it, but now he needs to calm it. He needs to address the morbidities of America—the trust deficit in the country's election system, the brutality of its economic order, the chaos of its cultural politics. Or else, Trump politics will linger around as a restless ghost. In defeat, the support for Trump swelled by 10 million votes, compared to 2016. Like Long COVID, there is Long Trump.

The Trump administration's disregard for the 'world order' opened opportunities for India's ambitions to be a 'leading power'. The transition from a US President (Barack Obama) who reminded India about its own Constitution during his visit to India in the first year of Modi's prime ministership, to a leader (Donald Trump) who never brought such topics up in his conversations with India was useful. Biden could dust up his old notebook and talking points on human rights, democracy, etc., but that will have limited impact on bilateral ties. India remains a topic of clarity in a confused America.

2

Hindutva Strategic Doctrine—A New Way for India?

'People want to know who is the real Modi—Hindu nationalist leader or pro-business chief minister?' Narendra Modi was once asked. He replied: 'I'm nationalist. I'm patriotic . . . I'm a born Hindu. So, I'm a Hindu nationalist . . . As far as progressive, development-oriented, workaholic, whatever they say, this is what they are saying. So there's no contradiction between the two. It's one and the same image.'[1]

Modi has been upfront about his adherence to Hindu nationalism, or Hindutva. Hindutva has at least a century's worth of literature, and an organization, the Rashtriya Swayamsevak Sangh (RSS), which was founded in 1925. Modi joined the RSS as an eight-year-old. The BJP, its political wing, has been in power in several states of India for several decades now; Modi himself was chief minister of Gujarat for twelve years before he became the prime minister of India in 2014. Most helpful of all in understanding the chief executive of the world's biggest democracy of 1.38 billion people and the fourth-biggest military power[2] are his own statements, such as the one above. But most commentaries on him, as he took over the reins in 2014, did not follow Maya Angelou's principle that when someone shows who they are, they must be believed.

Unlike the numerous interpretations of Modi that projected what other people expected him to do, this one is based on his own explanation, contextualized against his track record in office. Understanding him for what he is would be the most durable foundation for a robust India–US relationship. He was widely viewed as a pro-market globalist and a reformer, but one person who took him for what he said was American nationalist and Trump's key adviser in the 2016 election, Steve Bannon. In 2018, when this book was first written, practical evidence of a Hindutva Strategic Doctrine was emerging, but by 2021, when this second edition is being published, there is plenty of it, including a full-length treatise by External Affairs Minister S. Jaishankar, *The India Way*. It argues that a new phase of Indian strategy began in 2014, and elucidates its features. We shall come to that soon.

A general presumption informing scholarship on international relations is that there is a non-negotiable and unchanging precept of national interest. But the very notion of national interest itself is being re-litigated in both the US and India. For instance, secularism was considered to be in India's national interest until recently; immigration and trade were considered to be in America's national interest. The recasting of the notion of national interest in India that is underway can be understood with the frame of the Hindutva Strategic Doctrine.

What does India under Modi want from the world? It wants investment, technology and arms, but is resistant towards finished products or foreign ideas, including religions, an open global market, the right to self-determination, human rights, Western strands of democracy coming through missionaries, international bodies and non-governmental organizations (NGOs). 'We need Foreign Direct Investment but the new FDI is "Foreign Destructive Ideology", we have to protect ourselves from it,' Modi told Indian Parliament on 8 February 2021. This has been expressed through higher tariffs on imports and restrictions on global NGOs. Several global NGOs, including Amnesty International and Ford Foundation, stopped their operations in India post 2014. What does India offer in return? India is one of the world's biggest markets, growing at a steady pace. It is one of the biggest buyers of military hardware, and it is also a strategic counter to an increasingly aggressive China. It is the world's biggest democracy that the West can ally with. It produces talented and trained human resources that Western democracies can absorb without much concern. Modi would say India has three Ds going for it—Demand, Demography and Democracy.

What is a 'Hindu' way of understanding strategy, if there is such a thing? Western strategic thinkers have sought to understand India as Hindu for decades. In 1992, American scholar George Tanham tried to codify 'Indian Strategic Thought'. Written immediately after India had liberalized its economy and the West was beginning to see the country in a different light, Tanham's argument was that culturally, India is not equipped to think ahead and plan for the future due to a fatalistic and abstract understanding of life and relationships in the Hindu world view. 'The lacunae in strategy and planning derive largely from India's historical and cultural development.'[3]

He argued that the absence of long-term national security planning in India is due to its predominantly 'Hindu' philosophy. 'The Hindu concept of time, or rather the lack of a sense of time—Indians view life as an eternal present, with neither history nor future—discourages planning,' wrote Tanham. 'Hindus consider life a mystery, largely unknowable and not entirely under man's control. In this view, fate, intuition, tradition, and emotions play important roles, but how, how much and when is never clearly known. Man's control over this life is thus limited in Hindu eyes, and he cannot forecast or plan with any confidence.'

Tanham's paper was based on interviews with several serving and retired Indian civil and military officials and, therefore, it is safe to assume that many people within the Indian system shared this understanding.

There are Indian commentators who not only argue that India does not have a strategic culture, but also link that to Hinduism. For instance, Brahma Chellaney writes:

> India has an unusual history, having recurrently fallen prey to invaders of various sorts, yet having refrained from raising or conquering another civilization. That defensive, reactive character reinforced by the inherited social values of a Hindu society that gives credence to preordained destiny has defined India's national security approach. It remains the single biggest obstacle to an institutionalized, integrated, provident approach to national security planning.[4]

Hindutva, or political Hinduism, in its essence is about overcoming the real or perceived weaknesses of Hinduism. Participants at the World Hindu Congress in Chicago in 2018 received a box of sweets in their welcome kit containing two ladoos—one hard and one soft. 'The soft ladoo represented the status of Hindus today that they may be easily broken and swallowed while the future vision for the Hindu society should be like a hard ladoo—strongly bonded,' according to an organizer.[5]

Hindutva understands the religion not necessarily in the way interpreted by Tanham, though it alternates between lamenting the weaknesses of Hindu society and glorifying it. To the extent that the view of Hinduism being pacifist, fatalistic and lacking in a linear sense of time is true, Hindutva has been a conscious political movement to overcome these disabilities. M.S. Golwalkar, chief of the RSS from 1940 to 1973, ridiculed the idea that Hinduism is a pacifist religion. Every Hindu god is armed, he famously said.[6] Vinayak Damodar Savarkar, who developed the concept of Hindutva in his 1923 treatise by the same title, wrote on the Gandhian strategy for India's freedom struggle: 'It is to be won by the perverse doctrine of non-violence and truth [. . .] the Non-Cooperation Movement for Swaraj based on these twin principles was a movement without power and was bound to destroy the power of the country.'[7]

The notion of Hinduism as pacifist was inspired by Gandhi and imposed by Nehru, according to Jaswant Singh, former cabinet minister and India's interlocutor with the Bill Clinton administration when the first BJP prime minister, A.B. Vajpayee, was in power.

'With unthinking allegiance to Gandhi, the concept of "state power" then got emasculated, affecting its due and proper deployment in the interest of state and society, and at the correct time. Security got relegated to a much lower priority.' He called for a proactive and single-minded strategic culture for India.[8] His argument is based on the premise that Tanham uses, which is that India lacks planning and strategic culture. For this, he blamed 'ersatz pacifism' promoted by Nehru, and the 'unthinking allegiance to Gandhi'.[9]

Explaining the changes that the A.B. Vajpayee government (1998–2004) sought to bring in foreign policy, Sangh Parivar ideologue K.N. Govindacharya said, 'Embracing Kshatriya/Shakti (warrior) tradition of revolutionaries instead of the timorous Brahminical Bhakti (devotional) tradition is the main psychological makeover for BJP foreign policy'.[10] Hindutva, therefore, attempts to overcome this perceived pacifism and fatalism attributed to Hinduism, which is alleged to have influenced strategic planning and national policies.

Addressing a gathering of Indian–Americans in Washington, DC in June 2017, Modi said that his governance was aimed at overcoming the fatalism that has historically gripped Indian society. 'Even when a young child dies of disease, we would take it as god's will,' he said. But a new India and its young population are aspirational, he said. 'The rising aspiration is the biggest strength of Indian development. When aspirations get proper leadership [. . .] aspiration in itself is achievement. We are tailoring our policies to meet the aspirations of the people.' Modi said his aim was to create a 'technology-driven society [. . .] and technology-driven development'.[11]

The aim is to overcome limits, if any, imposed on India's progress, by its tradition or beliefs. At the inauguration of a line of the Delhi Metro Rapid Transport Corporation in the suburban city of Noida in Uttar Pradesh (UP) in December 2017, Modi said, 'Faith is important, but blind faith is not desirable.' He lauded UP Chief Minister Yogi Adityanath, a Hindu priest in saffron robes, for breaking the jinx that CMs who travel to Noida lose power soon. 'Modi said that due to his (Adityanath's) attire, a few people believe that the chief minister is not modern, but he has done what earlier chief ministers of UP have never done—travel to Noida.'[12] Speaking after laying the foundation for the Ram Temple at

Ayodhya on 5 August 2020, at the site of a mosque that was demolished by a mob mobilized by his party in 1992, Modi said it was a 'modern symbol of traditions'. 'It'll become a symbol of our devotion, our national sentiment. This temple will also symbolize the power of collective resolve of crores of people [. . .] an instrument to unite the country.'[13]

Prime ministers who preceded Modi have been astute in making amends to the country's foreign policy directions to make the best use of the fast-changing world around them, particularly in the last thirty years. However, they have been cautious to package it as incremental and timely improvement upon the long-held assumptions that guided India's role in the world. P.V. Narasimha Rao, A.B. Vajpayee and Manmohan Singh explained foreign policy changes within the context of non-alignment and strategic autonomy. These changes were essential, but they were in the spirit of a natural progression of what existed previously.

The first national BJP-led government under Vajpayee was particularly cautious as it went about making some remarkable changes to the country's foreign policy. 'On some issues there has always been a consensus in this country. And foreign policy is one of those. As far as foreign policy is concerned, nothing has changed,'[14] Vajpayee told the Lok Sabha in 1999, introducing the motion of confidence in his government that would go on to complete its full term. He then recalled his association with Nehru and Narasimha Rao, previous Congress prime ministers, on questions of foreign policy. Rao had chosen Vajpayee to defend India's position on Kashmir at the UN. 'It was astonishing for our neighbouring country. The opposition leader is defending the government's position on an international platform,' Vajpayee said, illustrating the broad consensus that existed across the political spectrum within India on foreign policy, promising to keep it that way.

In Prime Minister Modi's case, changing or appearing to change everything has been a constant feature sustaining him and his politics. Change is constant, as the cliché goes, but there is always a choice over what one emphasizes—change or continuity. Emphasizing continuity has been one of the key tools of conventional politics in India, but for Modi and even Trump, the emphasis has been on change. 'Discontinuous politics is helpful in challenging past practices and frozen narratives,' writes S. Jaishankar.[15]

So, what has indeed changed in terms of foreign policy under Modi? Several articles and books have appeared since he became prime minister in 2014, seeking to explain his strategic doctrine. C. Raja Mohan, in *Modi's World: Expanding India's Sphere of Influence*, argues that Modi's rise marks the emergence of India's Third Republic. From 1947 to 1990—independence to liberalization—was the First Republic. The Second Republic began with the end of the Cold War; and now, with the emergence of Modi and the BJP at the helm of affairs, we have the Third Republic. India's ambition to assume a 'leading power' status in the region is the notable feature of the Third Republic.[16] Mohan also makes the case that Modi has a 'non-ideological' world view and is guided by India's enlightened self-interest. 'Clearly, Modi seeks to transform India from being merely an influential entity into one whose weight and preferences are defining for international politics,' wrote Ashley Tellis, strategic affairs expert.[17] Elsewhere, Tellis sought to make a distinction between Modi and the larger politics of his party, the BJP.[18]

Now, with Jaishankar's explanation of the 'India Way', it is possible to understand the change in the country's strategic thinking under Modi. It is also illuminating to view these changes against the backdrop of the long-held Hindutva positions on these questions. Considering that the history of Hindutva is at least a century old, it will be more appropriate to call it the Hindutva Strategic Doctrine.

It is not that there have been no differences among Hindutva thought leaders on questions of self and strategy. Over the period, a school of thought can be identified in praxis and practice, which has acquired form and clarity with the BJP winning an absolute majority in the 2014 and 2019 general elections. A snapshot of Jaishankar's 'India Way' treatise could be handy before we elucidate the features of the Hindutva Strategic Doctrine.

According to Jaishankar, 2014—the year Modi became PM—initiated the sixth phase of the evolution of the Indian foreign policy. A number of global developments coincided with this phase, driven primarily by changes in the relative global standing of the US and China. He says that India's 'mandarins can no longer be impervious to the masses', and the country has become more nationalistic. But a more nationalistic India is also more globalist, and internationalist, as it seeks to have an expanding role in world affairs. India's globalization policies post 1991 have 'clearly gone astray', and it has ruined some sectors of the Indian economy. A new era of self-reliance is hence a course correction. It is moving from being a 'balancing power' to being a 'leading power.' India is shaking itself off from a 'Western paradigm' and inserting its own 'vocabulary and concepts' in global diplomacy. India must have its own narrative. 'Taking off on non-alignment, it is sometimes useful to speak of multi-alignment.' India is today leading the global debate on connectivity.

It is overcoming its baggage of being a 'soft state' and correcting the mistakes of the past when it could not act decisively against Pakistan sponsoring terrorism against India. India's military retaliations in Uri and Balakot against Pakistan for organizing terrorist strikes in India were a break from the past. Today's India is willing to pay the 'operational costs' of national interest. A 'strong and cohesive establishment' is essential for this pursuit, and the country is graduating from the bickering of democracy to 'discipline and formalism' in its internal affairs. It has a policy of 'generosity and firmness' in the neighbourhood. 'Powerful nations are understandably reluctant to put their options and interests at the judgement of others. That could be the case with India too as it gains in power and stature.'[19] Jaishankar's book is also an elucidation of how India is careful in maintaining multiple alignments with countries with varied interests in a fast-changing world, while keeping its own options open.

India offered an alternative way of thinking for the world that was in crisis, according to RSS Chief Mohan Bhagwat. In a speech on the 'role of India in global perspective' on 3 December 2020, he said the crisis of humanity was because of excessive individualism and materialism. Those who believed in liberal democracy rejected nationalism and said the whole of humanity was one. They hoped that market forces would drive progress. Now they were returning to nationalism. Humanity has made progress, but it has not reached where it ought to. The balance between materialism and spirituality has been lost; as has been the balance between individualism and social goals. The world has no bridge between this duality. India has the bridge that resolves this issue, which is called dharma. Religion may be a small part of it, but dharma is not religion. Dharma unites people. Everyone's activity is within bounds; everyone is stabilized. The balance between the interests of the society and the environment is maintained. If we create wealth with both hands, let's distribute it with a thousand hands. Money is to help others; strength is to protect others. India did not realize it has the power to offer this alternative vision to the world until recently. Now we have, and we are doing it. Every country has a purpose that is barred by time. India's purpose is eternal in the world, said the RSS chief.[20]

Strategic Autonomy

While Indian foreign policy has evolved over the decades, what has not changed is the concept of strategic autonomy, which is that India would not join any military alliance, would always keep its choices open and would choose what is good for it depending on the situation at a particular moment. Some commentators have derided strategic autonomy as a rigid ideological position that has prevented India from achieving more in the international arena. Some have said that India should have become an ally of the US several decades ago, and by not doing so, it has limited its potential.

Strategic autonomy has been at the forefront of discussions in the context of India's ever-tightening embrace with the US. As the two countries inch closer to one another, will India be able to maintain its autonomy of choice and independence? Will it become a satellite of the US, dragged by the latter into alliances and conflicts that it may not want?

Undoubtedly, the US is crucial to India's progress as a key source of technology and capital, and as the foremost destination for its students and job seekers in various sectors. Many advocates of continuing expansion of Indo–US ties say that strategic autonomy is useless and counterproductive. Why not join the US wholeheartedly and derive full benefits of being an ally of the most powerful military force and home to the best technology in the world?

The US shares its most advanced technologies and intelligence only with its closest allies. NATO allies and Israel are topmost in this pecking order. Only they had been given F-35 fighter planes, the most advanced of America's fighter planes yet, until Trump opened it up and offered it to the UAE. The Guardian-series Unmanned Aerial Vehicles (UAV) have been sold only to NATO allies till date, and now India has been offered them as a special gesture.

The counter to this argument is that, given the drastic changes in the US's position across several crucial issues, India might have done well by never aligning with it as an ally. The US had been pushing India to open its markets further to global trade, but turned against the same under Trump. The US under Barack Obama put tremendous pressure on India to ratify the Paris Agreement. But his successor announced a withdrawal from the pact and ordered an end to all measures for its implementation. Biden is back at it again, appointing a special envoy focused only on climate change.

Even before Trump unravelled US strategy, if one considers the last two decades of accelerated engagement between the two countries, the US has made abrupt U-turns on many foreign policy issues, much to India's discomfort. It has alternated between trying to befriend and confront China—something that continued under Trump and will continue under Biden; it has sought to ignore Pakistan, punish it and then woo it with money and weapons; following an earlier pattern, it sought to contain Iran under Trump and will now reach out to it again under Biden; and it has given conflicting signals on Afghanistan, switching between promising to stay engaged and threatening to leave. President Obama wanted India to take a tougher stand against the military junta in Myanmar while addressing the Indian Parliament in 2010, and then went ahead for a rapprochement with them himself.

Strategic autonomy has allowed India to have its own policies towards these countries to a great extent, in the midst of the flux that the US often contributes to.

However, strategic autonomy is not a phrase that Modi's key foreign policy advisers preferred to use in the initial years. For, it is a term that has come to mean some kind of friction with the US, and is also associated with Congress governments of the past. But in his speech at the Shangri-La Dialogue in June 2018, Modi said: 'It is a measure of our strategic autonomy that India's strategic partnership with Russia has matured to be special and privileged.'[21] The speech itself was an elucidation of the age-old policy of India's strategic autonomy.

Beyond Hesitations of History

'Today our relationship has overcome the hesitations of history,' Modi told the US Congress in an address on 8 June 2016. He was the fifth Indian prime minister to address a joint meeting of the US Congress.[22] This theme remains the centrepiece of a Modi strategic approach.

Masterful politicians excel in the art of saying things in a way so as to mean different things to different people. When Modi said that India and the US have overcome the 'hesitations of history', many eager supporters of bilateral ties instantly read it as a willingness to move closer to the latter. US policymakers and commentators who are friends of India and who have wanted to promote better relations between the two countries were elated by the speech. India's reticence to move militarily closer to the US has been a point that agitates American interlocutors the most.

American diplomats who deal with India are often taken aback by India's reticence to get involved in American projects in a third country—literacy in Myanmar or flood control in

Bangladesh, not to mention military involvement. Most of them talk about India's recalcitrance, what they see as unreasonable demands and unwillingness to join hands with the US in a more comprehensive way.

Strategic expert Tanvi Madan wrote that the Modi 'speech signaled and reflected a much broader embrace—an India–U.S. one that has been in the works for at least the last 17 years but has become much more visible . . . [under Modi].'[23]

In Washington, Democrats and Republicans, nationalists and globalists admired Modi in the initial years of his premiership. In the highly fractious politics of the US capital, one name that united a wide range of its actors was Modi, for individual reasons. His decision to unilaterally revoke the special constitutional status of Jammu and Kashmir; implementation of a new citizenship law that fast-tracks citizenship for refugees from neighbouring countries, pointedly excluding Muslims from it, and a raft of other internal policy measures, including economic and cultural protectionism, forced a rethink of him in DC. Under the Biden administration, these concerns will be more pronounced and we discuss that in the next chapter.

Modi's 2016 speech, which he delivered in the last year of the Obama presidency, was widely interpreted as a new Indian willingness to sign up with America as a partner. But, from an RSS ideologue's viewpoint, it was not India, but the US that was giving up its hesitations, seeing India's true worth and respecting India's autonomy because of Modi's leadership.[24]

So, is there a Modi Doctrine?

Modi, like other disrupters, likes to say that everything has started afresh under his leadership, which is a good marketing tactic. But unlike several other disrupters in world politics such as Trump, Modi is not a greenhorn to either politics or political philosophy. He has come up the ladder within a strong ideological movement. Modi has lived an entire life believing in, propagating and practising a political philosophy. Any Modi doctrine, therefore, will have to be located within the context of what I call a Hindutva Strategic Doctrine.

Hindutva thinkers have often lamented that Hindu timidity, mysticism and pacifism have held back the country's military and economic progress.

The Hindutva project—or political Hinduism—attempts to overcome so-called Hindu timidity in strategic and economic spheres. It has visions of the self, the enemy, how to fight the enemy and ensure progress for the self. While many commentators argued in 2014 that Modi had put Hindutva on the backburner and fought the general elections on the agenda of development, there is no such demarcation in his own world view, as is evident from the opening quote of this chapter—'there's no contradiction between the two. It's one and the same image.'[25]

India's Strategic Culture

Strategic culture denotes a country's ability and willingness to visualize long-term national interests and act in accordance with that vision so that it proactively changes the environment in its favour.

Strategic scholar Kanti Bajpai has classified India's contemporary strategic thought into three schools: Nehruvian, neoliberal and hyperreal.[26]

A Nehruvian approach considers war preparation and balance of power central to security and foreign policy as 'ruinous and futile' and military preparedness as defensive action and never a projection of power. For neoliberals, strategic partnership and confrontation are guided by hard-nosed economic calculations and the view that the future is led more by economic power than military. Hyperrealists have a more cynical view of the world. They think 'the surest way to peace and stability is the accumulation of military power and the willingness to use force. The governing metaphor of hyperrealists is threat and counterthreat.'[27]

Hindutva strategic policy is close to what Bajpai calls 'hyperrealist'. Hyperrealists do not think economic integration of countries necessarily leads to a more peaceful world. They feel 'conflict and rivalry between states cannot be transformed into peace and friendship (except temporarily, as in an alliance against a common foe); they can only be managed by threat and use of violence'. While neoliberals believe India must have alliances with all great powers, hyperrealists believe that New Delhi should put together an alliance in South-East and East Asia along the Chinese periphery.

Bajpai says that the Nehruvians consider war preparations ruinous 'because arms spending can only impoverish societies materially and create the very conditions that sustain violence and war; futile because, ultimately, balances of power are fragile and do not prevent large-scale violence (as the two world wars so catastrophically demonstrated)'. Neoliberals think that even if you build up the military, its utility is limited as 'in situations of complex inter-dependence, force is unusable or ineffective'. Hyperrealists believe that 'in the absence of a supranational authority that can tell them how to behave and is capable of enforcing those commands, states are doomed to balance of power, deterrence and war'.

How these three streams of thought evaluate India's three crucial relationships—with the US, Pakistan and China—is of significance here. For hyperrealists, 'the collapse or destruction of Pakistan is the only truly viable solution'. Nehruvians believe that 'for lasting peace, India should invest in long-run diplomacy'. Neoliberals think India's economic growth will bring Pakistan to it, and by joint ventures and trade, their mutual prejudices would begin to weaken.

Hyperrealists see China as the greatest military threat to India. Despite the 1962 conflict, Nehruvians do not consider China an existential threat to India. For neoliberals, China is about economic opportunities and the economic challenges it holds out.

In the Nehruvian view, the US is viewed with suspicion and is meant to be resisted. According to a neoliberal view, defying the US is self-defeating and a pragmatic deal with it should be negotiated. Hyperrealists believe in New Delhi being self-confident in its relations with the US and clear about its core interests. Bajpai quotes Chellaney's work again, 'An India–U.S. alliance is possible, particularly against the common enemy, China. India and the United States also have a common interest in combating Islamic fundamentalism and terrorism.'

Modi's predecessor, Manmohan Singh, pursued a hybrid of Nehruvianism and neoliberalism in strategy. Modi's foreign policy establishment—his advisers and Modi himself—has been categorical about a departure from the decades preceding the 2014 Lok Sabha election. The attempt is to move towards a Hindutva Strategic Doctrine, a hybrid of hyperrealism and religious nationalism. Here are eleven features of this doctrine:

1) The Hindu primacy in Indian civilization

'Twelve hundred years of enslavement continues to trouble our mindset. Often, when we meet a person of high stature, we fail to muster strength to speak up,' Prime Minister Narendra

Modi said, addressing the Indian Parliament on 9 June 2014, while speaking about the resurgence of the country's pride that his victory represented.[28]

Modi has repeatedly spoken about 'the 1200 years of slavery'. 'The Britishers ruled over us and prior to them, various others ruled us. Almost for 1000 to 1200 years, we were slaves,' he said, while addressing an Indian American gathering at Madison Square Garden, New York, on 28 September 2014.[29]

The implication is that the Islamic empires and kingdoms of India kept the country in slavery and the nation is waking up from that slumber only now, with his victory in 2014. The '1200 years of slavery' is apparently counted from 712 CE onwards when Sindh was conquered by Muhammad bin Qasim, an Umayyad general. The counting is wrong, though.

According to this imagination of India, the country was not liberated in 1947, when it won independence from British imperial rule. It was merely a transfer of power from foreign powers to Anglicized members of the Indian elite. In the Sangh Parivar's understanding of history, India has been ruled by a westernized, English–speaking elite since Independence. The BJP's 2014 election manifesto stated:

> After achieving independence, the leaders at the helm of affairs lost the spirit and the vision, which the freedom movement had evoked. They discarded the vision and adopted the institutional framework of administration created by the Britishers which was quite alien to India's world–view. It is unfortunate that these leaders could not comprehend India's inner vitality, which was the main force responsible for India's survival despite several attacks and prolonged foreign rule and thus, failed to rekindle the spirit of India.[30]

The idea that India is rooted in its civilization and the admission of its Hindu character cuts across political philosophies in India. In the midst of the struggle against colonialism, when Nehru wrote *The Discovery of India*, which till date remains an authentic non-sectarian explanation of the notion of India, he drew primarily from a Hindu cultural ambience. While the Nehruvian understanding of India and its civilization draws substantially from Hindu notions, religions and philosophies that developed in the subcontinent, it was also emphatic in stating that Islamic civilization was part of Indian civilization.

The Hindutva understanding of Indian civilization does not accept this view. The notion of 1200 years of slavery in India is a pointed exclusion of Islam from the civilizational heritage of India. This was not only campaign rhetoric, but extended to the prime minister's speech on the floor of Parliament.

The distinction between the Hindutva view and the secular view of Indian civilization is a fine, thin line that is easily blurred, particularly for scholars who are not tuned into the multiple political streams within India. Rodney W. Jones, a Washington-based scholar, writing for the Defense Threat Reduction Agency under the US Department of Defense on India's strategic culture, conflates all this into one straightjacket. His views cannot be treated as an official American understanding, but it is clear that such commissioned studies inform American state agencies.

According to Jones, 'Muslim governments adapted to Indian society by restraining forcible conversion, and by recruiting Hindus from urban and upper castes to help run government and from middle and lower castes to fill out military ranks, thereby avoiding incessant internal warfare and rebellion. But Muslim hegemony was imposed, and this mutual accommodation was inherently unstable.' In his view, the nationalist movement may have forced the British to leave India, but the fundamental problem in India remained that Muslims were viewed as 'the enemy'. 'The Muslim invader is a particularly potent example of an enemy in India's concept. In theory, Indian society had long absorbed alien intruders by their assimilation of its superior teachings, traditions and civilized values. Muslim beliefs and practices were less permeable and could not be absorbed and transformed.'[31]

Assuming that Jones may be correct in concluding that Indian elites historically considered Muslims as enemies, Hindutva strategic thinking sought to capitalize on it and popularize it as a mass movement, while the Nehruvian approach sought to question the premise and undo it to the extent that it existed, through its own politics and policy. In the Nehruvian idea of Indian nationalism, it was British rule that was foreign to India—which was defeated by a non-sectarian, secular unity of the country. In the Hindutva view, enslavement of India started 1200 years ago when Muslim invaders reached parts of what is today Pakistan. Though political independence was achieved in 1947, the centuries-old mindset of enslavement continues and needs to be overcome by the unity and resurgence of the Hindu community. Hindutva accepts Tanham's argument that Hindus are held back, but blames it on foreign rule. It rejects Tanham's argument that this is due to their lack of skill or genius—on the contrary, they believe that the Hindu genius has survived centuries of slavery and is now realizing its full potential.

In 2018, RSS chief Mohan Bhagwat sought to explain Hindutva's emphasis on Hindu unity and the place of Muslims in its scheme. 'We say ours is a Hindu Rashtra. Hindu Rashtra does not mean it has no place for Muslims. The day it is said that Muslims are unwanted here, the concept of Hindutva will cease to exist. Hindutva believes that the world is a family,' he said. Why then equate organizing society with organizing Hindus? 'Like an examination in which we solve the easy questions first and then pick the hard ones later . . . we will organize those first who admit they are Hindus . . . There might be people who consider us enemy . . . our objective is not to finish them but to take them along . . . that is Hindutva in the real sense.'[32]

2) Territory and Citizenship

> 'Mera aapka nata khoon ke rang se juda hai, aapke passport ke rang se nahin. Jitne adhikar Narendra Modi ke hain, utne aapke bhi [Our relations are based on the ties of our blood, not on the colour of our passports. All the rights that Narendra Modi has, you do too].'
>
> —Narendra Modi, addressing people of Indian descent in London, 13 November 2015[33]

> 'India shall remain a natural home for persecuted Hindus and they shall be welcome to seek refuge here.'
>
> —BJP manifesto, 2014

In the Hindutva Strategic Doctrine, the idea of what is foreign and what is not derives from the foundational principles of political Hinduism, i.e. Hindutva. The Hindutva view of territory transcends the modern nation-state of India that came into being in 1947, and imagines a cultural world where Hindu, Sikh, Buddhist and Jain heritages expand into the west and the east, areas that are part of other sovereign nations now. The BJP in power, under Vajpayee to a limited extent and under Modi more aggressively, promoted the idea of India as a cultural expanse that is spread across continents, through the Indian diaspora. Modi addressed large gatherings of people of Indian origin living in various countries over his tenure, canvassing their support for Hindutva nationalism in India.

In the Nehruvian understanding, people of Indian origin, wherever they are, were expected to live as dedicated citizens of those countries. It is interesting to note how this view of extraterritorial nationalism squares with the notion of 'sacred land' that forms the basis of the Hindutva philosophy. According to Savarkar, Hindus are defined as those who consider India their fatherland and their holy land. '[T]he tie of common holyland has at times proved stronger than the claims of a Motherland [. . .] Look at the Mohammedans. Mecca to them is a sterner reality than Delhi or Agra,' he wrote in 'Hindutva', the 1923 treatise on the philosophy of political Hinduism.[34] Savarkar had made a distinction between a 'nation' and a 'state,' however. Hindus 'do not advance any special claims, privileges or rights . . . over and above the non-Hindu sections of Hindustan. Let the Indian state be purely Indian. Let it not recognise any invidious distinctions whatsoever as regards the franchise, public services, offices, taxation, on grounds of religion and race.'[35] Golwalkar, who was RSS chief, argued for lesser citizenship for non-Hindus. The RSS no longer holds up this view.

The definition of Hindu nation excludes the Muslim and Christian minorities from its ambit—even if they are born in India and India is their fatherland, what they consider holy land is outside the boundaries of India—and hence their being Indian is less authentic and their participation is non-essential in the national project. But Hindus who live outside the territory could be considered part of the Indian nation because they consider it their holy land and fatherland, though they may not live in it.

Hence, according to Hindutva, people who live in the US as US citizens are no less Indians as long as they consider India their fatherland and holy land. By the same logic, the patriotism of Muslims living in India who might have never stepped out of the country could be questioned. Therefore, the notion of territory includes being in control and command of the sacred land—that is, India—on one hand, while imagining and promoting the community as a global enterprise on the other.

Prime Minister Vajpayee started this process of assimilating the Indian diaspora as part of a nationalist agenda. He even added a new category of territory to accommodate non-resident nationalists of India—*karmabhoomi*, or workplace. 'India is your *matrubhoomi*, America your *karmabhoomi*, and you must work for both,' he told Indian–Americans in 2000.[36] The idea has caught on in Hindutva diaspora politics. Modi described South Africa as Gandhi's *karmabhoomi* when he visited the country as prime minister.

'We are changing the contours of diplomacy and looking at new ways of strengthening India's interests abroad,' said Ram Madhav, a former general secretary of the BJP and RSS leader. 'They can be India's voice even while being loyal citizens in those countries. That is the long-term goal behind the diaspora diplomacy. It is like the way the Jewish community looks out for Israel's interests in the United States.'[37]

Manmohan Singh as PM reached out to the Indian–American community for support on the India–US nuclear deal, but Modi brought the weight of cultural nationalism behind the diaspora pursuit. 'By focusing on blood ties and by repeatedly addressing ethnic Indians [abroad] as *deshvaasiyon* [those who live in India], not *pravaasi Bharatiyon* [overseas Indians], Modi is extending the idea of nationhood beyond the constitutional parameters. His courting of overseas Indians as part of the Indian nation is both exceptional and unambiguous,' observes Ashutosh Varshney, political scientist.[38] Three parameters define territoriality in the Hindutva Strategic Doctrine— notions of *pitrubhoomi/matrubhoomi* (fatherland/motherland), *punyabhoomi* (sacred land) and *karmabhoomi* (land of action), the first two based on Savarkar's exposition, and the third one to account for the seemingly contradictory nationalistic politics of Hindu diaspora communities spread all over the world, but particularly in the US. In 2020, the prime ministers of Australia, UK and Canada wished Deepavali as did the president and president-elect of the US—showing the expanding presence of the Hindu diaspora in powerful countries of the world. In 2020, a minister in New Zealand spoke an Indian language, Malayalam, in the country's parliament. Since 2016, at least three practising Hindus have been members of the US House of Representatives, though they are critics of Hindutva. We shall discuss this in detail in the next chapter.

The 2014 BJP manifesto clearly declared that India was the natural home for Hindus anywhere in the world, and Modi enunciated this principle in campaign speeches. 'There are two types of people who have come in—infiltrators and refugees. Those who are refugees are our family. It is the responsibility of all of India, whether Gujarat or Rajasthan, to rehabilitate them with all respect,' he said.[39]

The Hindutva Strategic Doctrine imagines India to be a natural homeland of all Hindus anywhere in the world, and the Modi government and the BJP state governments over recent years have sought to translate this into policy. In the US, the Trump administration had sought to make this distinction between Christian and Muslim refugees who sought asylum in America. In India, this differentiation has now been legislated, as the Citizenship Amendment Act passed by Indian Parliament in 2019. People belonging to minority communities, that is, Hindus, Jains, Sikhs, Buddhists, Parsis and Christians, from Afghanistan, Bangladesh and Pakistan, shall not be treated as illegal immigrants, according to the law, which offers them a fast track to Indian citizenship.[40] The BJP state government in Madhya Pradesh has a special scheme to rehabilitate minorities—read, non-Muslims—from Bangladesh.[41] The Centre has said a countrywide National Registry of Citizens will be prepared, to identify citizens. The registry is currently operational in the state of Assam, following a Supreme Court order.[42]

3) Military society

'India is being threatened by China and Pakistan [. . .] with rising concern over internal security, we should give top priority to military education to students to make India strong. Current education system is business oriented [. . .] Foreigners have adopted our education system and our policy makers are imitating theirs [. . .] This should be rectified.'

—Mohan Bhagwat, RSS chief, while addressing the platinum jubilee function of Bhonsala Military School, Nashik (founded in 1937 by B.S. Moonje who mentored the RSS founder, K.B. Hedgewar), in 2012[43]

The role of the military in society has been a topic of heated debates in democracies, including the US and India. Both India and the US do not have conscriptions like Israel has. In the US, the dangers of a standing army and its implications for centralized power was a question before its founding fathers; in India, the debate, in the early years, was more about keeping the civilian authority over the military firm and unchallenged. The idea of citizen–soldier, someone who is willing to fight, not primarily for money but for a national purpose, has been around in the US since its founding. A standing army was considered a tool of oppression of the state; defence was considered a social responsibility, Phil Klay points out in a superb essay, 'The Citizen-Soldier: Moral Risk and the Modern Military'.[44]

The idea of an all-of-society approach to the defence of the country existed in the US as a signature of its democracy. A civil–military separation and hierarchy has been part of India's democratic evolution. The founding principles of the Indian Republic balked at the principle of militarization of society, which would find reflection in a statement by Arun Jaitley as defence minister in the first year of the Modi government in 2014 in Parliament, that reflected the pre-existing institutional wisdom. 'Military training to all the youth of the country may also lead to militarization of an entire nation. With our socio-political and economic conditions, it is highly undesirable, lest some of the unemployed youth trained in military skills join the ranks of the undesirable elements.'[45]

But the idea of compulsory military training through various routes remains an influential thought. In 2018, the Parliamentary Standing Committee on Defence headed by Major General B.C. Khanduri (retd.) of the BJP recommended five years of compulsory military service for those aspiring for gazetted jobs in the state and central governments.[46] In the same year, the Modi government had started discussions on a national programme to give military training to a million boys and girls each year. 'According to the proposal, the scheme will instill values of nationalism, discipline and self-esteem into the youth, which, in turn, will help make India a "Vishwaguru" (read a universal leader) and achieve Prime Minister Narendra Modi's vision of New India 2022.' As of end 2020, the proposal did not go any further.[47]

Earlier in this chapter, we discussed the fascination of Hindutva leaders for the warrior culture. This idea recurs throughout its history. In the 1970s, Vajpayee travelled to Ghazni in Afghanistan, from where Mahmud of Ghazni came and plundered Somnath temple in the twelfth century. He could succeed because of 'our internal splits . . . the king will fight, the *kshatriya* will fight . . . (but) we have banned the big section of our society from fighting,'[48] the future PM would conclude. 'Savarkar popularized the slogan "Hinduize all politics and militarize Hindudom", and urged Hindus to enlist in the armed forces in order to learn the arts of war.'[49] 'The militarisation and industrialisation of the Hindus must constitute our immediate objective,' according to Savarkar.[50]

Mass military training, bordering on conscription, development of military hardware and forward deployment of forces are part of the Hindutva conception of a militaristic India. The idea of citizen-soldier gives birth to the idea of militias that remain embedded in Indian society. This is connected to the notion of an enemy that is living within the body of the nation. Savarkar was upfront that Hindus must get military training to deal with internal threats to the nation.[51]

A corollary to a military society is a military state. The idea that a formidable military build-up cannot wait until the country progresses economically and socially is central to the Hindutva Strategic Doctrine. Proponents of Hindutva have argued for the last several decades that to protect the nation and claim its true place on the global stage, a strong and expanding military that projects power forward into the Indian Ocean rather than maintaining a defensive posture as designed by the Congress governments was necessary. The Bharatiya Jana Sangh (BJS), the political wing of the RSS prior to the BJP, also maintained that a strong military must precede the other development priorities. This was the inverse of the Nehruvian view. The Congress also believed that India would have to be independent and self-reliant in defence matters, but it gave precedence to economic development.

As early as 1962, a BJS resolution called for raising the strength of the Indian Army to 2 million soldiers and building an air force with 5000 planes.[52]

Preparedness is not limited to raising a professional defence force, but it is an all-of-society approach.

A militarist culture has now seeped into the Indian public discourse, accompanying the hyper-nationalism. A public willingness to glorify the army, overlook its faults and haunt anyone raising critical questions as 'anti-national' is far too visible. '[T]he whole issue of nationalism has been brought to the fore. The army as an institution has been accorded a halo—that it can do nothing wrong and nobody should criticise it,' writes H.S. Panag, retired lieutenant general of the Indian Army.[53] This militarization of society and politics can also be seen in the controversial statements of former Army chief and India's first Chief of Defence Staff Bipin Rawat, which have come under criticism from political scientists.[54] Rawat's appointment itself was controversial in 2016 when the Modi government handpicked him, ignoring three officers senior to him in the hierarchy.[55]

To attribute India's military modernization and the push for new weaponry to a Hindutva Strategic Doctrine might sound implausible at first glance. But the rise of Hindutva has also militarized social discourse.

4) India as a Superpower

'The Prime Minister [Modi] urged them to use this unique opportunity to help India position itself in a leading role, rather than just a balancing force, globally. Urging them to shed old mindsets, the Prime Minister said they should be quick to adapt to changing global situations.'

—A press release on Narendra Modi's address to heads of missions in New Delhi, 7 February 2015[56]

Hindutva is guided by a sense of the inevitability of India's rise as a global power. '[The] second essential of Hindutva puts the estimate of our latent powers of national cohesion and greatness yet higher. No country in the world, with the exception of China [. . .] is peopled by a race so homogenous, yet so ancient and yet so strong both numerically and vitally [. . .] The Americans [. . .] are decidedly left behind. Mohammedans are no race nor are the Christians,' wrote Savarkar.[57]

The Nehruvian model, which the proponents of Hindutva claim has been delinked from the civilizational foundation of India, failed to achieve this objective. 'Shedding old mindsets' has become a motto. India was content being a balancing power earlier, but now it wants to be a 'leading power', according to S. Jaishankar.[58]

It is not that the Nehruvian vision had no ambition regarding India's global role. It was more about being a voice for the colonized Third World countries, against imperialism.

Nehru's global ambition for India was not about turning the country into a military power or an expansionist power; rather, it focused on human development. Vijaya Lakshmi Pandit, Nehru's sister and India's ambassador to the USSR from 1947 to 1949, told the then US ambassador to Moscow that she and her brother believed that 'India's role in the family of nations should be modest and relatively humble'. She said that while most Indian leaders realized that their 'natural alignment' was with the West, they did not want to be caught in Cold War politics and Nehru felt that a nation 'still in swaddling clothes' should not talk about 'military preparation in the event of war'.[59]

What would be the vision for India today according to Nehruvian thinking? Former Union minister and Congress leader P. Chidambaram, while speaking at the K. Subrahmanyam Memorial Lecture on 6 February 2013, stated that the basis of a robust strategic culture must be economic growth and social inclusion, which could lead India to become a 'middle income country'. He was the home minister of India then. 'Some think that the value of growth is overstated and that we would be better off if we pursued not the goal of growth, but other goals such as cultural nationalism or debt-driven egalitarianism.'[60] He went on to say:

> Today, we have a choice. We have a choice between becoming the third largest economy of the world and a middle income country, or becoming one of the largest economies of the world that muddles along with the bulk of its people trapped in a life of low income, poor quality, high morbidity and great inequality. Needless to say, the two models of India will have very different consequences for national security.[61]

Both Nehruvian and Hindutva visions might account for linkages between the external, global environment and the internal one in the country, and reflect on how to manage the global situation to India's advantage. But these visions are dissimilar because of their divergent understandings of India's national interest and how it is advanced. For instance, they would both see the rise of global Islamist terrorism as a challenge to India's security. So, while the Nehruvian model would use the poverty-combating role of strategic policy and domestic policies that are inclusive and responsive to keep social divisions in check and make India insular to the lure of Islamism, the Hindutva Strategic Doctrine would favour eliminating Islamist threats through an assertion of a consolidated Hindu society and strong military tactics.

5) India as Vishwa Guru

'Swami Vivekananda's words have come true, I see it here. His dream was for India to become Vishwa Guru. I am seeing it here. Mother India has actually become Vishwa Guru.'

—Modi, addressing the Indian diaspora in Sydney, Australia[62]

Modi, Bhagwat and other leaders of the RSS family refer to the idea of India as Vishwa Guru or global teacher. This is a staple of RSS thinking. Vishwa Guru implies the entire world's acceptance of Hindu wisdom as universally relevant and important. What does it mean?

Swami Vivekananda had a vision for promoting Indian spirituality in the West. 'This is the great ideal before us [. . .]

the conquest of the whole world by India [. . .] Up, India, and conquer the world with your spirituality!' he said.[63] The freedom-fighter-turned-mystic Sri Aurobindo believed that India's national revival must spread the universal truth of Hinduism around the globe. 'The protection and upraising of the world of the Hindu religion, that is the work before us [. . .] This is one religion that can triumph over materialism by including and anticipating the discoveries of science and the speculations of philosophy,' he said in 1909.[64]

Vivekananda, Sri Aurobindo and Gandhi envisioned a post-industrial world that would come to appreciate the values of limited consumption, human–nature oneness and other ancient Indian thoughts. They critiqued Western civilization, driven as it were by industrialization and consumption. Current Hindutva proponents draw from all of them and claim the legacy of universal values and brotherhood in an extraordinary act of deftness. A Hindu vision of globalization and human development is what Modi delivered in Davos at the World Economic Forum in January 2018.

The change in India's position on climate change under Modi is instructive of this point. A Nehruvian understanding led India to talk about justice and fairness in the emerging climate regime; Nehru was an admirer of Hinduism, but he did not think its promotion on the global stage was his duty. His model sought to claim a global leadership position for India by advocating disarmament, global justice and a more egalitarian system internationally and domestically, mindful of cultural and religious diversity. The Hindutva view, on the other hand, saw climate consciousness as global acceptance of Hinduism's ancient wisdom, and Modi was quick to ratify the Paris climate treaty.

One has to read Modi's assertions about India's emergence as Vishwa Guru in conjunction with his references to the changing world situation. Global capitalism and liberal democracy are facing a major crisis of credibility and sustainability. Modi's recurring references to how the global situation opens space for India's leadership derives from a conviction in Hinduism's role in the changing circumstances. In a deft, 'utilitarian' deployment of Hinduism by Hindutva, the successful promotion of International Yoga Day under the auspices of the UN is another step towards this Vishwa Guru status—a point that Jaishankar elucidates in *The India Way*: 'Introduction of Indian vocabulary and concepts in global diplomacy.'

India's emergence as Vishwa Guru is also essential to dealing with the crises of modern society such as disease, stress, violence and drug abuse.

'The problems of modern lifestyles are well known. People suffer from stress-related ailments, lifestyle-related diseases like diabetes and hypertension. We have found ways to control communicable diseases, but the burden of disease is shifting to non-communicable diseases. Young people who are not at peace with themselves seek refuge in drugs and alcohol. There is ample evidence that practicing yoga helps combat stress and chronic conditions. If the body is a temple of the mind, yoga creates a beautiful temple,'[65] Modi said on yoga, a theme that repeatedly appears in his speeches, including at the UN.

Hindutva has historically had a deep-rooted distrust of capitalism and Western dominance. It embraced technology and accepted the notion of racially and religiously homogenous nationalisms that evolved with industrial capitalism, but had a more complex relationship with modern science and the rationality associated with modernism.

The Vishwa Guru notion of 'India's Manifest Destiny' can occasionally lead to brazen claims. For instance, while addressing a gathering of doctors and other professionals at the inauguration of the Sir H.N. Reliance Foundation Hospital and Research Centre in Mumbai, Modi said on 25 October 2014, 'We can feel proud of what our country achieved in medical science at one point of time.' He went on to say:

> We all read about Karna in the Mahabharata. If we think a little more, we realize that the Mahabharata says Karna was not born from his mother's womb. This means that genetic science was present at that time. That is why Karna could be born outside his mother's womb [. . .] We worship Lord Ganesha. There must have been some plastic surgeon at that time who got an elephant's head on the body of a human being and began the practice of plastic surgery [. . .] What I mean to say is that we are a country which had these capabilities. We need to regain these.[66]

It is the responsibility of Hindus to ensure that India becomes Vishwa Guru, according to RSS chief Bhagwat. 'If India were to become world leader [Vishwa Guru], Hindus will have to take responsibility . . . India is the only country for Hindus.' He called on Hindus to remain united. 'We do not want anyone to remain weak. We want them to become able and turn into givers from takers.'[67]

Hindutva does understand ancient wisdom of the land as a repository of power and believes that India is destined to command global leadership in the future—its Manifest Destiny—but it does not believe in eternal patience and timeless goals as virtues in strategic planning—the Hindu weaknesses, according to Tanham and Chellaney. While it has a tactical and operational understanding of how much the domestic political environment and the international system may allow the pursuit of such a global ambition with far more patience than Western strategists can comprehend, the Sangh Parivar's knowledge system has short timelines. As explained earlier, the entire idea of political Hinduism is about overcoming what is perceived as the weakness of Hinduism.

While India's march to become Vishwa Guru is part of a long-term plan, the nation must have no problem seeking technology and weapons from wherever it can and hence, consider America a legitimate partner.

Hindutva imagination is not about rejecting technology or communication, but about making a global presence of the Hindu civilization as an antidote to the present-day crisis of capitalism. Modi is a globalist, but not one who is guided by the principles of free market as understood in the West. He is a Hindutva globalist who seeks to overcome the failures of market-driven globalism.

6) India–Pakistan Friction as a Hindu–Muslim Problem

'If BJP loses in Bihar by mistake, then victory–defeat will be in Bihar, but crackers will be burst in Pakistan.'

—Amit Shah, while campaigning for the 2015
Bihar assembly elections[68]

'Speak to Pakistan in the language Pakistan understands.'

—Narendra Modi about the 2008 Mumbai terror
attacks when asked in 2013 what he would do if
he were the prime minister[69]

The propagation of Hindu ideals as a balm for bruised societies in the West facing brutal inequities of capitalism and marauding

Islamist terrorism is one side of the Hindutva strategic theory. When applied to domestic questions, it tilts towards racial supremacy.

While Hinduism as articulated by its non-Hindutva proponents did not imagine an enemy to define it, Savarkar's Hindutva breaks from Vivekananda's Hinduism by definitively identifying its enemies.

The idea of territory and community, in the Hindutva version of nationalism, does not overlap with the boundaries as defined by the modern nation state of the Republic of India, as discussed earlier. India is a cultural expanse, and the country as it stands today is only the centre of it. This seemingly inchoate, but fundamentally coherent, understanding of territory and community is most emphatically articulated in Hindutva's view of India's relations with Pakistan.

In this telling, Indian Muslims become inseparable from Pakistan, the epitome of Islamist nationalism that divided Mother India and continues to threaten it.

Hindutva strategists have understood Pakistan as an extension of Indian Muslims outside the boundaries of the Indian Republic and Indian Muslims as an inward extension of the outward enemy named Pakistan.

Jaswant Singh, defence minister under A.B. Vajpayee and one of the BJP's strategic thinkers, says about the partition of the subcontinent:

And thus was fractured the great unity of this ancient land; a divide could simply not bring any peace in its wake; it compartmentalized and then tightly sealed the Hindu–Muslim animosities; cementing festering grudges into near permanent hostilities; what was domestic (Hindu–Muslim) became international (India–Pakistan). We made global our domestic disagreements. For Pakistan it became a policy plank: 'perpetual and induced hostility towards India that became its premiere state polity'.[70]

In 1973, in his foreword for the BJS documents on defence and external affairs, former prime minister A.B. Vajpayee said that the Congress sought to end communal strife by letting Partition take place. 'The Hindu–Muslim conflict had only become enlarged into an Indo–Pak confrontation. Pakistan's aggression in Jammu and Kashmir State continued. In East Pakistan (now Bangladesh), Hindus were being decimated in a systematic manner. There was widespread discontent in the public mind regarding the Government's Pakistan policy, which in effect was only an extension of Congress's Muslim appeasement policy,' wrote Vajpayee.[71]

In a resolution in 1961, the BJS said in a paradoxically titled document, 'Recognition of Indo–Pak Interdependence'[72], how India was giving concession after concession to Pakistan without protecting its own national interest. It described Pakistan's policy towards India thus:

To keep demonstrating both in its external and internal policies that it can force India to give it more and more facilities regarding funds and land as well as in other respects, in order to attract the loyalty of the Indian Muslims to Pakistan. The purpose of this is to establish in the Muslim mind an ambition of Muslim rule. The continuous driving out of Hindus from Pakistan is part of this policy.

In 1961, the BJS raised concerns about rail links between India and Pakistan in the following words: 'The agreement regarding a direct rail link would increase the capacity of

Pakistan to send spies and arms into India, as also to mislead Indian Muslims, among whom a section has already started pro-Pakistan activities.'

In a resolution in 1962, the BJS said of citizens with 'doubtful loyalties', 'Citizens Defence Schemes should be enlarged and strengthened. Citizens whose loyalty is unquestioned should be allowed to keep arms [. . .] Persons with doubtful loyalties must be scrupulously excluded from defence industries and from all works related to defence and the army,'[73] an insinuation that there is a Fifth Column that could turn against India, which is reflected in Shah's statement on Bihar elections and Modi's on Gujarat elections from 2017, when he said that Pakistan was trying to make Congress leader Ahmed Patel the chief minister. Savarkar's Hindutva is clear as to those who could not be fully part of the national body—Muslims and Christians.

Pakistan is also an irreconcilable enemy that cannot understand any language other than of might and violence—which is reflected in Modi's statement at the beginning of this section— 'Speak to Pakistan in the language Pakistan understands.' This aspect of the Hindutva doctrine has remained intact for decades. In December 2008, Arun Shourie—an articulate member of the BJP leadership until he was sidelined by Modi—argued for a more aggressive retaliatory policy towards Pakistan to punish it for promoting terrorism in India. During a debate in the Rajya Sabha following the 2008 Mumbai terror attacks, he said:

'No war is won with minimal force. It is won by overwhelming the enemy [. . .] Not an eye-for-an-eye, not a tooth-for-a-tooth. That is completely wrong. For an eye, both eyes! For a tooth, the whole jaw! Unless India has that determination and that clarity, we will continue to bleed like this all the time.[74]

As prime minister, Vajpayee made a significant departure from this policy as he pursued peace with Pakistan and even facilitated the travel of Kashmiri separatists to Pakistan. How can we explain this? First, Vajpayee did not have the parliamentary majority to be a fully Hindutva prime minister. The BJP had gained power with the support of other parties and had to suspend its ultra-nationalistic agenda of pushing for a uniform civil code and withdrawing the special status given to Kashmir in the Indian Constitution. Second, he was constrained by his own partial commitment to the Nehruvian strategic thought at some level, a point that many proponents of Hindutva admit. Vajpayee was considered to be a 'soft face' of Hindutva. So was his key lieutenant, Jaswant Singh.[75]

The focus on combating the internal enemy is no less than dealing with the external enemy. In 1947, Golwalkar thought 'all Muslims should leave India'.[76] The RSS has since revised this position and its current chief Bhagwat has said there cannot be Hindutva that excluded Muslims, as noted earlier.

7) Kashmir: Where Hindu Nation Meets Jihad

'Today we are powerful and Pakistan is weak. That is the only solution to Kashmir.'

—Amit Shah, home minister of India[77]

Kashmir and many parts of India's eastern frontier were accorded special status when the Republic of India was born in 1950. These regions are predominantly populated by minority religious or ethnic groups who feared their rights and identity might be overwhelmed in a Hindu majority India. Separatism took root in several of these regions, turning violent in places, including in Kashmir.

One of the foundational principles of the BJS, the forebear of the BJP, was 'full integration of Kashmir to India'[78] by nullifying the special status the state was granted in the Indian Constitution. Since then, abrogation of Article 370 remained a contentious question in Indian politics. It was a key plank for the BJS, and later the BJP. Kashmir epitomized the appeasement of Muslims—we saw earlier in the BJS resolutions and statements from its leaders that they viewed alleged special concessions to Indian Muslims and an alleged soft line on Pakistan as part of an appeasement policy that the Congress pursued. In 2019, two months after winning an absolute majority in the lower house of Parliament, the BJP revoked the special status of Jammu and Kashmir, and reorganized it into two union territories under direct Central rule. Article 370 remains in the Constitution as dead letter. Not only separatist groups, even regional parties such as the National Conference (NC) and Peoples Democratic Party (PDP) are disengaged from any potential conversation on resolving the issue.

The Sangh Parivar and the Modi government reject any role for Pakistan in the resolution of Kashmir. Pakistan claims Kashmir, based on the two-nation theory that Hindus and Muslims are separate nations.

While Vajpayee made the most daring outreach to Pakistan on resolving the Kashmir issue by initiating talks with separatist leaders and Pakistan, and facilitating travel of the former to Pakistan and the part of Kashmir controlled by it, in one of its first measures, the Modi government ruled out any role for Pakistan in Kashmir. The Hindutva Strategic Doctrine allows no leniency to separatist leaders and does not believe that Kashmir is a political problem to be resolved through negotiations. The BJP's alliance with the PDP in Jammu and Kashmir from 2015 to 2018 June—the latter is a regional party that argues for more autonomy for the state—had a common agenda, but for the first time in the history of the conflict, the government at the Centre adopted a policy of not talking with separatists.

The BJP–PDP common agenda formed in 2015 said it would follow in the footsteps of Vajpayee and that 'the coalition government will facilitate and help initiate a sustained and meaningful dialogue with all internal stakeholders, which will include all political groups irrespective of their ideological views and predilections'.[79] That gave the state government—'coalition government'— the space to talk to separatists, a BJP functionary explained to me in February 2015 when the agenda was finalized. 'The Centre won't talk to separatists; the State government can, if they want to,' he told me.[80]

Over the first three years, the Modi government adhered to its position that it would not talk with separatists and there was no role for Pakistan in the resolution of Kashmir. In October 2017, the party appeared to change course and appointed former director of the Intelligence Bureau Dineshwar Sharma as its interlocutor for Jammu and Kashmir, after three years of massive military operations against militants and protesters. His role was quietly ended by sending him as administrator in Lakshadweep, India's island territory in the Arabian Sea.

Madhav, the Sangh Parivar ideologue, explained the Modi government's approach towards Kashmir thus:

> Militancy needs to be tackled with a tough hand, which we are doing. Public protest, such as stone pelting, is the second dimension of Kashmir problem, which has been strongly dealt with while ensuring there are no casualties. Third dimension includes businessmen, politicians, so-called

NGO groups, who are overt support mechanism for the militants and anti-India activists. We adopted a legal mechanism to tackle them—through the NIA [National Investigation Agency] and other agencies. The fourth is development activities. Now we added this fifth dimension [of sustained dialogue].[81]

Though Madhav has since ceased to be a BJP general secretary, this policy continues as Central agencies move aggressively against not only separatists, but also mainstream regional parties such as the PDP and the NC.

Greater autonomy for the state is a demand of both the regional parties. The Modi government is not open to the demand and thinks demands for autonomy echo Pakistan's position. During the 2019 Lok Sabha election campaign, Modi said the opposition Congress spoke the language of Pakistan on Kashmir. 'The Congress says Article 370 won't be removed. The language of the Congress's "Dhakosala Patra" [a term used by PM Modi to describe the election manifesto of the Opposition party] is the same as Pakistan's. They have promised to hold talks with chaotic forces in Jammu and Kashmir. Pakistan wants the same thing to happen,' he said.[82]

In August 2019, India stripped Jammu and Kashmir of its special status and its statehood. Severe measures were put in place to prevent any flare-up. The government said the move would promote investment in the region. Movement of people into Kashmir, which was restricted earlier, has now been freed up, raising fears of a potential demographic overrun of the region.[83]

In the Nehruvian construct, Kashmir is the crown of a secular country, a territorial and social embodiment of a multi-religious state—a Muslim-majority state with a culturally harmonized Hindu minority in a Hindu-majority country. In the Hindutva Strategic Doctrine, Kashmir is the place where Hindus are victims of Islamic oppression. Since 1989, 1,70,000 Hindus—who lived in peace amid Muslims for centuries—have been hounded out with the rise of separatism and terrorism. Kashmir epitomizes the victimhood of India's Hindu majority; it is here that Hindus are threatened, are fleeing and being harassed in their own homeland. It is here that the Muslim appeasement of earlier regimes that were guided by the meek and pacifist notion of Hinduism surrendered the interests of the nation.

The sweeping spread of global jihadism made the Sangh Parivar position acceptable—or at least tolerable—to the rest of the world. In the early days of insurgency in Kashmir, the US was ever willing to bring pressure on India about the issue. But the rise of Islamist terrorism across the world seems to have snuffed out global sympathy for Kashmiri separatism. The interest of Western countries in the Kashmir dispute has diminished. Pakistan tried to raise the issue in the UN several times since 2014, but no other country supported it. But in 2018, with continuing unrest and military retaliation in the Valley, the UN called for an international inquiry into the human rights situation in Jammu and Kashmir, for the first time in the history of the conflict.[84] The end of Kashmir's special status in 2019, followed by a clampdown on political activity, attracted little attention from the Trump administration, though the Democrats raised it with India. The Biden administration might be more vocal, but only slightly more, in expressing its view. India's ongoing and bloody encounter with jihad has come as validation of the Hindutva strategic thinking.

8) View of 'Expansionist China'

> 'China should shed its expansionist policy and forge bilateral
> ties with India for peace, progress and prosperity of both
> the nations.'

> —Modi, during the 2014 campaign[85]

Pakistan is more of a nuisance that can be dealt with once the
right amount of force is applied and national determination
is demonstrated. China, on the other hand, is considered a
bigger, more consequential and dangerous rival to India.

India's global ambitions, based on its civilizational wisdom,
when projected towards its eastern neighbours and into the
Pacific and the Indian Ocean—where India's historic links are
organic—come into conflict with China.

Savarkar has explained why, of all countries, China is the
only one that can rival India. 'China alone of the present comity
of nations is almost as richly gifted with the geographical, racial
and cultural essentials as the Hindus are.'[86]

Walter K. Andersen and Shridhar D. Damle write in
detail about the Sangh view of China as expansionist that has
evolved over decades. While Nehru represented the thought
that the shared experience of colonialism made India and
China potential partners in the world order emerging after the
Second World War, an opposite view was already in existence.
His deputy Sardar Vallabhbhai Patel, who is considered one
of their own by the Hindutva school, had thought of China
differently: 'Chinese irredentism and communist imperialism
are different from the expansionism and imperialism of the
western powers. The former has a cloak of ideology which
makes it ten times more dangerous.'[87] Golwalkar considered

China as a threat and wanted India to work for free Tibet as a precaution. 'For that, if it becomes necessary to cross our frontiers, let us do it without the least hesitation.'[88]

So when the Vajpayee government wrote to US President Bill Clinton that its 1998 nuclear test was to push back against China, and its defence minister George Fernandes described China as 'enemy number one', they were shaped by decades of ideological understanding. Hindutva believes that economic considerations and trade alliances cannot necessarily prevent a flare-up in the Indo–Pacific. The current American leadership in the Indo–Pacific would end sooner or later, the Hindutva school had predicted. America cannot be relied on for securing India's interest in the region to its east, and it will therefore have to seek its own alliances and military plans to deal with the threat posed by China.

The notion of free nations in Asia forming a coalition against Chinese aggression appeared in a Jana Sangh resolution in December 1959:

> What is wanted in the present crisis brought about by Communist China's expansionist ambition is that India must follow a resolute policy of herself fighting the aggression, seek the moral sympathy and cooperation with free nations of Asia [who are also feeling concerned at China's design and strategy] to create a United Front with them against Communist China's new imperialism.[89]

Governments prior to Modi's adopted a 'Look East' policy, which sought to build primarily on economic ties with the countries to India's east. The Modi government has replaced 'Look East' with 'Act East'. While the act of merely 'looking' might be considered passive, defensive and pacifist as a strategic approach, 'acting' connotes an active and forward-moving approach.

Savarkar argued that the Indian Ocean region was 'India's moat', implying that any transgressions into it could be a major threat. In his first foreign policy speech during the 2014 election campaign, Modi termed China an adversary with expansionist ambitions and criticized the Congress for being 'timid' in challenging it.[90]

Just as the rise of global jihad allowed Hindutva proponents a certain claim of validity regarding their own views on Islam, the aggressive posturing of China too appears to bear out Hindutva views. The Trump nationalism in the US also took a dim view of China, and considered it a threat to the US. Biden has limited scope of reviewing it, despite this long association with the promotion of US–China ties.

The Nehruvian notion that there could be common interests between India and China, both emerging powers, collapsed in the last decade. As China decided that its interests were not aligned with India's, there were no common goals to pursue. It began to demonstrate its global ambitions more assertively, often at the cost of India. The financial crisis in the West in 2008 was an inflection point in its behaviour globally. The collapse of India–China cooperation was illustrated most starkly as both parted ways on climate negotiations.[91] And since then, it has been a downslide.

The Hindutva doctrine sees China as a worthy rival, admiring its growth and success. Conversely, the Chinese model is close to what it would like to emulate for its own growth—a highly centralized and powerful state, embedded in civilizational pride, and pursuing its principles and interests aggressively within the country and outside to create a sui generis governance and developmental model.

But there are many tactical limits to any aggressive posturing towards China, one key factor being America's fluctuating attitudes towards Beijing, apart from India's own limitations. Modi's efforts to mend ties with China at a summit with Jinping in Wuhan in April 2018 and Chennai in October 2019 were guided by this reality. 'Exercises in pure realism,' according to S. Jaishankar.[92] We discuss this in Chapter 4.

9) US–India: Alliance of the Century

'For too long, India and the US have looked at each other across Europe and the Atlantic. When I look towards the east, I see the western shores of the United States. That tells us that we belong to the same vast region. It is a region of great dynamism, but also many unsettled questions. Its future will be vital for our two countries and the destiny of this world. And our relationship will be indispensable in shaping its course.'

—Modi, while addressing the Indo–US CEO Forum in
New Delhi in 2015[93]

The Hindutva doctrine's understanding of India's relations with the US is the one point that many of Modi's supporters on the right and the critics on the left agree on. They all agree that there is bonhomie between Modi and the US and that he has a special affinity for the country. However, the ideological foundations of this relationship in the Hindutva doctrine have not been sufficiently explored.

Values and interests are the two components of global ties, it is often said. The shared values between Hindutva and the West in general is a complicated topic—while Hindutva admires Western militarism and nationalism, it is less enthusiastic about Western institutions of democracy and governance. According to one Hindutva thinker, India's early leaders, 'instead of creating a socio-economic and political paradigm of governance drawn from the civilizational consciousness of India . . . tried to follow whatever was being practised in this or that Western country.'[94]

Hindutva has historically considered the US to be an imperial power. 'Jana Sangh has been consistently of the view that the superpowers USA and the USSR are in collusion or competition to carve out spheres of influence and to make India a "cockpit of intrigues".'[95] Consequently, the relations with the US were to be pragmatic and based on common interests—or common enemies—without undermining the strategic autonomy of the country. America's support for Pakistan and the Sangh Parivar's belief that it supported Christian missionary activities in India only added to a nagging distrust over decades. American Christian charity, Compassion International (CI), was forced to discontinue its activities in India in 2017 on the suspicion that it promoted religious conversion.[96]

Such instances do not mean that India and the US have no common ground. On the contrary, the prospects and the necessity of a strong India–US partnership are evident and the Hindutva Strategic Doctrine is committed to it. While the question of convergence of values remains complicated, there is a near total convergence of interests in two primary areas—combating the rise of China and Islamism.

Hindutva believes that in the fight against Islamism, the US and India are allies. In fact, this has been an argument that Jaswant Singh, India's interlocutor for talks with the US between 1998 and 2000, made to Strobe Talbott in 2000. Talbott was Bill Clinton's interlocutor for talks with India and Singh was Vajpayee's. This conversation took place immediately after Al-Qaeda bombed American embassies in Africa on 7 August 1998, triggering retaliatory bombing against bin Laden targets in Afghanistan—the early years of global jihad. Singh considered India to be a natural partner of the West and Israel in the fight against Islamism, seeing it as a civilizational clash.

Talbott writes in his book *Engaging India: Diplomacy, Democracy and the Bomb* that Singh was trying to convince the US that 'a nuclear-armed India was a natural ally of the United States in the struggle against Islamic fundamentalism'.

> I also found troublesome, the way Islam fit into Jaswant's world view [. . .] the way it seemed inherently at odds with his concept of Hindu civilization. By implication, while Parsees, Christians and others qualified as welcome additions to the Indian melting pot, Muslims did not . . . What concerned me, in hearing it from Jaswant, was what it implied about the BJP's ideology and therefore about the party's approach to governance . . . it meant that there were surely many who held more primitive and virulent forms of this view.[97]

Such a view may be more acceptable to the Republicans on the American side, but Democrats would not expend their political capital with India in confronting it. On the second aspect of convergence with the US, Chinese assertiveness, the Hindutva doctrine is more circumspect.

According to Ram Madhav:

> When the US Secretary of Defence Aston Carter called at the Shangri La dialogue this year [2016] for the emergence of an inclusive 'principled security network' that 'represents the next wave in Asia–Pacific Security', we immediately

lapped it up. Some scholars started saying that India would be not merely a participant in that 'principled security network', but will lead it. Nobody sat up and asked Carter as to what was the 'principle' that he was referring to. Carter is gone today, and with him the 'principle' that he was talking about. Trump's foreign policy is going to be violently different from that of Obama, Hillary and Carter.[98]

A third area of common interest is the presence of a large Indian diaspora in the US, which is a strong support base of Hindutva. The Hindutva doctrine seeks to galvanize the influence of Indian–Americans, Hindu Americans to be precise, and influence US state policies in India's favour.

India–US ties, according to the Hindutva Strategic Doctrine, are hence based on shared notions of an enemy rather than shared values. It is a different matter that both values and interests are being recast in both countries. There is also the view in the backdrop that liberalism is on the decline.

Proponents of Hindutva shared the Nehruvian scepticism of the West, but at the same time, maintained a more pragmatic approach. The retreat of a West-led world order is necessary for India's rise, but India wants to rise under the wing of the US, and not by questioning it. According to Jaishankar, 'Questioning the 1945 order is important, but a task to be handled with considerable delicacy.'[99] Hindutva strategy is not blind to western caution in its support for India. 'The broad approach was to keep India in play, and yet to also keep it in check. An unstable or weak India was as undesirable as a strong and domineering one. It was, in truth, a Goldilocks approach to the Indian porridge—not too hot, nor too cold, needing some effort to get it just right.'[100]

What India is looking for from the West, in the era of Hindutva, is not a subordinate partnership but a new equilibrium. '. . . there is also the fact that the evolution of the Indian polity has brought out its societal characteristics more sharply than before. As it begins to define itself more clearly, there would be an inevitable period of argumentation and adjustment . . . it will be about rebalancing as that is what nationalism in global affairs is hastening.'[101]

Hindutva is resolute in its pursuit of broad and deep collaboration with the US. That is India's route to progress and growth. Like other Asian powers, Japan first and China second, it wants India to fit in the global strategy of the US. In the next chapter we discuss this.

10) Israel as a Natural Ally

An alliance that the Hindutva doctrine has always pushed for, and the Modi government has taken forward, is the one with Israel. Arguing for full diplomatic relations with Israel, a Jana Sangh statement on foreign policy in 1973 said,[102] 'While India has consistently supported the Arab cause against Israel, the Arabs have reciprocated no such support to India in our disputes with Pakistan and China. Our Arab policy should be such as to make the Arabs understand that India's support cannot be taken for granted. Also, we should establish diplomatic relations with Israel.'

The Hindutva school has historically maintained that India's sympathies with the Palestinian movement were to get Muslim votes for the Congress party. In 1973, the party said, 'In this connection, it is obvious that New Delhi's West Asia policy is conditioned by the ruling party's obsession with the communal vote [. . .] The Jana Sangh urges the GoI to overhaul its West Asia policy.' Going by this logic, freed from the need to seek 'the communal vote', the BJP found the space to elevate relations with Israel as Modi became the first prime minister of India to visit Jerusalem.[103]

Addressing the UN General Assembly in September 2017, Israel's prime minister Netanyahu singled out Modi's visit, along with Trump's visit to Israel:

Hundreds of presidents, prime ministers, foreign ministers and other leaders have visited Israel, many for the first time. Of these many visits, two were truly historic. In May, President Trump became the first American president to include Israel in his first visit abroad. President Trump stood at the Western Wall, at the foot of the Temple Mount, where the Jewish people—or rather the Jewish people's temples—stood for nearly 1000 years, and when the president touched those ancient stones, he touched our hearts forever [. . .] In July, Prime Minister Modi became the first Indian prime minister to visit Israel. You may have seen the pictures. We were on a beach in Hadera, we rode together in a Jeep outfitted with a portable desalination device that some thriving Israeli entrepreneur invented. We took off our shoes, waded into the Mediterranean, and drank seawater that had been purified only a few minutes earlier. We imagined the endless possibilities for India, for Israel, for all of humanity.[104]

While the public display of affection for Israel is a component of Hindutva Strategic Doctrine, in yet another one of its contradictions, its proponents have also expressed admiration for Hitler and Nazism. Golwalkar, the RSS chief from 1940 to 1973, writes, 'To keep up the purity of the race and its culture, Germany shocked the world by her purging the country of the Semitic races—the Jews. Race pride at its highest has been manifested here [. . .] a good lesson for us in Hindusthan to learn and profit by.'[105] Both Golwalkar and Savarkar were also admirers of Zionism—the common point being their belief that only homogenous nations could be strong and prosperous.

Alongside the improvement of relations with Israel, India under Modi also deepened its ties with Arab countries, particularly the UAE and Saudi Arabia. With Israel and the UAE opening full diplomatic relations under a pact brokered by the Trump administration, one part of India's West Asian engagement has become less complicated. But another part, its critical ties with Iran, has become more complicated, and we discuss that in the last chapter.

In December 2017, India voted for a resolution in the UN General Assembly that criticized the Trump administration's decision to move the American embassy in Israel from Tel Aviv to Jerusalem, thereby recognizing the city contested by Palestinians as Israel's capital. Both this, and Modi's visit to Palestine are linked to the global leadership ambitions of the Hindutva doctrine. Blind loyalty to either Israel or America is detrimental to India's leadership prospects. Thus, India doesn't want to take sides in the Israel–Palestine disagreements, but play the role of a leader who has interests all over.

11) The Hindutva Rate of Growth

'I have said several times that my aim is to reform to transform. For me, reforms are those policies that transform the lives of ordinary citizens [. . .] we have taken a comprehensive package of reforms which go beyond mere economic reforms.'

—Modi, speaking to US business leaders at the US–India Business Council in Washington on 8 June 2016[106]

'In the name of openness, we have allowed subsidized products and unfair production advantages from abroad to prevail. And all the while, this was justified by the mantra of an open and globalized economy.'

—External Affairs Minister S. Jaishankar explaining the
Modi government's trade policy and doctrine of
self-reliance in November 2020[107]

The media, Indian and foreign, had characterized Modi as a market liberalizer in the early days of his premiership. By 2021, after six years of his rule as PM, this view has been tempered. Those who read him as a market liberalizer and a votary of open economy were extrapolating his pro-business measures as a state chief minister. They were entirely in the dark about the economic philosophy of Hindutva, which, as its other components, has evolved over decades. A more rigorous group of scholars has suggested that Hindutva does not have a clearly articulated economic vision. Walter K. Andersen and Shridhar D. Damle in *The RSS: A View to the Inside*, Vinay Sitapati in *The BJP Before Modi* and Dinesh Narayanan in *The RSS: And the Making of the Deep Nation*, tend to suggest so after surveying the range of opinions and practices that have emerged out of Hindutva leaders over the decades.

I would, however, argue that there is a defining core of Hindutva economic vision, though variations in theory and compromises in application are evident.

What is the Hindutva economic philosophy? In January 2018, Modi addressed the World Economic Forum in Davos where he sought the attention of the world's economic moguls to the fractures that have paralysed the world 'at various levels in various facets'. At the level of the individual, within nations, at the international level and between the present and the future. 'There is a divide between the requirements of today and the needs of conservation for future.'[108] He went on to offer ancient Indian thoughts on human interactions as a new template for globalization. He does not reject globalization, but critiques its current template.

Three months later, in April 2018, the RSS chief, Mohan Bhagwat, explained the Hindutva economic philosophy in rather lucid terms at the Bombay Stock Exchange. A commentary on Bhagwat's speech carried by the RSS mouthpiece, *Organiser*, said: 'Those who know RSS or study RSS are aware that RSS has been talking of an alternative economic model based on Indian genius and experience as both Communism and Capitalism have failed to solve the problems of the society in a holistic manner since 1960s.'[109] 'While West talks of survival of the fittest, we say upliftment of all, not some. We say a person should not just earn, but work as a trustee of wealth, and distribute wealth to the society. Live for others,' the RSS chief said.[110] Earlier in this chapter we discussed his views on the crisis of liberalism.

Modi's response to the question whether he is a Hindu nationalist or a pro-business chief minister at the beginning of the chapter is illustrative. Equally so are the quotes at the beginning of this section—on what reform and liberalization are according to his view, clearly making the case for a Hindutva model of market economy. This could be widely at variance with the checklist of measures that we usually associate with 'reforms'.

Modi has promoted Indian entrepreneurs and entrepreneurship, but to conflate it with any ideological commitment to market economy would be misleading. He has promoted business and trade in Gujarat, but to overlook the nationalist politics he has subscribed to all his life would lead to an incomplete understanding of a key figure in global politics today. His promotion of a national capitalist class too has to be seen in conjunction with the rest of his policies.

Numerous measures taken by the Modi government in the last six years are not aligned with the principles normally associated with a free market economy. These could actually be seen as market-distorting, statist and restrictive economic policies from neoliberal and classical liberal perspectives— whether it is demonetization, restriction on cattle trade, restrictions on drug prices and medical equipment, GST reforms or the expansion of tariffs, to name a few. This leads us to the conclusion that Hindutva understands and promotes market meritocracy and the rule of law within the framework of its notions of nationalism.

'Prime Minister Modi has made repeated statements about undertaking economic reforms [. . .] However, the rhetoric has far outpaced the reforms,' Senator Bob Corker,[111] the former Republican chairman of the US Senate foreign relations committee, said in early 2016, only two weeks ahead of Modi's speech to the US Congress where he spoke about 'overcoming the hesitations of history'.

What rhetoric was Senator Corker referring to? Modi spoke about reforms and economic growth during the 2014 campaign and fought on the promise of development. Senator Corker's remark in early 2016 was the turning of the tide in the American capital on the non-delivery of Modi's initial promise.

Modi did assure an environment conducive for business. But the fact is that he never promised or indicated that he would meet the expectations of the global industry in this regard. The expectations at the beginning were based on pending demands of US-based capital—to dismantle the existing intellectual property regime in India, to abolish compulsory licensing of drugs even if the situation warranted it, to dilute localization requirements in defence contracts and to dismantle public sector industries, or allow the hire and fire of workers and open up the market more, for global trade. Many people who claim to know Modi gave an impression that these were the things he would do as prime minister, as a reformist leader. These were what *others* said he would do. He never corrected them, because it suited him to create such an image.

When expectations of US investors and businesses were not met, Modi explained his understanding of 'reforms' to them with this criticism in mind. Reforms, he said, go beyond market. In that world view, demonetization and cattle protection are part of it.

A Hindutva view on interaction with the global market has always argued for technology and investment from outside, but not social, economic or religious ideas and finished products. Translated into policies, that means a 'pro-investment, but anti-trade posture.'[112] Though Modi would not state his market protection strategies in quite the way many other politicians across the globe would, the policy direction has been clear—it is to create jobs in India. The 'Make in India' initiative is the most vivid and forceful demonstration of this brand of politics—bring capital, bring technology, employ Indians, make in India, sell in India and abroad. The Atmanirbhar Bharat—Self-Reliant India—campaign that was launched after all countries ushered in nationalist responses to the COVID-19 pandemic was a further reinforcement of this idea. It is not isolationism, but an aversion to imports and an eagerness to export. The practicality of this formulation is a different question.

India has always been sceptical of unbridled market forces, and under Modi, it has only been more so. The idea of individualism-driven free market itself is foreign in the Sangh Parivar view. 'Generally speaking [. . .] a party resolved to rebuild Indian society on the basis of Bharatiya Sanskriti and Maryada [Indian culture and norms] as a modern and progressive nation cannot accept that an individual's right to amass wealth and spend on consumption should be absolute and untrammelled,' Vajpayee wrote in 1973.[113] In 1980, when the BJP was founded, Vajpayee said the party rejected the 'twin brothers of capitalism and communism'. 'One which ends equality and other freedom.'[114] The BJP and Congress governments, including one led by Vajpayee himself, opened the Indian market to a great extent in the last thirty years, but it will be difficult to argue that Modi's economic policies are out of line with the vision of a culturally oriented market as stated by Vajpayee four decades ago.

A routine template for understanding Hindutva politics is based on Hindutva versus development, the underlying assumption being that they are mutually exclusive. When Modi won in 2014, a dominant narrative was that he won on a development agenda and rejected Hindutva's religious nationalistic agenda. That is not true—for instance, in several speeches in the 2014 campaign, he spoke about cow protection. Ideologically, that distinction never existed in the Hindutva understanding. The entire philosophy has been that India's development is possible only when the Hindus assert themselves.

I have argued over the years that Hindutva does not delink Hindu nationalism and development. As the BJP became a ruling party, Vajpayee as prime minister and Modi as chief minister adapted Hindutva to the requirements of the global market without abandoning the ideas of development based on Hindu values. Reporting on the 2007 Gujarat assembly election, I illustrated the point that in Modi's politics there is no distinction between Hindutva and development. I termed this new adaptation 'Hindutva 2.0'.[115] So, far from replacing Hindutva ideology with development, as many people have wrongly interpreted Modi's style of governance and politics, what he puts forward is an argument that Hindutva is essential for, and leads to, development. His politics and governance have proven this beyond doubt. The 2017 Gujarat campaign by Modi drove home this point so strongly that Milan Vaishnav wrote in his assessment of the election results, 'As tempting as it is to view the BJP through the simple binary of *vikas* versus Hindutva, the truth is that Modi's project is to fuse the two into a seamless whole.'[116]

In the wake of the COVID-19 pandemic, India launched a new campaign for 'Self-Reliant India', or Atmanirbhar Bharat. Critics wondered whether this amounted to a throwback to the age of import substitution. But the concept is not about India delinking from the world market, but about India making for the world, according to Amitabh Kant, CEO of National Institution for Transforming India (NITI). He elaborated that the thrust of the government is to create sectorial champions in India on the lines of the South Korean electronics sector and the Japanese auto sector. Self-reliance does not mean India turning away from globalization, but India taking a centre stage of the global chain.[117] This approach is aligned with nationalism in economic policy—state promotion of national behemoths, promotion of exports but a resistance to imports.

In terms of the economy, the Hindutva growth rate is about fusing religious nationalism and the global market system to create a growth model unique to India. Traditionally, the Hindu right has had to deal with three dilemmas that have stunted its growth. First, the conflict between Hindu traditionalists and the market-friendly middle class; second, the hierarchical caste structure that endowed leadership to the minority upper castes, something that the majority lower castes began to resent increasingly as democracy took root; and third, the organizational question of how the RSS should relate to its political wing. Modi's Hindutva 2.0 overcame all these ahead of the 2014 elections.[118] But these conflicts have not disappeared for good and surface occasionally.

The fundamental deviation from liberal market in the Hindutva model for progress is collectivization and the commanding role of the state in all affairs. Free market, by definition, is individualistic—a person interacts with the market and the political system in his individual capacity, as a citizen who votes, as a consumer who buys, as an investor who invests, and so on. Hindutva argues that development can be achieved only by the collective energy and ambition of a community. The 2016 banknote demonetization was an unprecedented demonstration of this idea, using state power. Pratap Bhanu Mehta writes on the politics of the move: 'To work as a national project, all individuality, all questions of distributive consequences, have to be effaced. Every citizen will appear, alternatively, as a patriot or a criminal . . . When was the last time literally every citizen is being inducted into a behaviour change? This ability to translate a policy measure into a national project is unprecedented.'[119] The trend has progressed further in the following years—from social media posts to culinary habits and even the most intimate choice an individual makes, choosing a partner; all of these are increasingly under the thump of the state.

The parallel with the Chinese model here is not accidental. Modi has been an admirer of it, travelling to China several times as chief minister and seeking to fashion several of his policies accordingly. The Chinese growth model has been described variously as 'socialism with Chinese characteristics' and 'capitalism with Chinese characteristics'. In India, it can be called 'capitalism with Hindutva characteristics'.

The synergization of market and religious nationalism—Hindutva 2.0—represents a 'spiritualization of neoliberalism', Amitav Ghosh has argued in a compelling comparative analysis of Modi and Turkish President Recep Tayyip Erdogan.

The BJP (under Modi, like the AKP under Erdogan before it) was able to turn the tables on the secularists: it succeeded in presenting itself as more modern than its opponent, being less statist, less corrupt and less tainted by the past. That the BJP's prime ministerial candidate was a self-made man, not a dynastic scion, was frequently cited to suggest that he would bring a new dynamism to the country's politics.[120]

Baba Ramdev, a yoga-guru-turned-entrepreneur who supports Modi and is promoted by all BJP state governments, is exhibit A in the Hindutva model of growth. Ramdev has a huge following in India and abroad, and presides over the Patanjali group of companies that competes with multinationals in products ranging from soaps and shampoo to noodles and biscuits, and yoga pants. Ramdev routinely derides consumption of MNC products as unhealthy and unpatriotic, and his message has caught on with the rise of Modi.

This is how Swapan Dasgupta interpreted Modi's qualified support—or guarded critique—of market globalization in Davos in 2018:

Nominally, the audience comprised investors and global notables who influence the financial and political worlds. The speech, therefore, had to appeal to them [. . .] At the same time, there was a domestic dimension. For many Indians, the importance accorded to Modi at Davos was a source of immense pride and recognition of India's hard-earned place on the world's high table [. . .] The invocation of India's spiritual heritage and his critique of over-consumption may have had a niche global audience, but these themes were primarily aimed at Indians (not least within his ideological ecosystem) who are sceptical of India's rush to be integrated into the choppy waters of global capitalism.[121]

Today, not only is India a national market, it is a nationalist market. And the role of the state in that market is formidable. Foreign investment and trade need to operate within this nationalist framework. In this, the Modi government is hardly any different from those who preceded it. Foreign direct investment (FDI) in defence would be welcome, but when it comes to foreign control of ownership of the defence industry, it is unlikely to be acceptable. An Indian private company emerging as a global defence giant would be promoted by the government, but not foreign control of the Indian industry.

Conclusion

Is it helpful to analyse Modi using the prism of RSS thinkers and Savarkar? This is a very valid question that might cross the minds of many readers. As we started the discussion in this chapter with Modi's self-description, we shall conclude with his views on these thinkers and their views.

In his 2008 book *Jyotipunj*, Modi retold the life stories of sixteen men who inspired him—all of them RSS leaders. 'His mind was a mix of science, religion and culture. He said once that the advance of humanity depended on the advancement of science,' Moḍi wrote about Golwalkar.[122] On 28 May 2014, as prime minister, he paid homage to Savarkar before his portrait, and tweeted about the latter's 'tireless efforts towards the regeneration of our motherland'.

Hindutva will advance on the foundations of democracy and elections. Savarkar said the 'tenets of Hindutva were consistent with democracy.'[123] Winning elections fair and square, and acting within the Constitution, champions of Hindutva are recasting the idea of India. Elections and rule of law will continue; but the manner of elections and the nature of law are rapidly changing.

They might draw from the experiences of other countries. The paths of Erdogan and Iranian revolutionaries, both Islamists, are instructive. Two different versions of Islamism are supported by democracy in these countries. Iran's Islamic revolution took a course of confrontation with America, but Hindutva, despite its suspicion of Western values and Christianity, would never do that, offering a hand of friendship to the US, in such a fashion that it promotes its own principles of nationalism and advancement of national power. America, regardless of who is in the White House, will find this approach appealing. Ultra-nationalism leads to disengagement, but 'ultra-nationalism in India, in China, in emerging economies is how much more we go out and shape the environment around.'[124] India will also learn its lessons from the engagement of other Asian countries with the US, particularly that of China and Japan.

The concern that Indian democracy and its institutions will fray under the marching boots of Hindutva may be well-meaning but the trajectory is more complicated. Champions of Hindutva are seeking to enforce an institutionally crafted idea of the nation and its interests, which cannot be questioned without attracting the label of anti-national or foreign agent, and state action under fresh laws. The rancorous protests and multitude of political parties that characterize Indian politics could be transformed into a more disciplined, formal and constrained one. At least on this front, the idea is to reshape Indian politics like the US politics in its institutionally prescribed form. There is a notion of an American national interest mandated by the establishment that cannot be easily questioned. Institutions fall in line—a case in point is what happened to Edward Snowden, who blew the whistle on the massive surveillance of US agencies. The idea of building a modern nation state as a disciplined project is western, and Hindutva borrowed and retrofitted it for India. What makes this experiment more fraught in India is its diversity, which has no parallel in the world. What is ironic is the fact that such a monolithic idea of the national project is facing stiff challenges in western countries, particularly the US, in part due to the expanding diversity of populations.

The Vajpayee government, particularly his deputy prime minister, L.K. Advani, whose protégé Modi used to be, sought to change the vocabulary of Indian strategic thinking by talking of 'hot pursuit', 'strong state' and 'zero tolerance (to terrorism)'. But Vajpayee also made path-breaking overtures to Pakistan, got himself photographed in skullcaps and hosted iftar parties at the prime minister's residence, in a clear attempt to rise above the politics of Hindutva and as a signal to Muslims. Nehruvians approvingly hoped, and Hindutva apologists disapprovingly grudged, that he was a closet Nehruvian, despite his deep Hindutva roots.

If you see similarities in the Hindutva doctrine and Nehruvian notions, the fact is that there are. The Hindutva doctrine presupposes certain features about the self and the enemy. An ideologically programmed decision-making would lead to a set of different policy outcomes, which could in turn influence the policy of your enemy too. The advantage for Hindutva Strategic Doctrine is the 'current global situation', marked by the continuing threat of Islamism, the rising challenge from China and the crisis of capitalism. This situation dramatically increased the acceptance of Hindutva as a governing principle domestically in India, and internationally as an ally of the global liberal order led by America.

Whether Modi is pragmatic or ideological is a false binary. Leaders are largely both. Modi's engagement with the world will have the Hindutva Strategic Doctrine as a touchstone, though there could be tactical compromises that are part of any politics.

At any rate, there no point in trying to understand any ideology as a static monolith. It is possible that Hindutva is gradually adapting itself to the logic of demography and democracy, and other calculations. During his lecture series in 2018, Bhagwat was asked about Golwalkar referring to Muslims as enemies in his *Bunch of Thoughts*. Bhagwat said: '. . . every statement carries a context of time and circumstance . . . his enduring thoughts are in a popular edition in which we have removed all remarks that have a temporary context and retained those that will endure for ages. You won't find the (Muslim-is-an-enemy) remark there.'[125] The RSS has edited Golwalkar to fit him in its twenty-first-century plans. Talking at the centenary celebrations of the Aligarh Muslim University in December 2020, Modi said: 'The country today is moving on a path where nobody should be left behind because of their religion . . . What belongs to the country belongs to every citizen. Everybody should get it.'[126] The speech was widely seen as a desire on his part to mark a new beginning with the Muslims. Whether his own constituency would be amenable to such a shift is a different question.

The argument in this book is not at all that because there are certain notions that are articulated by a list of leaders, that will be the only prism that we must use to understand it. This is not an argument about the inevitability of anything.

Far from it. The point about these arguments is that there is an intellectual ecosystem that has sustained the rise of Hindu nationalism in India, and a sense of that ecosystem is essential to understand the political process that is currently underway in India. Any interpretation delinked from this will be inadequate and misleading.

3

India in America

'I am a big fan of Hindu, and I am a big fan of India.'

> —Donald Trump, addressing a meeting of Indian–
> Americans as a Republican candidate, October 2016

'. . . one of the last events I hosted at the Vice President's residence was a Diwali reception (in 2016). Here I was, an Irish Catholic Vice President opening my home for a holiday traditionally observed by Hindus, Buddhists, Sikhs, and Jains, and that night joined by Muslims, Christians, and Indian Americans of various backgrounds representing the diversity of the diaspora [. . .] I've always felt deeply connected to the Indian American community because of the values we share: duty to family and elders, treating people with respect and dignity, self-discipline, service, and hard work.'

> —Joe Biden, in an op-ed published in October,
> during the 2020 campaign for presidency[1]

'The Indian community has done so much for our community [. . .] Your family structure and your Hindu culture have created an amazing system, particularly when it is blended with the American culture, which is that you can do anything that you want [. . .] When you look to the future of America, you look to the Indian community.'

—Chuck Schumer, Democrat, Senate Majority Leader[2]

There are certain long-standing notions in the mainstream of US thinking regarding India, along with a tendency to essentialize India as Hindu. In a written commentary, Biden is careful to emphasize the religious pluralism of India, but in extempore remarks, it is commonplace for politicians to use India and Hindu as synonyms.

For more than a century, many American laws and lawmakers, and a considerable segment of the country's popular culture and society at large, saw India as Hindu, partly due to ignorance and prejudice and partly as strategy. Essentializing India as Hindu served contradictory purposes historically—justifying racial prejudice and validating spiritual admiration, and counting Indians/Hindus as the other and the ally simultaneously or alternatively, depending on the time and place. Indians in America, divided as they are by caste, religion, language and disparities in education, largely accepted the term 'Hindu' as a unifying marker, as a counter to the racist derision they faced and as claimants to the high culture of eastern spirituality that has significant western following and admiration.

Of concern are two questions—how has this changed in the era of Hindutva that dovetails with an unprecedented era of Indian–American political activism, and increasing divides within the US; and how does this notion affect America's strategy, i.e., its idea of self, enemy and allies? India–US ties have cultural, strategic and economic components, interacting and changing over time. In all three components, there are convergences and divergences. Horizontally across these three verticals, a post-pandemic world will see energized and more robust India–US ties. By 2020, India is not merely a distant partner, but part of its living body, for the US. A half-Indian, who spent her childhood vacations in Chennai and likes her idli sambhar, and tikka, whose name is so authentically Indian—Kamala, or Lotus—is the Vice President of the US. It is a different matter that her presence in the White House creates complications in US politics and within the Indian diaspora, which we will also discuss in this chapter. All told, India–US ties are on the cusp of emerging as the defining partnership of the twenty-first century—a vision several American leaders, including Biden, and Indian ones, including Modi, have outlined. Understanding the motivations of this partnership in both societies and their mutual interaction is critical for its progress and nurturing. This chapter makes that effort.

Hinduism in America

It was in the US that Swami Vivekananda enunciated the idea of Hinduism, codifying an overwhelming diversity of culture and myriad beliefs for the benefit of a foreign audience. 'Of the Swami's address before the Parliament of Religions, it may be said that when he began to speak, it was of the religious ideas of the Hindus; but when he ended, Hinduism had been created,' writes Sister Nivedita, the Swami's closest disciple, in her introduction to his collected works.[3]

In 1893, when the Swami addressed the Parliament of Religions in Chicago, the total number of Indians—who were all called Hindus though there were Muslims and Sikhs among them—in the US was less than 2000. American capitalism was in a crisis, in the era termed the Gilded Age by Mark Twain. Hinduism as interpreted by him was a far cry from the Hindutva that Savarkar invented exactly three decades later, in 1923. Votaries of Hindutva quote Vivekananda and Savarkar in the same breath, but usually not the former's views on other religions: 'We Hindus do not merely tolerate, we unite ourselves with every religion, praying in the mosque of the Mohammedan, worshipping before the fire of the Zoroastrian, and kneeling to the cross of the Christian.'[4] Vivekananda's American lectures presented India as the land steeped in a spiritual ethos and, as opposed to Savarkar, this remarkably avoided the notion of enemy.

Strategy, however, is not only about the self, but about enemies and allies as well.

Historically, due to ignorance and racism, the religious identities of non-white people did not count for much in the US. Many Americans could not even distinguish between Islam and Hinduism in the early twentieth century. This could be seen almost immediately after Indian immigrants began arriving in America in trickles. A US Congressman from California, who was a campaigner against 'Hindu' immigration to the West Coast in the early twentieth century, claimed 'those of us who come into contact with the Hindus, and I think it is universal, regard them as a menace'.[5]

For a better idea of what he knew of Hindus then, note this exchange in a congressional discussion:

Mr. Church: They have their religion; in fact, it seems to be about all there is to a Hindu, his religion.

The Chairman: Is that the Mohammedan religion?
Mr. Church: As I understand.[6]

If this was the understanding of a lawmaker who wanted to make a law on Indian immigration to America at the time, vestiges of this attitude have not entirely disappeared over the next century, from American society. In the 1990s, racial offenders in a series of incidents abused their brown targets as 'Hindus', no matter whether they were Muslim of Pakistani origin or Buddhist from Sri Lanka. 'The word "Hindu" referred to all desis.'[7] If Muslims were catalogued as Hindus in the early twentieth century, 'Indians continued to be classified as Hindus in the 1920, 1930, and 1940 censuses'.[8] As the population of Hindus attained a threshold to form a community, it began to present itself as a distinct religious group. This effort gained strength in the aftermath of 9/11, when all brown people became suspect to some white Americans, this time as Muslims, due to a combination of ignorance and paranoia.

It is not a coincidence that the Hindu American Foundation (HAF), a professionally run and American-grown organization of Hindus, was started in 2003. A curious subtext to many of these campaigns was an effort to differentiate Hinduism from Islam. Several Muslim organizations also expanded their public outreach to dispel wrongful notions of their religion being violent. As it happened, Hindu mobilization in America could present itself as an extension of mainstream Indian nationalism, while the Indian Muslim diaspora's civic and religious activities became disconnected from it. Indian Hindus and their temples and religious congregations became the nucleus of the diaspora community, in a way that mosques and other Islamic centres could not, as they were visited by people from multiple countries. Indian Muslims could not run solely or predominantly Indian mosques in America; but Indian Hindus could and do run Indian temples, at least predominantly, and even solely.

The Hindu temples and centres too are not only visited by people from India. A study by Devesh Kapur and others estimate that at least 10 per cent of the nearly 3.65 million people of Indian origin in the US have come from a third country, born to people of Indian origin who left India decades ago. Most of them are Hindus. The disconnect of minorities from the larger Indian–American community is also recorded in the same study. Kapur et al. catalogued 966 organizations in America linked to the Indian–American community. Twenty-four, i.e., 2.5 per cent of them, were caste-based, but an overwhelming number of the total were Hindu organizations.

> Almost half of Indian-American organisations were religious organisations. This contrasts with Mexican immigrants whose primary membership of organisations were hometown associations. There were 481 religious organisations in the data set; three-fifths of which were Hindu organisations or Hindu temples [. . .] The number of Indian-American organisations for Christians and Muslims was small, at 3 per cent and 2 per cent respectively [. . .] This is likely because Indian-American Christians and Muslims may join broader religious congregations in the United States that don't specifically serve immigrants from India.[9]

This leads to a situation in which the Hindu groups form and sustain deeper connections with India, while the Muslims and Christians from the country are increasingly linked to Indian politics and mobilization in America as dissenters. A broader identity is convenient for its bearers and beholders—Indian and Hindu, often used interchangeably, subdues regional and linguistic diversities of the diaspora. The Dalits are not part of this largely upper caste milieu of the Indian diaspora. This fragmentation of Indian communities in the US has been more intense since Hindutva mobilization began to get Indian state patronage in the US, since 2014.

The Modi government has attempted to essentialize India as Hindu before foreign audiences, guided by its Hindutva Strategic Doctrine. On 22 September 2017, the Ministry of External Affairs uploaded an e-book on its official website titled *Integral Humanism* to explain the thoughts of RSS ideologue and BJS founder Deendayal Upadhyaya. The then External Affairs Minister Sushma Swaraj described the book as a product of the 'hard work of MEA officials'. Patriotism is a religious obligation, the booklet said. 'Anyone who abandons Dharma, betrays the nation.' It talked about Vedas and Hindu scriptures as 'our scriptures', and equated India with Hinduism. 'This is the essence of Hindu thought. Bhartiya thought. Deendayalji named this thought only integral Humanism.'[10]

This move was questioned in the Indian Parliament and the booklet was subsequently removed from the ministry's website.[11] Soon enough, the government went one step further. It began appointing Hindu missionaries as officials attached to Indian missions abroad. With official passports, offices and support staff, the mandate of these demi-diplomats designated as 'Yoga and Indian Culture Acharyas' was to serve as experts in Sanskrit, yoga and Hindu scriptures, to spread Indian culture essentialized as Hindu. 'This is the vision of the current government, but previous governments did not have this,' Mokshraj, a PhD in the Vedas from the Rajasthan Sanskrit

University, attached to the Indian Embassy in Washington, told me in March 2017.[12] In 2018, the World Hindu Congress in Chicago had Vice President Venkaiah Naidu and RSS chief Mohan Bhagwat as key speakers. Issues ranging from the need for Hindus to procreate more and the dangers of missionaries, and love jihad—a derogatory label for interfaith romance— were topics of discussion.

Hindu Activism

Indian activism in the US has been shaped by the discrimination the community has faced in the country. The discrimination has essentialized all desis as Hindus for more than a century now. So, the responses to it often swing to a place where the Hindu community in America volunteers—they don't necessarily need to be recruited—for a project to defend anything Hindu. And they are also willing to buy into, and in fact add to, the narrative that equates being Indian with being Hindu and being Hindu with being Indian. If anything happens in India, be it communal riots, lynching in the name of cow protection or caste violence, the reflex and default response of most Indian–Americans is to defend India's reputation. Quite often, this leads to defending activities of the Hindutva brigade; conversely, criticism of the Hindutva agenda gets attacked as anti-India or Hindu-phobia, or defamation of India, Hinduism or both.

Such campaigns quite often and successfully benefit from the hypocrisy of American policy, the Christian origins of America's own principle of religious freedom and the strategic importance of India–US ties. American advocacy of religious freedoms abroad is inspired by two political factors at home— the first, primarily on the Republican side, are the Christian evangelical and charity organizations that want to operate in other countries; the second, primarily on the Democrat side, is the human rights and values camp. The Christian missionaries were the original promoters of the human rights agenda in US foreign policy.[13] Both streams have their own hypocrisies and the Hindu groups, speaking and campaigning as American citizens, question them. Often, their advocacy benefits Hindutva groups in India.

There are many organizations in America that are affiliated to the Sangh Parivar, but our brief focus here will be on the HAF, precisely for the reason that it is not allied to Hindutva nationalistic groups or organizations in India in any formal or technical way. The attempt, hence, is to examine how and why the Hindu–India equivalence becomes almost axiomatic for a large mainstream of Indian–Americans, who do not find anything contradictory about championing minority rights in America, while overlooking or even promoting the rise of Hindutva in India.

Negative essentialization of India as Hindu is based primarily on stereotypes about caste and gender in India. The HAF's campaign has been about contesting such stereotypes with a humane interpretation of textual Hinduism, which often leads to decontextualizing it from the actual practice of the religion on a daily basis and sanitizing it. It argues that caste or gender violence is only as much relevant to the teachings of Hinduism as the Crusades are for the teachings of Christianity. The HAF has pushed back against the negative stereotyping of India as backward. It has alternatively proposed a positive essentialization of India as a Hindu spiritual place of virtue where democracy, pluralism and market economy exist in an eternal union—a formulation that sounds very pleasing to the mainstream American self-perception. The HAF operates in the minority, civil rights activism space in the US—not as a conservative religious group—and consequently gets easily aligned with the Democrats. The overall Indian–American alignment with the Democrats is against their economic interests, argues Kapur and others in their study, and is a reaction to the preponderance of Christian evangelicals in the Republican Party.

The HAF is at the forefront of many campaigns for minority rights in America, including those of Muslims. It denounced the Trump administration's move to impose a travel ban on Muslim-majority countries. 'We are not only a Hindu organization, but also a civil rights group,' Samir Kalra, a second-generation Indian–American and a key functionary of the HAF, told me. The organization sees India as the 'spiritual homeland of the Hindus' and hence, its ties with India are more pronounced, but it does not feel obligated to champion Indian causes in America.

The HAF's focus is on fighting prejudices against Hindus and Hinduism widely prevalent in America. Kalra said that their organization tried to 'contextualize' reports on Hindus and their faith. For instance, regarding the often violent, Hindutva-promoted cow protection movement in India, the stand it takes is this:

Throughout the world, laws are often formulated based on the moral and cultural norms or judgments of a country's population. It is illegal to sell dog or cat meat in the U.S. [. . .] Similarly, in India, Hindus view the cow as a generous, ever-giving source [. . .] Hindus treat the cow with the same respect accorded to the mother, as the cow is a vital sustainer of life, providing milk and a means of ploughing the earth to grow crops.[14]

Kalra goes on to emphasize that the cow received such status as a 'result of the historical need of early agrarian Hindu civilization' and 'cow protection laws have thus evolved from these cultural and moral precepts and not any anti-Muslim sentiment.' He is also emphatic in condemning violence in the name of cow protection, arguing that 'such incidents run contrary to Hindu teachings regarding the sanctity of all life and ahimsa, or non-harming, and Hinduism's history of mutual respect and pluralism'. He points out that the cow protection laws do not impinge on the religious rights of others. In a document, the HAF says:

> At the time of India's independence, the founders of the modern state sought to codify as policy the uniquely Indic ethos of compassion towards animals and the practical reality of the wealth cattle represents for people in a primarily agricultural society. Cow protection laws are thus rooted in and evolved from economic, cultural, and moral precepts, pre-dating the modern Republic of India, and do not stem from any animus towards Muslims and Christians.[15]

These assertions can be questioned on merit. For instance, a large number of Hindus in India actually eat cow meat (unless one wants to count anyone who eats cow meat as non-Hindu); the argument against the violent cow protection movement has not been that it is against the religious beliefs of Muslims; and beef production in India is a by-product of its agriculture sector as there is no cattle rearing for the sole purpose of meat. But suffice it to say that HAF's argument could be an appealing explanation for the American audience—that the cow protection movement in India is not contrary to the principles of a democratic, multi-religious society.

The HAF also defends anti-conversion laws enacted by Hindutva governments in India that target minority religions as it opposes conversion *from* Hinduism, though it supports conversion *to* Hinduism, echoing the Hindutva view on the topic. It also has a widespread campaign for the propagation of Hinduism in America, but opposes Christian missionary activities in India, curiously making the argument that poor, uneducated people in India are gullible to the machinations of evangelists.

The Biden campaign had found the Citizenship Amendment Act 'disappointing',[16] but the HAF defended the law and the implicit assumption in the law. 'Indeed, India is the sacred homeland of the four Dharmic/Indic traditions—Hinduism, Buddhism, Jainism and Sikhism [. . .] The specific mention of adherents of the four Dharmic traditions in the CAA is [. . .] recognition of India as the sacred geography and homeland of these traditions and their respective adherents.'[17] It then goes on to suggest neutral language to define the beneficiaries. 'Any specific outlining of groups is prone to inadvertent exclusion.' It does not mention the Rohingya Muslims fleeing genocide in Myanmar; and cites country-specific and religion-specific extension of asylum and citizenship in the US itself[18] in support of the CAA in India. The HAF canvases support for the construction of a Ram Temple at the site where a Muslim place of worship stood until 6 December 1992, when it was destructed by a mob gathered by the BJP.[19] When India revoked the special constitutional status of Jammu and Kashmir in August 2019, the HAF was quick to seek support of the US. 'We urge the US to fully support India's internal sovereign decisions on Kashmir and to continue to exert pressure on Pakistan to end its support of cross-border terrorism, so the Kashmir conflict can be resolved once and for all,' Kalra said.[20]

The Indian–American community is still divided along caste and linguistic differences and is often debilitated by the humongous egos of its numerous self-styled leaders. Modi's engagement has helped cement some of these divisions and build an Indian identity, difficult to distinguish from Hindu identity though it may be. Even so, it is quite a long way from achieving the success of the Jewish–American community. The Jewish model is what politically active Indian–Americans aspire towards. Along with constituting 1 per cent of the US population, Indian–Americans amounted to 1 per cent of the members in the US Congress after the 2016 elections, the highest proportion in history. It is curious that the election that brought Trump to power also resulted in the highest representation of Indian–Americans in the US Congress. 'With 2 per cent of the country's population, the Jewish community has 10 per cent of the members of the U.S. Congress. That is the kind of aspiration we need to have,' said M. Rangaswamy, a California-based tech entrepreneur and founder of Indiaspora, a bipartisan body of Indian–Americans.[21]

Jason Isaacson, director of international affairs at the American Jewish Council (AJC), is a great supporter of India–Israel–America triangular ties. At the 110-year-old organization's headquarters in Washington, he spoke about their attempts to coordinate with Indian–Americans, 'We will work together, to demonstrate the benefits of what is really a trilateral relationship, between India, Israel, and the U.S.'[22] The AJC had pulled its weight in support of the India–US civil nuclear deal. 'There is less hesitation in India on embracing Israel. It started before Modi, and it is a bipartisan position in India, but it is more public under Mr Modi, that Israel is a natural ally of India and there are mutual benefits.'[23]

About the ambition of several Indian American initiatives that try with limited success to emulate the Jewish model of intervention in American politics, Isaacson said, 'The way you can be effective in this society is—gather people together, make an agenda, raise funds, hire staff. If you are going to have a community that has a political voice, it has to be treated as a business. America is welcoming to that kind of political activity. But you will have to take that job seriously.'[24]

'We the People'

'The friendship between the United States and India is built on shared values, including our shared commitment to democracy [. . .] both the American and the Indian constitutions begin with the same three very beautiful words: We the people,' President Trump said while appearing with Prime Minister Modi at the Rose Garden, White House, on 26 June 2017.[25]

India–US relations are often described as a convergence of values and interests. These are not static, and Trump and Modi are two leaders who have set off a new inquiry into these concepts in the US and India. They sit at the top of powerful political forces that are trying to re-litigate principles that have evolved over centuries in America and have been held for decades in India. They are leaders of populist revolts against the national consensuses that have held sway for long in their countries. They, in fact, created these revolts, as much as they are the creations of these revolts. In India, this populism is sustainable as Modi's emphatic re-election in 2019 and his continuing popularity in regional elections show. In the US, the process is more contested as the defeat of Trump in 2020 shows. Trump got 10 million more votes in 2020 than his 2016 tally.

This ongoing re-litigation involves fundamental questions about citizenship, individual and collective rights, particularly religious rights, terms of engagement between state and citizens, balance of power between various branches of government, role of the media, and so on. At a conceptual level, what is being debated is national identity itself—who are we?

As discussed earlier, this question—who are we?—is often answered by asking another question—who is our enemy? The process of asking and answering these questions can often take the form of violence against the perceived 'other', the so-called 'enemy'. Both the Indian and American constitutions have 'we the people' written in their preambles. The debate renewed by Trump and Modi in their respective countries is who constitutes the said 'people'. The process continues with the re-election of Modi in 2019 and despite the defeat of Trump in 2020.

As PM, Modi had met Vice President Biden. The variation in emphasis in their respective characterization of the first conversation they had after the 2020 election was noticeable. 'We reiterated our firm commitment to the Indo–US strategic partnership and discussed our shared priorities and concerns—the COVID-19 pandemic, climate change, and cooperation in the Indo–Pacific Region,' Modi said. 'I also conveyed warm congratulations for Vice President-elect Kamala Harris. Her success is a matter of great pride and inspiration for members of the vibrant Indian American community, who are a tremendous source of strength for Indo–US relations.' A read-out from Biden's office noted that he looked forward to working closely with the prime minister on 'shared global challenges, including containing COVID-19 and defending against future health crises, tackling the threat of climate change, launching global economic recovery, strengthening democracy at home and abroad, and maintaining a secure and prosperous Indo–Pacific region.' Biden 'expressed his desire to strengthen and expand the US–India strategic partnership alongside the first vice president of South Asian descent.'[26]

Biden's emphasis on democracy is against the backdrop of American concerns about challenges to it in India. 'Throughout 2019, government action—including the CAA, continued enforcement of cow slaughter and anti-conversion laws, and the November Supreme Court ruling on the Babri Masjid site—created a culture of impunity for nationwide campaigns of harassment and violence against religious minorities', the US Commission on International Religious Freedom said in its annual report in 2020. The annual report of the US State Department on religious freedom uses neutral language while cataloguing the religious violence and discussing CAA.[27] When Trump was visiting India in February 2020, communal riots in Delhi led to the death of 43 people, a majority of them Muslims. Allegations of police partisanship in the investigation followed.

In the US, white supremacists have triggered violence in recent years; racial and class tensions have been on the rise. In 2020, a new wave of protest for racial justice swept the US, after the gruesome killing of an African–American man caught on camera shook the nation. In the five months up to October 2020, 'at least 950 instances of police brutality against civilians and journalists during anti-racism protests' were recorded. Police forces in several cities appeared to be permissive towards white supremacists.[28] Gun-carrying militias marched in several cities against lockdowns to control the COVID-19 pandemic. Around a thousand people are killed by the police every year; African–Americans twice at the rate of white Americans.[29] Millions marched in the streets in support of Trump's claim that the 2020 elections were manipulated by the Democrats. The year 2019 was the most lethal for domestic violent extremism in the United States since 1995, according to the Department of Homeland Security. In sixteen attacks, forty-eight people were killed.[30] Indian–Americans have not been immune from this turbulence.

One Indian–American on a temporary H-1B work visa, Srinivas Kuchibhotla, was killed in a case of racial hatred in Kansas days after the Trump presidency was inaugurated in 2017. Thirty-two-year-old Kuchibhotla, along with his friend Alok Madasani, had gone to a bar after the day's work, where he was shot, allegedly by a fifty-one-year-old US Navy veteran who shouted, 'Get out of my country,' before pulling the trigger. Kuchibhotla died later, while Madasani, who was also shot, survived.[31]

Adam Purinton, the man who pleaded guilty of murdering Kuchibhotla, told the police that he mistook his victims for Iranians. 'The fact that he targeted Kuchibhotla and Madasani based on the mistaken assumption that they were Iranian rather than Indian, makes the incident all the more tragic,' the HAF said in a statement.[32]

Both in India and America, the ongoing re-litigation of national identity and principles is not based on a commonly agreed set of facts. Rather, it seems facts are being invented and misrepresented, including in cases where historical records and scientific evidence might be to the contrary. In India, the majoritarian project is to undermine the country's Islamic heritage; in the US, the re-engineering of history is a conflict between those who want to remove the remnants of its racist past—which is not entirely past, incidentally—and those who want to preserve and even eulogize it. This internal debate on democracy is also testing the resilience of institutional checks and balances, the bedrock of both democracies. In the US, while mainstream media and the judiciary to some extent have taken upon themselves the burden of fighting for the protection of the national consensus on identity, rights and the limits of executive power, in India, the situation appears to be mixed. A significant section of Indian mainstream media seems to not be averse to amplifying anti-Muslim propaganda, as also branding critics of government policies 'anti-nationals'. The media hysteria in India communalized even the reporting on the COVID-19 pandemic, with several platforms accusing Muslims of deliberately spreading it.

The judiciary in India, which has been, by and large, a bastion of democratic rights, has in recent years seemingly supported a hypernationalist narrative. The judiciary, particularly the Supreme Court (SC), has shown no great hurry in settling several questions originating from executive and legislative actions that pertain to the constitutional scheme of things. The revocation of the special status and the reorganization of a state into two union territories in August 2019 was an unprecedented act in the history of the country. The SC has not examined its constitutional validity more than a year later and in December 2020, 140 petitions on this question alone were pending in the SC. Two former chief justices of India (CJI) have been appointed to political posts since 2014, after their retirement—one as governor of Kerala, and another a member of Parliament. The judiciary has come under severe criticism from Indian civil society and members of the bar. According to A.P. Shah, former chief justice of the Delhi and Madras High Courts, 'For the past few years, particularly since the Bharatiya Janata Party-led government took power at the Centre, the performance of the judiciary has deteriorated to disappointing lows. It no longer stands on the pedestal of chief protector of freedoms: the government has done so much damage to personal liberty, but the courts, and especially the Supreme Court, have watched this indiscriminate and often, literally, violent trampling of dissent like mute spectators . . . This is hammered home in incident after incident, and case after case . . . The list is disappointingly long and getting longer still.'[33]

In the United States, the judiciary is increasingly a field of partisan contest between conservatives and liberals. Voting on nominating SC justices in the US Senate has become an extremely bitter and partisan contest between the Republicans and Democrats. Many of the conflicts within society are due for judicial review and settlement in both India and the US over the next few years, and the role of the judiciary will be critical in both countries. Speaking about the shared values of democracy serving as a binding glue to India–US ties, it must therefore be remembered that they are being recast.

India does not invoke any intense feeling among Americans. In the new wave of nationalism unleashed by Trump's 'America First' politics, there are instances where India appears as an ally, but there are also contexts in which it is the other. This duality is most noticeable in the immigration debate. How does it impact Indians in America? Whom we call 'Indian–Americans' in this discussion include both American citizens of Indian origin and Indian citizens in America on visas. It is important to understand who these people are, and what their engagement is with politics in America and India.

Immigration Debate: India as Ally

From his hilltop perch on the eastern side, across the San Francisco Bay, Vinod Dham has a bird's eye view of Silicon

Valley. When the lights come on, the headquarters of Google, Facebook, Apple, Uber and Intel—where he once led the invention that revolutionized computing, the Pentium chip—are clearly visible. The story of Dham's journey, from chasing DTC buses in Delhi in the 1960s as an engineering student to the Fremont mansion where he lives now, is relegated to the background as software geniuses and social media moguls dominate the world's digital imagination. The mansion, with an eight-ton Buddha stone sculpture from Mamallapuram in the garden, is testimony to Dham's status in Silicon Valley—the higher up the hills that surround the Valley your house is, the higher up you are in the pecking order of its cut-throat social hierarchy.

Until the early 1990s, it was the Chinese that dominated the tech sector in the Valley. Dham tells me how multiple forces of nature worked to create the formidable Indian presence in the Valley that has become a cornerstone of India–US ties today. Infosys was created in 1982, but it was not until the mid-1990s that it began to spread its wings. 'There were software people sitting in India, there were hardware people sitting in America. These computers were not connected then. Then happened the perfect storm. By mid-1990s, American corporations began to be worried about Y2K,' recalls Dham.

The fear was what would happen when the clock turned to the new millennium in 2000, because computer coding and programming were not pre-written for that change. 'A lot of Indian engineers were brought from India to fix the code. American corporations realized how smart the Indian engineers were. Not only that they were fixing it, but they were also writing the code. That was the first leg of the perfect storm,' says Dham. The second leg was the spread of the Internet that was happening simultaneously—the browser took off in 1995. Earlier, computers were linked only within the company. By 2000, the Silicon Valley and Bangalore were connected in a seamless network.

The third factor was the bursting of the dot-com bubble. 'Companies collapsed like cards. CEOs had to look for ways to save money. They looked around and saw this vast reservoir of Indian IT talent,' he says. Simultaneously, the 1998 nuclear explosion conducted by India changed its profile in Washington, DC. Most considered India a disrupter of the nuclear order; some conceded that a country of India's size and ambitions would do this. But either way, America could no longer ignore India. It is not a coincidence that the first breakthrough in India–US relations, with President Bill Clinton weighing in clearly on India's side in the Kargil conflict in 1999, forcing Pakistan to withdraw and then making a trip to India, happened around the same time. So, by the turn of the century, India was a significant presence in the East and the West Coast of America, the nerve centres of its governance and new economy, respectively.

India wants policies that allow freer trade in services in the American market. It believes that opening the doors of other countries, particularly the developed ones, where skilled Indian workers can be allowed to go and work, is the future of its trade. India continues to push for more opportunities for its competitive workforce.[34] India had the largest number of migrants living abroad—17.5 million, followed by Mexico (11.8 million) and China (10.7 million), according to the UN World Migration Report–2020. The United States is the top destination country, which now houses 50.7 million international migrants. India is the top recipient of remittances, receiving $78.6 billion, followed by China ($67.4 billion) and Mexico ($35.7 billion).[35]

Letting people from other countries into America is the most sensitive part of the 'America First' debate started by Trump and inherited by Biden. Who is allowed to come to the country has been a critical component of American identity ever since its foundation. Over the decades, changes have taken place and now the US issues 1 million permanent residency permits, or green cards, every year, two-thirds of which go to the category of family unification. Family unification allows those who are already in the US to bring in their relatives, creating what is derisively called 'chain immigration'. There is strong resistance to this in America now. It is the only country that allows this.

A category that India has a huge stake in is that of skilled temporary workers who come to the US with non-immigrant status. India's $150 billion outsourcing industry is hugely dependent on it. The immigration approach pushed by Trump was that *only* highly skilled talent must be allowed to come in, while immigration in general must be discouraged, particularly of those with limited or no skill. The Trump administration pushed for changes in legal immigration in favour of the more skilled, by raising floor salaries of H-1B workers and other executive measures. A significant portion of Indian–Americans came to the country on the H-1B programme over the last three decades.

Another intractable immigration question that America is grappling with is the status of an estimated 11 million people who are in the country without documents, i.e., illegally. A Pew study estimated in 2014 that around five lakh of these were Indians. 'Asia, encompassing South Asian nations such as India as well as East Asian countries including China, was the birthplace of 1.4 million U.S. unauthorized immigrants, or 13% of the total in 2014,' the study said.[36] Public opinion in the US is clearly in favour of legalizing the status of those who are already in the country, but Trump linked immigration to the economic distress of a large segment of the people. The 'America First' politics of Trump so complicated this question that it will take a miracle to resolve this now.

Of all the American policy gridlocks, the one on immigration reforms remains the most intractable of all. But there are some indications of where it could be headed.

A piece of legislation proposes to change America's immigration system from family-linked to primarily skill-linked. RAISE or Reforming American Immigration for a Strong Economy Act, 2017, sponsored by Republican senators David Perdue (who lost his seat in January 2021) and Tom Cotton, proposes to cut immigration by 41 per cent in the first year and by 50 per cent by the tenth year, shrinking the overall intake of people into America.[37] The proposals include giving weightage to English proficiency and reducing the number of refugees admitted annually to 50,000, half the current number. The US has a lottery system to promote diversity in America, allowing immigration from less-represented countries such as Nepal and Ethiopia, which the proposed law seeks to do away with.

The proposal for skill-based immigration per se could find greater support, including among Democrats, but the host of allied issues entangled in the American immigration debate makes any forward movement extremely difficult. Since they comprise a significant portion of new entrants into the US in the last two decades, Indians have a huge stake in the debate. The Biden administration plans to increase the number of refugee intake, which will be resisted by the Republicans.

According to the United States Citizenship and Immigration Services (USCIS), which maintains a country-wise list of H-1B visa applications, but not allotments,

21 lakh Indians have applied under the programme. That makes for around two-thirds of the total applications of 34 lakh in the last eleven years until 2017. The second largest cohort of applicants was from China, at 2.96 lakh.[38]

As noted earlier, two events around the millennium—the taming of the Y2K bug by Indian tech talent, and India's nuclear test—put India and Indians at the centre of planning for CEOs in the West Coast, and strategic pundits in the East. Then came 9/11 and the rise of militant Islamism. Even though India had never presented its nuclear capability as a 'Hindu bomb', dealing as they were with the admittedly Islamic nuclear bomb of Pakistan, and the immediate threat of Islamist terrorism, American strategists perhaps made that assumption. American strategists had for years sought to think of India as Hindu, as we noted earlier. There were good strategic reasons to reinforce that in the new millennium, even before Modi's rise to power.

The pitch that Jaswant Singh made to Bill Clinton's envoy Strobe Talbott in 1998 gained renewed traction after 9/11. Nobody even needed to state it. Indian–Americans had become a key cementing force of the India–US ties. So, American companies and strategists began to see Indians as allies—they were a cheaper, smart workforce and from a democratic military power. And in the emerging global scenario, India was a strategic partner. Of course, for American labour, Indian workers were not allies. This duality was reflected in Trump's 2016 campaign—he supported allowing talented people from India to come in more numbers at one point and took up the case of American workers displaced by H-1B workers at another point in the campaign. Therefore, Indians (or Hindus) appear as both the other and allies in the framework of heightened nationalism in the US.

Two studies on Indian–Americans in recent years—'The Other One Percent' by Devesh Kapur et al. and 'Desis Divided' by Sangay Mishra—warn against the assumption that there is a monolithic 'Indian–American' identity.[39] Both studies establish the diversity among the Indian diaspora in America—in terms of their background in India, and their economic and social status in America. Kapur's study goes a step further and also questions the notion that Indian–Americans are inclined towards Hindutva. There is enough academic evidence, therefore, to restrain us from plunging into any notion of a unified Hindu or Hindutva politics in America. That caveat must be kept in mind while we discuss Indian–American politics.

The rising profile of Indian–Americans was visible in the 2020 elections, but 2016 was the first remarkable turn in the process. Trump became the first presidential candidate to address an Indian–American rally, on 15 October 2016. 'I am a big fan of Hindu, and I am a big fan of India,' he said in his speech at the event. 'Big, big fan,' he added for emphasis, confusing the right word to describe Hinduism and conflating Hinduism with India, intuitively endorsing the Hindutva Strategic Doctrine.[40] The rally was labelled 'Humanity against Terrorism', and what it means—or was supposed to mean— was illustrated with unmistakable clarity in a series of 'cultural programmes' that preceded the arrival of Trump on stage. In one, two couples enacting a Bollywood-style romance were interrupted by Islamist terrorists, only to be overpowered by American soldiers.[41] Bollywood actor Anupam Kher's monologue on the plight of Kashmir's Hindu Pandits who had to flee the Valley after being targeted by Islamist terrorism was played repeatedly. With a choked voice and moist eyes, against a grave black background, Kher described the sufferings of

Hindus in Kashmir, who were chased, raped, killed and who were now ignored by the 'intellectuals' and 'advocates of multiculturalism'.[42] This conjured up the vision, in faraway America, of a Hindu nation under threat from Islamist forces.

Immigration Debate: India as the Other

The Indian success in Silicon Valley did not end discrimination or racism against Indians in America. In fact, the large-scale immigration of Indians into America made them an immediate target of resentment caused by an overall distress among the American working class in the same period. The murder of Srinivas Kuchibhotla was an extreme expression of that resentment, which was a significant component of Trump's campaign. Steve Bannon, who became chief executive of Donald Trump's campaign and was his strategist at the White House for the first seven months of his term, is a virulent opponent of the H-1B visa programme. Breitbart News, the right-wing website that he used to run, campaigned against the visa programme, and while interviewing Trump in November 2015, he had lamented that two-thirds of Silicon Valley CEOs were South Asians.[43]

It is not that Trump politics created this resentment. Anu Aiyengar, now a managing director at JPMorgan Chase & Co., while being interviewed for a job at a major Wall Street firm at the turn of the century, was told by her interviewer, 'You have three strikes against you [. . .] How can I hire you? You are the wrong gender, wrong color and wrong country.'[44] This kind of discrimination—in your face and blatant—may not be usual, but it is real for many.

Shefali Chandan runs the website Jano, which publishes historical material on Indian–Americans. The discrimination faced by them over the decades is a key focus.[45] After reading her informative piece in *Swarajya* magazine[46] on the history of laws in the US that discriminated against Indians, I interviewed her. A fan of Hillary Clinton, articulate and opinionated, she said she was a great admirer of Modi and Hindutva politics in India. As it turned out, her admiration for Modi was deeply shaped by her experiences of racism in America. How had she experienced racism in America? 'It took us a while before we wondered whether there was a trend in our being seated next to the toilet, quite frequently, when we went to a restaurant,' she said. She was minutely perceptive of the discrimination that Hindus and Muslims faced in America and was fiercely opposed to Trump.[47]

So, how does Modi help, I asked her. 'The success of my country is the biggest pushback against discrimination,' she replied, going on to add that Modi would take India to prosperity and power. While she was extremely critical of the ultranationalism of Trump, she believed Modi's politics was about harnessing the country's pride for its progress. 'Hindus got a raw deal in India until Modi was elected [. . .] Sonia Gandhi was more keen to appease Muslims.'

Had she noticed caste discrimination in India? Chandan grew up in Mumbai and came to America in the early 1990s on an H–1B. 'In my house, all my life, I have not heard anyone say that we are better or someone is less human because of their caste. I have not felt that caste was a part of my identity while growing up,' she said, lamenting that the first thing she gets asked in America about India is caste. Her support for Modi is also drawn from her opposition to the 'socialist' policies of the previous governments. Socialism is the next question that Indians are likely to be asked about in America, after caste and gender—an easy and wrong label that Americans stick on

India is 'socialist.' This uneducated opinion is not limited to the non-educated. We discuss this point elsewhere too.

V.A. Shiva Ayyadurai is an Indian–American scientist and entrepreneur, a Dalit born in Mumbai, the city where Chandan grew up. He registered and voted for the first time in 2016. Despite supporting Trump, he does not like to be called a Republican. 'I hate this labelling business. The Republican establishment and the Democratic establishment are hand in glove to dupe the public,' he told me. He supports Modi and Trump because 'they are revolutionaries'. 'I have studied Leninism and admired Che Guevara,' he said. With multiple degrees from MIT and a controversial claim to being the inventor of email, Ayyadurai was, in 2009, hired by India's Council of Scientific and Industrial Research (CSIR) to develop a business model for a new company, CSIR Tech, which was to establish businesses using research conducted by the country's many publicly owned laboratories. He left that position after running into conflict with the CSIR hierarchy. He has dabbled in politics, as a Democrat and a Republican in Massachusetts.

Ayyadurai's great-grandfather had left Madurai district in Tamil Nadu for Myanmar in the early twentieth century as an indentured labourer. Through almost an entire century, three countries and three generations, the Tamil language and memories of brutal caste oppression survived. Ayyadurai came to America as a seven-year-old in the early 1970s, and each time he returned to India, what struck him were the brutalities of caste. 'Stories at home were about how my parents suffered, and I was deeply interested in understanding it all.'

Ayyadurai says American liberals might accept him as a brown-skinned success story to a limited extent, but not as an inventor or a wealthy entrepreneur. 'There is an insidious model of racism that liberals in America practice [. . .] How could that Indian desi get that wealthy? How dare he do that? That is where Trump and I connect at a spiritual level.' He admires Modi for multiple reasons, among them, the caste angle.

> Narendra Modi is a revolution [. . .] I support Leninism in many ways [. . .] the CPI in India had become the left wing of the Congress party. Modi has done some extraordinary things. He broke down the despicable caste system of the Congress Party. What the hell is the Congress party? It is a dynasty. Here it is the Bushes, the Clintons and a few families that control politics. There it was Nehru, then Indira, then Rajiv, etc.[48]

Ayyadurai believes that for true merit to thrive and discrimination to end, Modi and Trump are the best bets for both the countries and for Indian–Americans. Dalits such as Ayyadurai, like Muslims, are invisible in Indian–American mainstream activities. Ayyadurai says he is at the receiving end of elitism in India and America; Chandan, on the other hand, had a privileged upbringing in India, but is at the receiving end of racism in America. They devise their responses to nationalism, racism and elitism in the US accordingly. Indian–Americans are overwhelmingly upper caste. Only 1.5 per cent of Indian immigrants in the US are Dalits or people of lower caste, according to Kapur.[49]

Indian Americans have faced discrimination that existed in the US, but they have also carried caste discrimination to their new homes. 'India's engineers have thrived in Silicon Valley. So has its caste system,' the *Washington Post* said in its headline for an October 2020 story that recorded widespread and deep-rooted caste discrimination in the US tech industry. The issue came to the spotlight after a Dalit engineer complained of sustained discrimination and harassment at the hands of his upper caste supervisors at Cisco. The issue led to California regulators suing Cisco under the Civil Rights Act of 1964 and California's Fair Employment and Housing Act. The lawsuit said 'higher caste supervisors and co-workers imported the discriminatory system's practices into their team and Cisco's workplace'. The employee received less pay and fewer opportunities, and when he opposed 'unlawful practices, contrary to the traditional order between the Dalit and higher castes, [the] defendants retaliated against him,' the lawsuit said.[50]

Another Dalit engineer told the *Post* that in more than a hundred job interviews for contract work over twenty years, he got only one job offer when another Indian interviewed him in person. When members of the interview panel had been Indian, he said, he faced probing questions to figure out whether he was upper caste. There apparently exists a 'Tam-Bram pat' on the back to check whether the person is wearing the sacred thread of Brahmins.[51]

After the Cisco case was widely reported in July 2020, nearly 260 more complaints emerged in three weeks, according to Thenmozhi Soundararajan, a Dalit activist and executive director at Equality Labs. Allegations included caste-based slurs and jokes, bullying, discriminatory hiring practices, bias in peer reviews, and sexual harassment. They were from Facebook, Cisco, Google, Microsoft, IBM and Amazon. All these companies have a stated policy of not tolerating discrimination.

In 2018, Soundararajan had led a survey of 1200 people, which reported large scale caste discrimination. '[. . .] people who responded [. . .] were in the assembly lines for a Campbell soup factory in Central Valley, as well as people who work for Google, Facebook and the other big tech companies,' she had said. The survey 'unfairly essentializes and villainizes Hinduism,' the HAF had said.[52] 'California's lawsuit against Cisco uniquely endangers Hindus and Indians,' according to the HAF, which has come out strongly against it.

Racial prejudices are certainly a catalyst for the resentment against foreign workers that the Trump movement harvested as political gains, but also real are the economic grievances of the American workers, which include highly skilled professionals. How these grievances will be addressed under a Biden presidency remains an open question. With more and more jobs being automated, the challenge is no longer strictly about getting the immigration policy right.

Leo Perrero is an American IT professional who used to work at the Disney World amusement park in Orlando, Florida. He earned more than $1,00,000 a year and led a happy life. His bosses liked him and things were pleasant. It all changed one day in 2015, when he, along with dozens of people, was called for a conference where they were told they no longer had their jobs. They were going to two Indian companies that would bring people from India.

'My co-workers and I felt extremely betrayed by Disney,' Perrero told a congressional committee. 'They were going to simply cast us aside for their financial benefit. Later that same day (of the layoff) I remember very clearly going to the local church pumpkin sale and having to tell the kids that we could not buy any because my job was going over to a foreign worker.'[53] To add insult to injury, the sacked workers were required to train their replacements to be eligible for a severance package. 'I started to think what kind of American was I becoming? Was I going to become part of ruining our country by taking severance pay in exchange for training my foreign replacement? How many other American families would be affected by the same foreign worker that I trained? Sadly, I choose the money over America.'

Perrero made national headlines when he broke down at the hearing titled 'The Impact of High-Skilled Immigration on U.S. Workers' on 25 February 2016 and caught the attention of the future President, Trump.[54] He appeared with Trump at the presidential campaign several times where the latter repeatedly declared that he would end the abuse of the H-1B system.

Perrero and most others who lost their jobs have not been able to find new jobs in IT. He joined his family's small business that pays him much less than what he used to earn.

India's position used to be that the H-1B visa debate is a trade issue rather than an immigration one. The US trade representatives included provisions regarding movement of people to the US in some trade deals. The Trump administration condemned this practice of the earlier administrations. In any case, it was against open trade and open immigration both.

The question of temporary workers and immigration in general is fundamental to ongoing debates in American politics and this debate has life independent of Trump's rise. Ronil Hira, an associate professor at the Howard University in Washington, DC, has researched the H-1B visa programme widely and has become its strident critic. He argues that there is no shortage of labour in IT and therefore, it should be treated as an immigration issue and not a trade one. He says had there been a shortage of talent, it would have reflected in an increase in salaries. That had not happened until the Trump administration enforced higher salaries as a precondition for H-1B visas.

Hira's research on the salaries of Indian H-1B workers brought to the US by Cognizant and HCL that got the

Disney contract shows that Cognizant paid its H–1B workers a median salary of $61,131, while HCL paid $67,300. 'The Disney workers were being paid about $1,00,000 per year plus generous benefits. Those H–1B workers are being paid 33–39 per cent less than the Disney workers,' he told the congressional committee.[55] Salaries are not the only saving to the company. The employer holds the H–1B visa and therefore can easily terminate a worker. If terminated, the foreign worker is 'out of status' and must leave the country immediately.

'That threat alone is enough to scare away many potential whistle-blowers. But there are other tactics used to intimidate and bully H–1B workers into indentured servitude, including employment bonds (literal indenture) and the threats of liquidated damages lawsuits,' says Hira. 'Professional jobs have been an important rung on the ladder to the middle class. Computer occupations in particular have been a traditional path from working class to the middle class. Exploitation of the H–1B and other guest-worker programmes is shutting that pathway down.'

The criticism against H–1B is no longer limited to Trump's 'America First' politics. For instance, Ro Khanna, the Indian–American Democrat who represents Silicon Valley in the US House of Representatives, is at the forefront of efforts to legislate new regulations on the programme. 'I [. . .] strive to reform the H–1B visa programme to ensure that corporations cannot displace American workers in favour of cheap, foreign labour who they can easily control and underpay. Silicon Valley's leadership in the world of technology was achieved in large part thanks to immigrants who came here on H–1B visas. For that I am grateful, but we must fix this programme by restoring it to its original intent, protecting all workers from systemic abuses by profit-driven companies, and preserving the limited H-1B visas for high-skilled foreign workers.'[56]

This position has wide support across the political spectrum in the US, and is not far from what Trump has been saying and doing. Biden has come to accept this position on temporary work visas, even while his condemnation of the Trump administration is absolute on other allied questions of immigration, particularly regarding asylum seekers and family-linked immigration. The section on 'temporary visa system' in Biden's election platform said: 'High-skilled temporary visas should not be used to disincentivize recruiting workers already in the U.S. for in-demand occupations. An immigration system that crowds out high-skilled workers in favour of only entry level wages and skills threatens American innovation and competitiveness. Biden will work with Congress to first reform temporary visas to establish a wage-based allocation process and establish enforcement mechanisms to ensure they are aligned with the labour market and not used to undermine wages. Then, Biden will support expanding the number of high-skilled visas and eliminating the limits on employment-based visas by country, which create unacceptably long backlogs.' Trump or Biden, Democrats or Republicans, this seems to be a default American position increasingly.

Passing legislation is not easy in the US, given the fragmented positions of lawmakers on any given question. Therefore, changes to the H-1B programme, which is made by congressional law, are not easy. But there are measures that the executive could take to regulate it. During the Trump administration, denial rates for H-1B petitions increased significantly, 'rising from 6% in FY 2015 to 24% through the third quarter of FY 2019 for new H-1B petitions for initial employment.' Between 2010 and 2015, the denial rate for 'initial' H–1B petitions never exceeded 8 per cent.[57] Approval rates improved by 2020, possibly due to the fact that prospective applicants began to self-eliminate in response to the more stringent conditions. The Biden administration will be less hostile towards visa seekers in the administration of the programme.

The idea that those who are offered the highest salaries must get the visa first remains alive, however, in Biden's politics. Such a direction will increase the pressure on the current business models of many Indian IT companies that have thrived on business with the US. During the Trump presidency, US firms such as Amazon, Qualcomm, CTS and Deloitte cornered a significant share of work certifications. 'Indian firms continued to recruit H–1B workers, but the numbers pale in comparison to their hirings before 2016.'[58] Indian companies or American companies, an overwhelming majority of H–1B visas are obtained by Indians year after year. The US has issued more than 1.7 million H–1B visas since 2009, 65 per cent of them to Indians.[59] In September 2019, there was an approximately 5,83,420 H–1B authorized-to-work population. This number is excluding those who have moved to the queue for Permanent Residency (PR) or Green Card. That is yet another question that we discuss a bit later here.[60]

While such regulatory changes forced by the changing nature of politics in the US are gradually changing the character of Indian migration, there are other looming technological ruptures. The business model of outsourcing—which is at the core of India–US trade in services—is coming to an end, according to close observers of industry and technology trends. Dham says that the Indian offshoring model was built primarily on cost arbitrage, the fact that an Indian programmer or coder was available at a lower cost than an American. That was an opportunity presented by historical forces. Today it has plateaued 'not because of Trump, but because of technology', he says. 'Some of us have been telling the Indian companies that a business model based on labour arbitrage—"I will take 60 dollars from the American outsourcer, will keep 30 and give 30 to my employee"—is beginning to break down.' This is primarily due to rising automation. He believes both automation and artificial intelligence (AI) could provide new opportunities for Indian IT talent in America.

Vivek Wadhwa, an Indian–American technology-entrepreneur-turned-academic, confirms that the new frontiers of technology, robot-driven manufacturing and AI, offer the next big opening to Indian IT professionals.[61] 'The value addition Indian companies could do now is artificial intelligence. The highest paid people in Silicon Valley as of today are data scientists—people who can programme these neural networks that enable computers to learn. They are basically mathematicians and statisticians who understand computers,' Dham said. Trump or not, the American immigration system will get tighter for low-skilled workers in the coming years, whether or not it allows more skilled immigrants. With technological advancement pushing more skilled people to compete for jobs below their skill levels, the less skilled will find survival increasingly difficult in the American job market.

'America First' nationalism is forcing politicians to understand issues from the perspective of the country's workers as opposed to its companies. Trade in services with India and American FDIs in India have been seen traditionally from the perspective of American corporations. But the rise of Trump politics changed that, and the relationship is now being seen from the perspective of American labour too. Trump's politics triggered the debate, and the Democrats had no option but to join the bandwagon. This trend is likely to outlast Trump's presidency.

Chicken Nationalism

If trade in services involves Indians coming to America and altering the demographics of the country in the process, and American jobs moving to India through outsourcing contracts, trade in goods has equally become a contentious American question since the rise of 'America First' nationalism. India has a significant surplus in trade with the US and this is a concern not merely for Trump, but for Democrats as well. A particular thorn in the flesh for India–US ties has been the poultry trade. From 2007, India has not allowed American poultry into the country, citing concerns of avian influenza. America argued that there could be no countrywide ban based on avian influenza concerns. When India refused to budge, the US took the case to WTO in 2012. On 19 June 2015, the organization ruled against India. America has moved the WTO again, alleging non-compliance by India and seeking permission to impose a penalty tariff on imports from the country. By mid-2018, India relented and began allowing chicken parts from America, though in small quantities. The last word on this has not been said yet, however.

Political climates in America and India are both unsupportive of trade in goods, but the poultry trade is a curious example—it could be seen as how economies around the world could complement one another through trade or how developing markets become a tool for advanced markets. Also, how avoidable disputes could damage symbiotic relationships.

A little digression into America's global chicken presence shows us why trade cannot merely be understood in terms of surpluses or deficits. The US is the world's largest chicken producer and its chicken consumption per capita—now at 91 pounds—has increased nearly every year since the mid-1960s, while red meat consumption has steadily declined.[62] Nineteen per cent of its poultry produce is exported. It is estimated that Americans eat chicken ten times a month, but not more than twice do they eat chicken thighs or drumsticks. They prefer chicken breasts, a culinary habit that formed when chickens were raised in farms and their legs and thighs were more muscular. Called 'dark meat', chicken thighs and legs continue to carry the stigma of being tougher to chew even though those of factory-farm chickens aren't.

When birds were sold whole, until fifty years ago, there was nothing to be done about these preferences. Ever since companies began selling them in parts, differential pricing entered the picture. Breasts command the highest price, wings and drumsticks much lower, often a few cents per pound. Since the market is so biased against 'dark meat', chicken leg parts are nearly waste for the poultry industry. And we are talking of large quantities—in 2015, almost 9 billion broiler chickens were produced in America. Since culinary preferences decided by culture vary across the world, parts America does not want have a huge market abroad, and the expansion of global trade allowed chicken farmers to access these markets. Chicken feet are a delicacy in China, and chicken legs are considered superior in Russia as well as in India.

In 2008, America exported $854.3 million worth of chicken meat to China and Hong Kong, half of it feet and wings. In 2009, when China threatened restrictions on American chicken feet, in a trade confrontation, an American 'poultry economist' reassured the readers of the *New York Times*,[63] 'We have these jumbo, juicy paws the Chinese really love.' But China did ban poultry import from America in 2015, citing avian flu concerns. After Trump took over, it reopened its market to beef from the US—also banned in recent years—but not poultry. Chicken legs have been at the centre of the US–Russia diplomatic tussles too—in 2014, in response to American sanctions, Russia banned the import of American chicken. Chicken is one of the few items that America used to sell to Russia and it has flapped its wings alongside weightier diplomatic issues. 'When Putin came to visit the US, he and Obama were talking about nuclear proliferation one second and then poultry the next,' an industry expert told *LA Times*.[64]

America and Russia have fought over chicken legs several times in the post–Cold War era. The first Bush administration supplied Russia with tons of chicken parts as food aid immediately after the collapse of the Soviet Union, which came to be known as 'Bush legs'.[65] It squeezed the domestic poultry industry and Russians began to see it as a mark of its humiliation. Putin made self-sufficiency in poultry a national priority. Russia is now almost completely self-sufficient in pork and poultry meat as a result of anti-Russian sanctions, Putin said in June 2017.[66] China restarted poultry imports from the US in 2020, after several years, following a trade deal with the Trump administration.

The Indian poultry industry is up in arms and they fear American dumping into the Indian market would kill the sector. However, given the vast untapped potential of the Indian market and the throwaway price at which chicken parts could be bought from America, there could be a creative solution to this issue.

The Trump administration's drive to reduce American trade deficit has brought India into sharper focus in the US's trade agenda. India is the ninth biggest trading partner of the US and by the end of 2017, had a trade surplus of around $23 billion with the US, in goods and services combined.[67] 'The Obama White House never once mentioned trade deficit with India as a matter of concern. In fact, the discussions always were about the success in growing trade,' a US administration official said on the condition of anonymity in the initial days of the Trump administration.[68] Trump indeed raised these concerns with Modi.

The President's National Trade Policy Agenda for 2017 said, 'In 2016, voters in both major parties called for a fundamental change in direction of U.S. trade policy [. . .] because they did not all see clear benefits from international trade agreements. President Trump has called for a new approach [. . .] '[69] It reiterated Trump's four-point campaign agenda—'defending national sovereignty over trade policy, strict enforcement of U.S. trade laws, using leverage to open foreign markets and negotiating new and better trade deals'. This is for the first time that we have it all spelt out in a document, clearly going against all traditional U.S. positions on trade,' Moushami P. Joshi, international trade lawyer with Pillsbury Winthrop Shaw Pittman, a leading Washington law firm, told me about the Trump administration's National Trade Policy Agenda.[70] 'The emphasis on opening market for U.S. agriculture products and intellectual property are of particular significance for India and created tensions between the two countries that continue into the Biden administration.'

The US demand for the tightening of India's intellectual property rights (IPR) regime got louder under Trump. The United States Trade Representative's (USTR) office brings out an annual Special 301 Report, which is a stocktaking of intellectual property protections across the world. It categorizes countries based on Section 301 of the US Trade Act of 1974, hence its name. India is routinely criticized in this report. New Delhi never cooperates with its preparation as it considers the report a unilateral measure by the US to exert undue pressure on India.

In the wake of Modi's coming into power, there was much speculation in the US by his pro-market supporters that he would dismantle India's existing IPR regime. In July 2017, however, the government told Parliament that in this issue, the Modi government would follow the United Progressive Alliance (UPA) government's policy—that the Special 301 Report issued by the US was a 'unilateral measure' to pressurize countries to enhance IPR protection beyond WTO rules. The WTO has its own dispute settlement mechanisms, and India and the US have wrestled in that system on and off. But the USTR continues to keep its own process, which India finds problematic. 'Special 301 is an extra territorial application of the domestic law of a country, which is inconsistent with the established norms of the WTO,' according to the Modi government.[71] The Trump administration used that against India, and called India a troublesome partner.

The Trump administration made some threatening moves against China in IPR-related disputes based on the Special 301 section, which India opposes in principle. It also tagged India for allegedly inadequate protection of intellectual property. IPR is an issue that American companies, more than their workers, are agitated about. Modi's nationalist politics would not exactly like to allow foreign companies to profiteer off Indian consumers; and his populist politics would require providing affordable pricing for Indians. Since 2015, American medical companies and the Indian government have been locked in multiple regulatory issues, the most important of them being the prices of artificial stents used in human hearts.

Modi's and his predecessor Manmohan Singh's pitch—that India is an exciting market—has been accepted by American capital for which India is today a key destination. As the Modi government eased eighty-seven FDI rules across twenty-one sectors between 2014 and 2017, American investors lapped up the opportunity. India and the US aim to build on the big growth in trade in goods and services that has happened between 2005 and 2015 and reach $500 billion in bilateral trade by 2024, a five-fold increase from 2014.[72]

Trade tensions between the two countries spilled over under the Trump regime. The US invoked Section 232 (b) of the US Trade Expansion Act, 1962, to impose duties on steel and aluminium, affecting several countries, including India. The latter took the issue to the WTO. The US, in turn, challenged India's export subsidy programmes. The US terminated the Generalized System Preferences (GSP) for India which allows many exporters to enjoy lower tariffs on specific exports to the US. The price restrictions imposed by India on medical devices imported from America and the Indian government's position that certain types of international companies must keep the data of Indian consumers on servers physically located in India have riled up the trade bureaucracy and companies in America. These decisions by the Modi government are all in line with the strident nationalism of the Hindutva doctrine. Price control on medical devices is a typically sensitive topic for America. The US policymakers believe that if the Indian model of price restrictions is allowed to stand, other developing countries will follow suit.[73] In June 2018, India announced its decision to increase import tariffs on thirty items from the US. Under the 'Buy American, Hire American' policy of the Trump administration, nearly 1,00,000 Indians who were dependent spouses of H–1B visa holders were at the risk of losing their work authorization. The H–1B processing system itself has been tightened already, with frequent hold-ups, review of each renewal application of the visa as if it were a fresh application, etc.

With tensions mounting on the trade front, both countries continued working towards a Free Trade Agreement (FTA). The Trump administration was eager to shift away from multilateral trade deals and cut bilateral ones with partners. Even by the last days of the Obama administration, in 2016, India had shifted from its earlier position that IP issues must be part of the multilateral Trade-Related Aspects of Intellectual Property Rights (TRIPS) forum and agreed to discuss US concerns with it in a bilateral format in the Trade Policy Forum. India continues to maintain, however, that its IP protection regime is compliant with all TRIPS commitments. The US does not agree with this and has continuously sought better IP protection. Meanwhile, with a consecutive electoral win and against the backdrop of the COVID-19 pandemic, the Modi government also tightened its position on global trade agreements. It decided to walk out of the RCEP, a decision that Jaishankar explained as a step, partly, to undo the damage done by globalization of the economy. India and South Africa joined hands to campaign for relaxation of TRIPS provisions to deal with the pandemic.

Ahead of Trump's visit to India in February 2020, the expectations were that both countries could arrive at a Mini Trade Deal as they continued the pursuit for an FTA. India offered to liberalize poultry trade and some concessions in agriculture, but largely its instincts to protect its farm and rural sector ensured that a common ground could not be reached.[74] The pandemic fanned protectionism and nationalism on both sides. Trump publicly threatened India to ensure the supply of hydroxychloroquine, a cheap malaria drug that it produces and was wrongly considered a potential treatment for COVID-19 in April 2020. India released supplies to the US.[75] Modi announced a new era of Atmanirbhar Bharat—self-reliance—echoing import substitution, which also entails more modes of protection for domestic industries. We have discussed this in the chapter on Hindutva Strategic Doctrine.

Will Biden overturn the protectionism of the Trump era? Can he, and will he, switch back to the Obama era agnosticism regarding trade deficits and focus on the strategic aspects of global ties? Answers are available. 'During the presidential election campaign, one of the candidates pledged to put American workers first, procure American goods to fulfil government orders, and take a tough stance on China's trade practices. It was Joe Biden, not Donald Trump [. . .] trade was the one area where Biden borrowed his Republican rival's rhetoric, promising a "Buy American" approach with echoes of the "America First" agenda that powered Mr Trump to victory in 2016.'[76] Could he be more lenient to India considering the China challenge? That depends on how his approach to China itself would be. That question is discussed in a separate chapter later. Within the broader agenda of economic nationalism in the US and India, a subset of techno-nationalism has emerged as a strong component. The US and China are locked in a battle for supremacy in frontier technologies that will shape the twenty-first century, and India has a significant stake in it. India has also become highly sensitive about protecting its data sovereignty, alongside other components of sovereignty that have been eroded in the era of globalization.

Drones and Fighter Planes

While trade in general is not a great place of convergence between India and the US, trade in defence has greater potential. It is a point of convergence of American strategic interests, India's defence needs, the interests of American manufacturers and their labour. The two countries signed the 'New Framework for the India–US Defence Relationship' in 2005, when Manmohan Singh was prime minister and George W. Bush was President. Since then, there has been a significant uptick in defence trade. The framework was renewed in 2015, under Modi and Obama.

In 2015, during Obama's visit to India, the two countries announced a 'Joint Strategic Vision for the Asia Pacific and Indian Ocean Region'. During Modi's visit to Washington in June 2016, India was designated a 'major defence partner' by the US. This is a unique designation that has been created especially for India, and has led to two distinctive benefits for New Delhi. Earlier, India's requests for sensitive technologies were treated with a presumption of denial, but now the default mode is one of approval. The Obama administration made this change in the Export Administration Regulations (EAR) of the US. 'The EAR establishes a presumption of approval for export licensing, which increases the efficiency and reliability of licensing decisions,' a report jointly submitted by the secretary of defence and secretary of state to relevant congressional committees in July 2017 stated.[77] 'The EAR includes an authorization for India to be a Verified End User (VEU) for commercial and military exports, which negates the necessity of individually validated licenses for approved VEU applicants.'[78] Though this joint report was supposed to be an annual affair, it was produced only once.

Recent modifications in the US export control regime make cooperation in large manufacturing projects easier and also enable exports, at least in theory. The Obama administration had ensured India's admission to the Missile Technology Control Regime (MTCR), paving the way for the Trump administration to approve the sale of twenty-two Guardian Predator drones—the number was raised to thirty by 2020—to India. If India and America manage to reach an agreement on the price and other underlying conditions of the deal—negotiations continue as of 2020—that will be a significant leap in ties. In July 2018, the Trump administration further eased the sale of sensitive technologies to India by moving it to the Strategic Trade Authorization (STA)-1 category. The commerce department placement of India in this category puts India at par with Britain, Australia, Canada, Poland and Norway.

> Since 2008, the United States and India have concluded more than $15 billion in defense trade, including the transfer from the United States to India of C-130J and C-17 transport aircraft, P-8I maritime patrol aircraft, Harpoon missiles, Apache and Chinook helicopters, and M777 light-weight Howitzers. India operates the second largest C-17 and P-8 fleets in the world . . . [79]

The designation of India as a major defence partner is a good talking point when it comes to formulating joint statements and governmental reports, but expectations of any dramatic shift in arms trade could be misplaced. That is because the final call on all arms trade is by the US state department, which is guided by other laws. For instance, the state department objected to the sale of armed drones to India even after it was designated the major defence partner, before it was overruled by former Secretary of State Rex Tillerson.

Trump pushed for the liberalization of US arms sales to partner countries, bound less by grand strategic calculations and guided more by commercial and domestic political considerations. He sought to flip the equation between commerce and strategic rationale in favour of the former. This approach led to easier access for India to American sellers. India has always been wary of the strings that come attached with American weaponry, though the US security establishment and the Congress will not easily accede to major changes in existing laws to further Trump's ideas.[80] Biden's traditionalism could mean more weightage to strategic considerations in arms sales— for instance, how would they affect the regional power balance?

India's desire to move from a 'buyer–seller' relationship to a collaborative relationship first found institutional expression in the 2012 Defense Technology and Trade Initiative (DTTI). Modi's slogan 'Make in India' amplified it. However, the rhetoric associated with it has caused a nationalist blowback from America already, where lawmakers and other officials are wondering whether this is a trade restrictive policy in motion. The transformation of the 'buyer-seller' relationship into something more than that also has a more consequential implication. The US is eager to have interoperability with the Indian military. The US enters into what are called 'foundational or enabling agreements' with its defence partners. These agreements govern the nature and scope of US defence partnerships. Partners enhance the capabilities of the US military in distant places through sharing information, platforms and logistics. On 27 October, only weeks before the 2020 presidential election, India and the US signed the Basic Exchange and Cooperation Agreement

(BECA) during the third 2+2 dialogue of defence and foreign ministers of the two countries. This is the fourth and the last of the foundational agreements that both countries have concluded, starting with GSOMIA (General Security of Military Information Agreement) in 2002, LEMOA (Logistics Exchange Memorandum of Agreement) in 2016, COMCASA (Communications Compatibility and Security Agreement) in 2018, and now BECA. The competitive advantage of the US military is maintained primarily by the advanced technologies that the country develops continuously. The US sells military equipment to other countries with strict control over their deployment and use. For instance, consider the B777-300ER aircraft that India bought from Boeing recently for the use of VVIPs, which were delivered in 2020. The sale of advanced communication and security systems on the aircraft—which are not commercially available—is made seamless by foundational agreements.

'Make in India' in defence is a key component of Modi's plans to take manufacturing to 25 per cent of the gross domestic product by 2022, from the current 18 per cent. The move to develop a military hardware manufacturing base in India has been a key component of the Hindutva Strategic Doctrine for years. It is combined with the objective of creating more jobs in the country, but the idea of self-reliance in defence matters is equally central.

But, as mentioned earlier, the 'Make in India' policy triggered an alarm bell in America even before the 'Buy American, Hire American' slogan of Trump—followed now by Biden's 'Buy American . . . Make it in America'—had become the mainstream US thought on economy. 'Does the Make in India Campaign program discriminate against U.S. and foreign manufacturers and imports?'[81] Congressman Matt

Salmon from Arizona asked during a congressional hearing in early 2016, while the Trump campaign was on the ascent.

When the US and India announced the civil nuclear deal in 2005, US experts were discussing a nuclear renaissance in the energy sector. The calculations based on oil prices and the power demands projected during those times made sense for expanding the nuclear sector massively. 'Then there were setbacks. First came the global financial crisis, which flattened the demand for electricity. Then fracking flooded the market with cheap natural gas. Renewable energy—especially wind power—also got more competitive.[82]

Earlier in 2017, Westinghouse, which was building new nuclear power plants in South Carolina and Georgia, went bankrupt due to massive cost overruns. The first American commercial contract between India and the US was to be with Westinghouse. In India, renewable energy is getting cheaper and more accessible, while nuclear power remains costly, not to talk of its attendant risks. Given the churn of the energy economy dynamics, the basis of the civil nuclear cooperation between India and the US lies in shambles. Meanwhile, Trump latched on to the export of fossil fuel, including crude and natural gas. Modi was quick to seize this opportunity. Trump cared little about climate change, the political argument in favour of nuclear energy expansion and limits on fossil fuel trade. India's fossil fuel import from America soared under Trump's presidency.

For Here, or to Go?

It is possible to suggest that a triple selection created the unique population of Indian–Americans, Kapur and co-authors argue: 'First, India's social hierarchies and historic discrimination selected certain groups like Brahmins and other "high" or "dominant" castes for education [. . .] Second, the rationing of seats in higher education enabled a high-stakes, examination-based selection from within the already selected group [. . .] Third, the U.S. immigration system selected within this doubly-selected group.'[83]

But privilege and dispossession both come into play in Indian–American imaginations. This paradox is pronounced in the lives of the H-1B crowd. They are typically susceptible to being in a permanent state of suspended animation, due to their temporary visa status. The social and political milieu that shaped them in India, over the last three decades, included the rise of Hindutva, assertion of backward caste political parties and expanding reservations for backward castes. In the southern states, upper castes had to cede considerable political space decades earlier, but the rise of Indian backward castes as a national phenomenon happened along with liberalization through the 1990s. The Indian political order was shaken by alliances between assertive lower castes and minorities such as the Muslims through the 1990s and later. The Indians who came to America through the 1990s gained their education through either government-subsidized engineering colleges or as a result of the dramatic expansion of private professional colleges after liberalization.

The implementation of the Mandal Commission recommendation in the early 1990s, reserving 27 per cent of all government jobs for traditionally disadvantaged castes, or the Other Backward Classes (OBCs), created new fissures in Hindu society. In 2005, the Manmohan Singh government expanded reservations for OBCs into higher education too. Both occasions witnessed massive and violent protests from upper caste groups in India. Proposals were floated on how to ensure greater participation of backward castes in the private sector, the new field of upper caste power in India, during the UPA decade from 2004–14. The Congress regime also opened a debate on affirmative action for Muslims, who, according to a comprehensive socio-economic survey, were proven to have living standards far lower than several Dalit communities. The Indians who came to America in the last three decades, while being privileged on many counts, are also in exile from the homeland where they were the ruling class for centuries. It is likely that they believe the alleged appeasement of Muslims and lower castes put them at a disadvantage economically as well as politically in India. While the predominantly upper caste Indian immigrants moved to the US for greener pastures, memories of their relative disempowerment in India did not vanish. Hindutva's calls for restoring the glory of the nation and the idea that the country's progress has been withheld by 'appeasement' politics of earlier regimes, are hence particularly appealing for them. This closely echoes one of the sentiments that drive a segment of American nationalism—the yearning for the restoration of white dominance in politics and culture. There was a corresponding heightening of caste prejudices among the Indian–Americans as well. The expansion of affirmative action quotas in higher education for OBCs during Manmohan Singh's regime led to discussion forums of Indian IT professionals that exposed caste prejudices and the 2014 election was a second inflection point, according to Raghav Kaushik, an upper caste engineer who spoke to the *Post*. 'A lot of the previously repressed ideas, now South Asians feel more emboldened to say it out loud.'[84] The generation of Indian–Americans coming of age in the era of nationalism in the US may process this legacy differently, however.

It takes an unusually long time for Indians to get permanent residency in America, making the wait agonizing and unsettling. Green card allotment has a country-wise cap, which is currently disadvantageous to India. 'Right now, there's a mother in Greenland whose unborn child will be able to obtain permanent residence in America before someone from India who is already here and has been working here for years.'[85]

A Pew study estimated that the average waiting time for an Indian to obtain a green card in America under the employment category was more than twelve years, the longest for any nationality, but Indian–American activists consider it to be even longer. It is estimated that around two-thirds of the 85,000-plus H-1B visas granted every year go to Indians. Activists calculate that there are 1.5 million of them in the green card queue as of today. Of the million-plus green cards issued by the US every year, around 1,40,000 are employment-based—the category that most Indians already in the US are eligible for. But according to the existing system, only about 9800 of these can go to immigrants from any particular nation. Each year, at least 50,000 new Indians—and their families—join the queue, creating an ever-bulging backlog of applicants.

Indians are also the fastest-growing ethnic group among undocumented immigrants in America. A Pew study in 2016 estimated that there are around 5,00,000 undocumented Indians in America.[86]

Through 2018, the number of Indians in American detention centres swelled as the Trump administration cracked down. The American legal system is such that deporting unauthorized residents can be a lengthy process, but still, more than 12 million people were 'deported'—

either removed or returned—from the US during the Clinton administration. More than 10 million were removed or returned during the Bush administration. And more than 5 million were removed or returned during the Obama administration.[87] Despite his rhetoric on deporting people, under Trump, it slowed down.[88]

Though they come on temporary work permits, or H-1B, the American immigration system allows them to turn their statuses to permanent residents and, later, citizens. Only the company that brings them can apply for it, though, which is yet another contentious point in the murky immigration debate in America.

Consequently, a good chunk of Indian Americans seem to be people whom French scholar Olivier Roy characterized as falling between the 'old country' and the 'new country', a state of uncertainty and frustration that forms a fertile ground for anger and reaction.

The reading by Indian–Americans of the propaganda about the pride generated by Modi with regard to India has to be understood in this context. No other story can explain it better than that of Srinivas Kuchibhotla, who was killed by a white racist. His widow Dumala is from Andhra Pradesh, where the BJP is yet to establish its presence in significant measure.

In an eloquent Facebook post on 28 February 2017, a few days after her loss that had become an international news story, Dumala said this of the admiration of Modi and his politics she and her slain husband shared:

> He [Kuchibhotla] always cared about what was happening around him, and he was very proud of Mr Narendra Modiji and India. He was sure that India had finally found the leader that could make India shine. This might seem unreal,

but I know because there wasn't a day that ended without
him watching the news or reading multiple newspapers
before going to bed [. . .] I wish I could meet [. . .]
Mr Modiji and share his joy posthumously.

She tagged the prime minister on the post. Here is a woman
who lost her husband to violence instigated by nationalism in
America, finding in Modi's ultranationalism the project that
would make India great.

The popularity of Hindutva among Indian–Americans has
inspired heated debates in the recent past. This is not the place
for entering into such a debate, since a lot has been written and
said on the topic already. The focus of this discussion is how
Indian–American advocacy is promoting a particular image of
India and its strategic significance in America's global plans.
But suffice it to say that any form of pro-India sentiment, even
when it is blatantly communal and anti-Muslim, could pass off
as legitimate support for the progress of India when it is in the
context of a foreign land.

It is interesting to note what Tarak Nath Das—a much
revered figure in the history of India's freedom struggle, leader
of the Ghadar Party and an early immigrant to the US—wrote
to Lala Lajpat Rai early in the twentieth century, congratulating
him for the formation of the Hindu Mahasabha:

I regret very much that since the ascendancy of Mahatma
Gandhi, the Congress has been reduced to a communal
organisation to promote Moslem interests against the
interest of all the people of India. I do not believe that
there can be a genuine Hindu–Moslem unity by catering
to the Moslems and by sacrificing the sound principle of
Nationalism. I have seen enough of the Indian Moslem

patriots in all parts of the world, and I happen to know
something of their international work on the basis of Islam
First and use India for the cause of Islam.[89]

'We Are Allies'

As America's domestic politics and strategic calculations
identified India and Hindus as allies and others according to
their convenience, the Indian and Indian–American attempt
has been to firmly place themselves in the ally space. Due
to the global situation, more and more people among the
American policy elite consider India an ally. Continuously
endorsing India, regardless of the version of Indian nationalism
that plays out at a given moment, is also the best self-validation
for American strategists, who are facing the worst crisis of
credibility since the collapse of the Soviet Union. India is
the only significant country outside the western orbit where
market economy and democracy coexist, all its limitations
apart. At a time when the American idea of itself as the
champion of democracy and free market and the inevitable
coexistence of the two are being seriously challenged in the
homeland itself, India's success is essential for America's self-
validation. There is an incentive to overlook any regression
in India as much as there is for overlooking and ignoring the
brutal and insensitive nature of America's own political and
economic system, towards its own poor and the dispossessed.

An estimated 36 million people in America are connected
to, or sympathetic to, Hinduism, through multiple means, but
primarily through the practice of yoga. That is 10 per cent of
the country's population. India as the 'spiritual homeland' of
Hinduism has an appeal to them. The HAF presents Hinduism
as a peace-loving religion, and then extrapolates it into the

practice of statecraft and affirms the Hindutva Strategic Doctrine.

> . . .. over their vast history, Hindus have never invaded another land in the name of religion. It is also clear that, for centuries in Southeast Asia, it has been this Hindu brand of absolute pluralism, which has provided the ideal environment for peaceful coexistence and prosperity for at least eight major religions, including Hinduism, Buddhism, Judaism, Christianity, Islam, Sikhism, Jainism and Zoroastrianism.[90]

The wide-ranging support for Modi among the Indian–American community was reflected in the American foreign policy establishment too, in the initial years of his regime. Always sceptical of India's traditional positions of non-alignment and strategic autonomy, the US state department seems to agree with any narrative that predominantly blames Nehru and the Congress party for all the problems in India. It is a different matter that the Hindutva doctrine is neither non-statist nor a repudiation of strategic autonomy. India as a caste-ridden, backward Hindu society has been a prevalent stereotype among Americans, educated and uneducated; India as a communist, socialist country is another. The Hindutva Strategic Doctrine echoes and challenges these stereotypes opportunistically, and advances an alternative model of understanding.

American policymakers want to understand India, but in general, the anxiety in policy circles has been to do so from the perspective of American businesses and strategic interests. While this is an entirely legitimate and even predictable approach, it often mistakes or misrepresents the complexities of India, and leads to simplistic and often erroneous conclusions.

'In fact, the only place you can go to find a poor person of Indian heritage is India. I am confident that, as India gets better governance, it will emerge as one of the richer countries in the world,' lawmaker Sherman said at a congressional hearing.[91]

The primary contact with India of many American policymakers is through the largely upper caste professionals and business leaders who are generally not appreciative of the Nehruvian economic model, its emphasis on redistribution and socially inclusive policies such as reservations. American policymakers have little interest or capacity to engage with the domestic politics of India, but conveniently absorb the fact that India's attitude towards the market economy has been hesitant. It is a different matter that their hopes that Modi is a believer in market economics has been belied considerably after his policies began to unroll. This statement from Sherman, a left-leaning lawmaker, is indicative of the simplistic assumptions about India that still guide Americans—though they would no longer talk about maharajas and snake charmers!

Indian–Americans prosper in America for complex reasons. Kapur and Chakravorty's study on Indian–American exceptionalism point to its foundation—that there is a selection process that recruits the best and the brightest Indians to America, which makes their impressive rise possible. But the notion of Indians as backward-looking, Hindu Communists is widespread in America. Post liberalization, that image has been modified to a certain extent, but it has not entirely vanished. I personally encountered one such view, at a Trump rally in New Hampshire in 2016. 'Hindu socialist,' a middle-aged man said as he charged at me, before the woman I was interviewing calmed him down.

Nothing would augment Indian–Americans' fight against prejudice in the US than a self-proclaimed Hindu nationalist who is feted by the American security and military establishment. Modi's Madison Square address in New York in 2014, touted as an assertion of India, had elements of reinforcement of American prejudices and an eagerness to fit into this framework. 'And brothers and sisters, what you have done here is no short of a miracle. We are consuming the same food and water that you grew up on. If you can, then why can't we? So we too can achieve the same miracles. See the talent of this nation.' In the speech that portrayed India as a dysfunctional place where nothing happened due to '1200 years of slavery', he promised better policies. He thanked Indian–Americans for showing the world what Indians were capable of—not 'snake charmers' as popular stereotypes portray them as, but 'mouse charmers', for their success in information technology.[92] Conversely, any criticism of Modi is rejected as 'socialist and Leftist', which is the most convenient abuse for Americans of all stripes, progressive Democrats included.

The lure of India's consumer and defence markets, and the strategic environment that calls for closer India–US cooperation, makes the acceptance of such ahistorical theories easier for traditional American diplomats, who prefer to deal with stable dispensations abroad. The new variable that is added to the matrix of American foreign policymaking is America's own nationalism, whipped up by Trump, and at least its economic part adapted by his successor in the White House.

Steve Bannon was one of the few American observers to read Modi's 2014 victory as a populist revolt against establishment elites, while the American establishment read it mostly as an expression of popular desire for more market reforms and globalization. The contest between globalism and nationalism is far from over in the US, though Biden's long career in politics puts him firmly in the first camp. The contest between the two camps will continue, within both parties. The Biden administration is full of personnel who are largely globalists, but they are themselves responding to the changing political winds of the US. The policy towards India becomes a rare point of convergence for the globalists and the nationalists in the US, for different reasons, and at times with varying priorities and details. Essentially, in today's America, the Democrats and Republicans, the populists and the establishment, the conservatives and the progressives all appear to broadly agree on one thing—that India–US relations are critical for them. It needs to be added here that policies of the Modi government over the last six years have left them a tad disappointed. The pluralist warriors and market worshippers now think their enthusiasm for the regime change in India in 2014 was premature.

There has been continuity in India–US relations in the last two decades, starting with the breakthrough after America lifted the post-nuclear test sanctions in 2001. As Jaishankar notes in his treatise, India is seeking a new equilibrium with the West. India–US ties continue to have volatile ups and downs. One phase, comprising one decade, stands out, from an India perspective. I have called it the 'breakout decade', starting with Vajpayee and ending with the first UPA government of Manmohan Singh. The pitch for an alliance with the US had begun with a speech by Prime Minister Vajpayee within four months of the 1998 nuclear test. At the Asia Society in New York, Vajpayee declared that India and the US were natural allies.

The decade from 1999 to 2009—starting with the Kargil War and ending with the first UPA government led by Manmohan Singh—was characterized by an ideological pro-Westernism, with both the BJP and the Congress showing an ideological affinity towards the US. But the reasons of both were dissimilar, like the nationalists and progressives in America who look to friendship with India from varying perspectives. The Congress, with its Nehruvian–neoliberal hybrid filter, saw in America the necessary ally in its pursuit of domestic economic and social goals and a defensive security posture; the Hindutva–neoliberal outlook found in the US the perfect ally to boost 'leading power' ambitions and domestic social politics.

The end of UPA-1 also coincided with the 2008 economic collapse, which forced the Obama administration to recalibrate its global posturing and positioning, and which had a direct bearing on India's strategic calculations. Towards the end of UPA-2, American observers had begun to complain about the 'drift' and 'indecisiveness' in New Delhi, overlooking the Indian perspective. By the end of the Obama administration, India was complaining about the US's tepid approach towards India and the President's inability to deliver on issues dear to it, such as the NSG membership. But the American drift, from the Indian perspective, had begun with the 2008 crisis that Obama inherited as he stepped into the White House. Both countries were wishing for 'decisive' leadership from the other side by the end of the Obama administration and the Manmohan Singh premiership.

The nationalist era under Trump and Modi had synergies in their respective civilizational idea of nationhood, and the unambiguous belief that their common enemy is Islamism. At the same time, their similar approach to domestic economy to provide jobs for their respective populations, their desire to strengthen their country's standing in the world, and so on, cut both ways. The search for new equilibrium in the

India–US ties will continue as both countries are trying to figure out their own self-identity and interests.

India does not seek a formal military alliance with the US. It has been very cautious in its commitments and obligations. The closest India came to a military commitment was during the initial years of the Breakout Decade, under Vajpayee's premiership, when New Delhi considered committing Indian forces to the invasion of Iraq.[93] After internal deliberations, the Vajpayee government sent its regrets to the Bush administration. America has been very frustrated and often angry with India for its reluctance to march in step with the US on a wide range of issues. India prefers to maintain its 'strategic autonomy'.

As a mechanism to overcome this dilemma, a study sponsored by the Council on Foreign Relations and published in 2015 suggested a 'joint venture' model for India–US ties. The authors of the study noted:

> Just as joint ventures in business bring together parties to advance a shared objective without subordinating their many other interests, so should India and the US pursue their shared ambitions without assuming that each will— or even should—see eye to eye with the other on every matter. Reframing ties in this way will better explain how convergence on the need for open sea lanes, for example, may not presume agreement on climate change, and how convergence on the Asia-Pacific may not presuppose like-mindedness on the Middle East.[94]

The US has been pressing India for a formal agreement on defence intelligence-sharing, an item that has been mentioned in the Defense Framework Agreement signed between the two countries in 2015. The issue has figured repeatedly in bilateral talks, but signing an agreement is a political decision that the prime minister needs to take. In 2003, India did sign a defence intelligence-sharing pact with the US, but it was not renewed on expiry in 2008, when A.K. Antony was the defence minister. He had also refused to sign off on a 2+2 format of consultation between the defence and foreign ministers of both the countries. Trump and Modi had decided to kick off this format. As defence minister from October 2006 to May 2014, Antony did not travel to the US even once.[95] The first 2+2 dialogue between India and the US took place in September 2018 and the second one in 2020, just weeks before Trump was defeated by Biden.

Through the intense churn in both the US and India, both countries are likely to move closer and closer, even when they spar with each other. There is a surplus of accumulated capital in the US that needs stable markets. In his initial years as prime minister, Modi appeared to provide stability for American capital, with less distractions of democratic cacophony compared to the Manmohan Singh era. But the social policies of the BJP government and its Hindutva agenda appear to have disrupted the country's social balance. However, India's attraction as a huge market will continue for the US for a while. India will want US capital and technology, but it will also want to set terms. That is a bit too ambitious an approach, and there is a lot of ground to be covered for both countries to arrive at a common ground. Such issues were listed by the outgoing US ambassador Kenneth I. Juster in January 2021 as 'frictions and frustrations' on the Indo–US trade and investment front. He also made references to Delhi's decision to buy Russian defence equipment, and the Make in India and Atmanirbhar campaigns, the 'growing restrictions' by India on market access for certain US goods and services, 'increasing tariffs', 'new limitations' on the free flow of data, and a 'less-than-predictable regulatory environment for investors'.[96]

Crises—India–US partnership is *Forged in Crisis* as Rudra Chaudhuri's book title suggests—can provide sudden opportunities and momentum. COVID-19 was one such, and the bilateral cooperation between India and the US could achieve new heights, meeting the new challenges of the world.

A Divided Diaspora

Modi's entry on the scene, harnessing the political potency of the Indian–American diaspora as part of the Hindutva Strategic Doctrine, has provided them with an opportunity to mobilize support for him and his agenda, by presenting him in a manner that suits American sensibilities. One strategic strand is to place themselves on the right side of America's nationalist politics. Simultaneously, the communal polarization in India has been transported to the US. To cite one example, the Alliance for Justice and Accountability (AJA), a coalition of progressive organizations in the US, called for protests against mob lynching in the name of cow protection in India, taking inspiration from the 'Not In My Name' marches in several Indian cities in 2017. Protests were held in Washington, DC, San Diego, San Jose and New York. Among the handful of protestors who gathered in Washington, not a single one was Hindu. Every one of them was Muslim. In 2019, the protest against the CAA was widespread across cities in the US and American university campuses, and this time, Hindus were participating in large numbers. In 2020, during the farmers' protest, Indian groups in the US criticized the Modi government. Several American lawmakers also raised questions on all these issues.[97]

Reflecting on the creeping communal polarization among Indian–Americans, Salim Sheikh, a participant in the protest, said in 2017: 'Until some years ago, 90 per cent of my friends were Hindus. Social gatherings used to be mixed, but gradually the distance began to grow. Perhaps, my Hindu friends have become busy along the way.'[98] Sheikh, who grew up in Ahmedabad and has been a resident of Washington for nearly three decades, said that after the 2014 election in India, this polarization has deepened and a kind of unofficial excommunication of Muslims from the Indian–American stream is near total. As we noted in earlier paragraphs about the caste divisions among the community, religious divisions too are significant.

After the Modi government came to power, the Indian embassy in Washington, DC stopped the annual Eid gathering for the Indian Muslim community. The Embassy celebrates Diwali, Christmas, Hanukkah and Baisakhi, but Eid, no longer. In 2018, Trump reinstated the White House iftar after a break, but curiously, only foreign diplomats were invited. American Muslims, including Trump's supporters among them, were not called.[99]

Indian–Americans are traditionally Democratic voters according to available evidence, but Trump's repeated attack on 'Islamic terrorism' was one of the reasons that enabled him to carve out a constituency among them. Surveys suggest a shift of Indian Americans from the Democratic camp to the Republican side, though an overwhelming majority continues to be with the first in 2020. Around 22 per cent of Indian–Americans supported Trump pre-poll, according to the Indian American Attitudes Survey (IAAS), while 68 per cent (or 72 per cent of registered voters in the study) supported Biden. Compared with the 2016 post-poll National Asian American Survey (NAAS), Biden was nine points lower than Hillary Clinton's 77 per cent; and Trump was six points higher than his 16 per cent in 2016. The 2020 Asian American Voter Survey had Trump at 28 per cent among Indian–Americans, a 12 point jump from the 2016 post-poll survey.

The Indian–American ambiguity towards Harris has been louder. Only less than half, 49 per cent, were 'more enthusiastic' about the Democratic ticket because of her candidacy, while 15 per cent were 'less enthusiastic' because of her candidacy; and only 45 per cent Indian–Americans were 'more likely' to vote because one among them was a candidate. All this in a cohort in which support for Democrats was overwhelming otherwise. How does one explain this?

Harris was born to parents who married interfaith, and she herself has married interfaith. India's official policy has also leaned towards narrowing 'Indian–American' to 'Hindu American', going against the grain of the Democratic Party, which prefers wider categories to negotiate a landscape of increasing diversity in the US. The Democrats underscore Harris' identities as African–American and South Asian, a category that Hindutva groups abhor. 'Indian–American', as a typical hyphenated American identity, assumes a certain homogeneity across diverse linguistic and religious groups from India, and adds respectability to dual national loyalties, which is an accusation against minorities in India. However, double hyphenated identities throw not only diaspora politics, but even India's visa policy into a tailspin. Harris is African–Indian–American, or African–South Asian–American. American citizens of India–Pakistan mixed parentage find it impossible to travel to India, due to visa restrictions put in place during the UPA government, after a Pakistani–American used his US passport to gain easy entry into India and plan the Mumbai terror attack of 2008. David Headley was a US double agent. The efforts to tap diaspora resources for advancing India–US ties also sought to streamline the community as an extension of domestic cultural nationalism, by emphasizing its Hindu identity. That interfaith marriages would weaken the Hindu society is now a popular notion. At the World Hindu Congress, which was attended by Indian vice president Venkaiah Naidu and RSS chief Mohan Bhagwat, in Chicago in 2018, there was a poster exhibition on love jihad; in India, there are now laws against interfaith marriages.

The rise of Harris as US VP and global responses to domestic developments in India—the farmer agitation in 2020, the CAA in 2019 and mob lynchings in 2018—all demonstrated the limits of a partisan consolidation of Indian diaspora communities. The rise of Hindutva has accentuated the pre-existing divisions within the Indian–American community on religious, caste and generational lines, in part mirroring trends within India, besides pushing it to delink from the larger South Asian identity. Attempts by groups to corner Indian–American lawmakers on Hindutva questions and the India–Pakistan conflict have created a self-defeating dynamic. American-born Indian–Americans appear to be taking a hard look at developments in India in light of the nativist politics around them. Indian–Americans may well be culturally rooted, but that does not automatically make them puppets of Hindutva cultural politics in the US. Those who might gladly support cultural nationalism in India need cultural diversity in the US for self-preservation, and ally with the Democrats. Biden supporters are largely Modi supporters too. They might occasionally find common cause with the

Republicans on the question of Islam, but will remain suspects in the highly Judeo–Christian world. In an inverse situation, Christians who are unlikely supporters of the majority cultural politics in India, appear to be enthusiastic about it in the US. Engagement with the diaspora can be beneficial for India, but aggressive efforts to navigate it can be counterproductive.

The Trump administration had limited interest in taking up issues of global commons such as human rights or climate change in its international engagements. There is a perception that the Biden administration will try to reassert American pre-eminence and leadership in the world, leading to new avenues of tensions with India. What if it makes Kashmir or other domestic issues of India part of the bilateral engagement? Jake Sullivan has said the Biden administration would balance interest and values in dealing with India.

In the event of a conflict between the two, interests will prevail over values. India's attempts under Modi in the coming days would be to front-load the interest component in its engagement with the US.

At any rate, the US's ability to be the rule-maker of the world has reduced. Today, China, India, Russia, and Turkey all seem less likely to converge on liberal democracy than they did in 1990. These countries and many others have developed economically and technologically not in order to become more like the West, but rather to achieve a deeper independence from the West and to pursue civilizational and political goals of their own.[100]

Even when the US was pushing for a global agenda of order, human rights and rule of law, it had dealt with political dissent and aspirations of racial justice with utmost brutality and legal innovations that are comparable to authoritarian regimes. Confronted with a fresh, intense struggle over America's identity and interests, the US establishment is revisiting the toolkit of purge and punishment within its society. It is trying to discipline and formalize its own democracy by examining the loyalties of citizens, and scrubbing public discourse to ensure that they are aligned with a sanctioned understanding of national interest. Even a person as high as the president of the US is immune to such scrutiny. When India presents the ongoing restructuring of its twentieth century domestic consensus as measures to deal with twenty-first century challenges such as separatism, terrorism, climate change and threats to democracy, which moral perch has the US got to preach from? 'Then, as now, it was weak countries whose oppressive behavior attracted the most attention [. . .] No delegation of European powers came to Washington to discuss the treatment of Native Americans or to make representations concerning the status of African Americans,' writes Walter Russel Mead.[101] It is a question of power and self-perception of countries. 'In one month, our government has issued statements on events in US (capitol riots), Sri Lanka (devolution), Pakistan (Temple attack) etc . . . and also told half a dozen countries they have no right to comment on Indian "internal matters" (farmers protests, CAA, J&K, etc),' noted Indian strategic affairs expert Suhasini Haider in a tweet on 7 January 2021. While there are moral and practical restraints on the US's ability to be the beacon of global democratic standards, it also has enough moral and practical arguments to countenance any alliance, as it did during the Cold War. 'Saving the planet from a climate catastrophe and building a coalition to counter China are causes that many Wilsonians will agree both require and justify a certain lack of scrupulosity when it comes to the choice of both allies and tactics,' under the Biden regime.[102] One must, however, be cognizant of the fact that no US policy maker is losing sleep over what is happening in India on any given day.

4

China: The Dragon in the Frame

'For decades, they have ripped off the United States like no one has ever done before [. . .] They were able to get away [. . .] because of past politicians and, frankly, past presidents. But unlike those who came before, my administration negotiated and fought for what was right. It's called: fair and reciprocal treatment.'

—President Donald Trump, 30 May 2020[1]

'China is going to eat our lunch? Come on, man [. . .] I mean, you know, they're not bad folks, folks. But guess what? They're not competition for us.'

—Joe Biden on the campaign trail in May 2019[2]

The COVID-19 pandemic brought about tumultuous changes in international politics in 2020. China, where the pandemic originated, faced flak for its handling of the crisis in the initial months, but soon enough, it appeared to be in control, the spread of the virus tamed at home and its economy in recovery mode. While the pandemic turned out to be yet another occasion for China to claim superiority of its economic and political model, it also exposed the weaknesses of the American political and economic system. COVID-19 triggered a fresh round of debate on liberalism. Most significantly, the pandemic contributed to the fall of Trump, who had looked unassailable before the outbreak. 'China wants a different president,' Vice President Mike Pence had said as Trump went all guns blazing against it.[3] The 2008 economic crisis was the turning point in Chinese assertiveness, but the world was still unsure whether it had given up Deng Xiaoping's command, 'hide your strength and bide your time.' Through the launch of BRI in 2013, and Xi breaking his promise to Obama and militarizing the South China Sea features, Chinese assertion was growing strident and in 2020, Xi took it to new highs. There is no hiding of strength for a China that has concluded that its time has come.

The aftermath of the pandemic fuelled more nationalism in politics in many parts of the world, certainly in China, India and the US. Even in his defeat, Trump so sharply put the spotlight on China as the key challenger of the US in the twenty-first century that Biden and the Democrats have agreed to broadly follow it. This agreement may only be at the broad level,[4] as commentator Seema Sirohi points out. The Democrats are generally more inclined to give China the benefit of doubt. Some observers find Joe Biden lacking in strategic clarity when it comes to China.[5] His rather sterile view of China expressed in the statement above is genuinely his, but he would be amenable to persuasion. At the broad level for sure, 2020 brought about a rare consensus in US politics that China is an urgent problem to be addressed, if not necessarily confronted.

As for India, 2020 was a year of reckoning in its relations with China. In a first in forty-five years, both sides lost soldiers in a border clash. At least twenty Indian soldiers and an unknown number of Chinese ones died in Ladakh in June, leading to massive mobilization of forces by both sides. The Chinese action of occupying disputed territories so damaged the bilateral relationship that it is now at its 'most difficult phase' in the last thirty–forty years, according to Jaishankar, India's foreign minister. The Chinese action remained inexplicable. China gave India 'five differing explanations' and 'literally brought tens of thousands of soldiers in full military preparation mode right to the LAC in Ladakh'.[6] Ashley Tellis has linked the Chinese action to India's decision in August 2019 to carve out Ladakh as a federally administered territory, along with the ending of the special constitutional status of the state of Jammu and Kashmir.[7] Hindutva Strategic Doctrine had opposed the relative autonomy that J&K had enjoyed within the Indian Union.

'You can't have the kind of situation you have on the border and say let's carry on with life in all other sectors of activity. It's just unrealistic,' according to Jaishankar.[8] The Chinese push that commercial ties remain unaffected by all the turmoil on the border is no longer considered viable by India, which tried to make a symbolic statement by barring 267 Chinese apps in India. But the much talked about idea of decoupling from the world's second biggest economy and manufacturer is not an easy ask. Walter Anderson had argued in 2018[9] that the Modi government had 'decoupled' the strategic and economic aspects of the relationship with Beijing, while acknowledging the strident Hindutva position on China. Ending that decoupling may well be possible, but the decoupling of any national economy from the global economy, more so from the Chinese economy, is easier said than done. Even the desirability of it is not a settled question.

'Trying to fully decouple, as some have suggested, from China [. . .] is unrealistic and ultimately counter-productive. It would be a mistake,' Antony Blinken, US Secretary of State[10] had said earlier. It was the US that chaperoned China on to the global stage; Trump would say that the US built China into the power it has now become. China was 2 per cent of the world's GDP in 1980; in 2020, it is 20 per cent. But for the US, China would not have achieved what it has. The US alone cannot stop China in its tracks; but if the US does not challenge China, no one else can or will. The future course of China, and its place in the world, will largely depend on Washington's China policy.

The US has relative advantage over China, one could argue. China will lose 200 million working age adults and add 300 million senior citizens by the middle of the twenty-first century, while the US will continue to add a working age population of migrants, and remain the hub of innovation. Biden's views themselves reflect this approach that the paramountcy of American power will not be challenged by China. Trump got the China threat right, but not many appreciate him for this. An opposite view may be more popular even today in the mainstream of American thinking. ' . . . Trump has turned what Beijing perceived as a long-term risk into an immediate crisis that demands the urgent mobilization of the Chinese system,' according to one opinion.[11]

As it was winding up, the Obama administration's view was that the US–China relationship was 'the most important bilateral relationship in the world'. 'It's indispensable to addressing just about any issue that we care about.'[12]

Trump and Modi both understand the China challenge as a deeply ideological one, but they had to come to terms with the reality of its strengths. They had both described China as an expansionist power during their election campaigns in 2014 and 2016 respectively, but President Xi was among the first world leaders they both received after taking over as chief executives of their respective countries.

Three months after he took over as prime minister, in September 2014, Modi, in what was publicized as a new style of diplomacy, took Xi to his home state of Gujarat, and posed with him on a swing overlooking the Sabarmati River; by 2020, Modi and Xi had met eighteen times, including for three highly visible informal summits. The tensions on the border, however, brought in a new level of friction between the two countries. In early April 2017, more than two months after he took over as President of the US, Trump feted Xi at a resort owned by him in Florida. By the end of Trump's tenure, there was evidence for those who argued that a trade war with China would not be useful in dealing with the challenges it posed. Harsher opinions would say 'China has won the trade war'. In 2020, China's trade surplus with the US and the world grew further.

The 'America First' policy of Trump created a new narrative, with resolve and clarity, challenging the sanguine view that had been held by the Obama administration. In early 2020, Trump asked four of his most senior national security officials to explain current US policy on China to the American people. Over the summer of 2020, they did so in a series of speeches and before the 2020 elections, the White House published these speeches that cumulatively outlined the approach towards China.[13] An overview of this document is helpful to understand the default file that has been bequeathed to Biden, who as vice president in the Obama administration, was party to an opposing point of view. Biden has said during the campaign that he was 'Vice President and not President' earlier, signalling that he would not be bound by his own tenure as VP.

During the first year of Trump in office, India and China got entangled in a military face-off, in Doklam, a tri-junction between India, China and Bhutan. In the last week of June 2017, after Modi and Trump met at the White House, they issued a joint statement which echoed—nay reproduced—the Indian objection to the Chinese-led Belt and Road Initiative (BRI) infrastructure project. It said India and America support 'bolstering regional economic connectivity through the transparent development of infrastructure and the use of responsible debt financing practices, while ensuring respect for sovereignty and territorial integrity, the rule of law, and the environment.'[14] India had abstained from the BRI Forum in Beijing in May 2017, citing sovereignty concerns as the project passes through parts of Pakistan-occupied Kashmir (PoK). India had also pointed out that the financing of the project could turn out to be unviable. The India–US joint statement used similar language.

Contentious Equations

In the last week of November 2009, Prime Minister Manmohan Singh visited the US as the first state guest of Obama, who had taken over as President earlier that year. I was part of the media team that travelled with Singh. The first African–American president in the White House was an endless topic of conversation in the US, but a remarkable point that I noticed only after the election of Trump in 2016, with the benefit of hindsight, is the fact that Singh was the first non-Hindu prime minister of India. Sikhs constitute only 1.9 per cent of India's population, and were the target of massive mob violence following the assassination of Prime Minister Indira Gandhi at the hands of her Sikh bodyguards in 1984. Singh's rise to the top, therefore, marked a significant milestone in Indian democracy.

So here, the world's biggest democracy's first minority prime minister, who had just won a massive mandate for a second term in office, was meeting the first African–American president of the world's oldest democracy. This is not the occasion to venture into a detailed discussion on this, but the fact that Trump and Modi followed them, riding a wave of majoritarian right-wing religious nationalism in both these democracies soon after, is perhaps no coincidence.

Obama, who had deferred to Singh, hosted for him a lavish banquet at the White House on 24 November 2009. In 2020, Obama would single out Singh for wholesome praise in his memoir.[15] The White House spent half a million dollars on the dinner—the most expensive state dinner of Obama's presidency. But Singh had a particular agenda on his menu. Obama had already visited China earlier the same month, and the terms of engagement that he appeared to be setting with Beijing raised serious apprehensions in New Delhi. Of particular concern was a joint statement by Obama and President Hu Jintao on 17 November, in Beijing. It had a paragraph that alluded to a US–China joint role in South Asia, in India–Pakistan relations and their impact on Afghanistan, where Obama had committed to end the war that had begun in 2001. The joint statement said:

> The two sides [China and America] welcomed all efforts conducive to peace, stability and development in South Asia. They support the efforts of Afghanistan and Pakistan to fight terrorism, maintain domestic stability and achieve sustainable economic and social development, and support

the improvement and growth of relations between India and Pakistan. The two sides are ready to strengthen communication, dialogue and cooperation on issues related to South Asia and work together to promote peace, stability and development in that region.[16]

India has traditionally been opposed to third-party involvement in India–Pakistan relations, though it would like Washington to do more to control Pakistan's promotion of insurgency and terrorism targeting India. In a remarkable episode in American intervention, the Kargil War was resolved at Blair House, a guest house across from the White House where the American President hosts foreign dignitaries. There, President Clinton arm-twisted Pakistan prime minister Nawaz Sharif to order the withdrawal of the country's army from Indian territory. So, while India welcomed and accepted external interventions that are in furtherance of its own interests, as a matter of principle, it is opposed to any role for a third country in India–Pakistan affairs. A US–China joint intervention is even worse.

The China–Pakistan closeness was increasing at the time. Singh took up the issue with Obama and explained the outcome during a press conference before taking off from Washington, DC. 'The reference to South Asia in the US–China Joint Statement is not aimed at mediation by any third power [in Indo–Pak dialogue]. I am satisfied with what President Obama has assured me,' Singh said. He said India would deal with China independent of the US, but he had, during discussions with Obama, spoken about China's 'greater degree of assertiveness'. 'But I did not seek any help from the US. We just reviewed the world situation and I am confident that with true, purposeful negotiations between our two countries, we can resolve contentious issues.'[17]

Now, the idea of a US–China common approach towards Asia in particular and global politics in general is as old as the diplomatic breakthrough between the two countries when Nixon was President of the US. While America and China have had diverging views on the future of Asia and the world, they appear to agree on one principle—they need to work together to find common ground. The US–China Shanghai joint statement on 27 February 1972, at the conclusion of Nixon's visit, stated the respective positions of both countries on issues ranging from Japan's role, Korea's future and the ongoing war in Vietnam.

What is germane to our discussion is the fact that in that very first document itself, America and China noted that they had a joint role to play in India–Pakistan ties and in the affairs of South Asia. Their views on the issue were not identical, but similar.

The Shanghai statement said of Washington's view:

Consistent with the United Nations Security Council (UNSC) Resolution of December 21, 1971, the United States favours the continuation of the ceasefire between India and Pakistan and the withdrawal of all military forces to within their own territories and to their own sides of the ceasefire line in Jammu and Kashmir; the United States supports the right of the peoples of South Asia to shape their own future in peace, free of military threat, and without having the area become the subject of great power rivalry.[18]

Beijing's views were worded differently:

[I]t firmly maintains that India and Pakistan should, in accordance with the United Nations resolutions on the

India–Pakistan question, immediately withdraw all their
forces to their respective territories and to their own sides
of the ceasefire line in Jammu and Kashmir and firmly
supports the Pakistan Government and people in their
struggle to preserve their independence and sovereignty
and the people of Jammu and Kashmir in their struggle for
the right of self-determination.[19]

Chinese words are more hostile towards India here, but only
months earlier, Beijing had ignored a push by the Nixon–
Kissinger duo to open a front against India while it was fighting
Pakistani military in the newly formed Bangladesh. The relevant
point is that the US seeks to fit India and China in its strategic
calculus depending on Washington's priorities and compulsions
at a given moment. Nixon, who was pompous, vituperative and
had a limited understanding of the world, was pushing China to
attack India in 1971, though America had supported India with
arms supplies during the 1962 conflict with China. India helped
the US install equipment in the Himalayas that would monitor
Chinese nuclear activities in the 1960s.

A US–China joint strategy on South Asia surfaced yet
again during Bill Clinton's presidency, following the nuclear
tests by India and Pakistan in 1998. On 27 June, Presidents Bill
Clinton and Jiang Zemin issued a joint statement, responding
to the tests that had taken place only a few weeks earlier:

Recent nuclear tests by India and Pakistan, and the
resulting increase in tension between them, are a source
of deep and lasting concern to both of us. Our shared
interests in a peaceful and stable South Asia and in a strong
global non-proliferation regime have been put at risk by
these tests, which we have joined in condemning. We have

agreed to continue to work closely together, within the P-5, the Security Council and with others, to prevent an accelerating nuclear and missile arms race in South Asia, strengthen international non-proliferation efforts, and promote reconciliation and the peaceful resolution of differences between India and Pakistan.[20]

The Indian government—then led by Prime Minister A.B. Vajpayee—was furious. An official statement by the ministry of foreign affairs said, 'India categorically rejects the notion of these two countries arrogating to themselves joint or individual responsibility for the maintenance of peace, stability and security in the region . . . The US–China joint strategy reflects the hegemonic mentality of a bygone era in international relations and is completely unacceptable and out of place in the present-day world.'[21]

The Chinese Jigsaw

While the June 1998 statement was an instance of the US and China trying to find common ground in preventing a nuclear flashpoint in South Asia, and keeping in check two nuclear powers that destabilized the post-World War II global nuclear order, America had tried to pre-empt the rise of Communist China on the world stage by trying to push India up decades earlier. To what extent did India want to be part of the US–China rivalry is a question that confronted the country almost immediately after Independence. In 1950, the US proposed that it could support India as a permanent member of the UN Security Council, a tactical move to deny the Chinese mainland, which was now under the sway of communism, a seat at the global high table.

Whether the US would have taken such an offer to its logical conclusion remains an open question, but Nehru did turn it down. 'India, because of many factors, is certainly entitled to a permanent seat in the security council. But we are not going in at the cost of China,' Nehru wrote in 1950 to his sister Vijaya Lakshmi Pandit, who was then the Indian ambassador to the US.[22] The Trump administration cited US ties with pre-Communist China as the template to adhere to, and continuously sought to make a distinction between the regime and people in China.

For all his rhetoric against China, and the Hindutva Strategic Doctrine that sees China as the most consequential rival to India's superpower ambitions, the notion of sharing the Asian theatre with China is not alien to Modi's politics either. 'I have been saying for more than a decade that the 21st century belongs to Asia, and I have said this well before the economic analysts and financial experts highlighted the emergence of BRICS countries,' Modi said in November 2011, during one of the four visits he made to China as chief minister of Gujarat.[23]

George W. Bush thought the US must support India as a counterweight to China. This view had begun to take shape in the American foreign policy establishment while Clinton was still in office. Before the end of his tenure, Clinton gave up on sanctions imposed against India after the nuclear tests. He sought a new beginning with the country in the last year of his presidency with a visit in 2000. The same year, administration normalized US trade ties with China, paving the way for its rise as a global economic power. Around the same time, when the Bush campaign was underway, Condoleezza Rice, who would later become the national security advisor (NSA) under the Republican president, spoke about dealing with the

'China challenge'. 'India is an element in China's calculation, and it should be in America's too. India is not a great power yet, but it has the potential to emerge as one.'[24] This was the Bush world view that laid the foundation for the India–US civil nuclear deal in 2005.

Figuring out the Chinese jigsaw has been a challenge for America, as much then as it is now. In 2005, just two months after the India–US civil nuclear deal was announced and was widely cited as a move to restrain China, Robert B. Zoellick, deputy secretary of state, outlined the Bush administration's China policy thus:

> We are too interconnected to try to hold China at arm's length, hoping to promote other powers in Asia at its expense. Seven U.S. presidents of both parties [. . .] worked to integrate China as a full member of the international system. Since 1978, the United States has also encouraged China's economic development through market reforms. Our policy has succeeded remarkably well: the dragon emerged and joined the world. Today, from the United Nations to the World Trade Organization, from agreements on ozone depletion to pacts on nuclear weapons, China is a player at the table.[25]

It is also noteworthy that India and China signed their landmark agreement on Political Parameters and Guiding Principles for the Settlement of the India-China Boundary Question in April 2005, just three months before the Indo-US nuclear deal.

Zoellick, who would later become the World Bank president, did not mince words when he said that Chinese trade practices and its military build-up were less than reassuring. 'Many countries hope China will pursue a "Peaceful Rise," but none will bet their future on it,' he said. The ideal format for US–China cooperation would be one of 'responsible stakeholder', he added.[26]

This enunciation is indicative of the dilemma in the US—how to deal with China? The question stems from an underlying, fundamental question—is China a status-quoist power or a revisionist power? Trump's National Security Strategy (NSS), released in December 2017, identified China as a revisionist power that was trying to upend the world order, giving an impression that America under its nationalist president had finally concluded the debate. But a hurried conclusion may not be accurate. China is indeed a revisionist power, but the US's own fidelity to order has come under a cloud since the rise of Trump. Moreover, there have been instances where China and America have joined hands to fiercely protect their P-5 pre-eminence, as both—in fact all permanent members of the UN Security Council—closed ranks against India's Dalveer Bhandari in the 2017 election to the International Court of Justice.

An influential section of conservative thinkers in the West believe that to maintain the world order and prevent chaos, the dominance of the five permanent members of the UN must continue. So, regardless of their critical views or concerns about China, they are willing to accommodate it. This is how historian Niall Ferguson explained this thinking to me:

The difficulty about international order is that it requires some element of hierarchy. You can't have the UN General Assembly run the world. That is why the permanent members of the Security Council exist. The advantage of the P-5 is that it has legitimacy, because it has been around

for a while. And if you try to reinvent it, it will be very hard
for any new institution to acquire that legitimacy.[27]

While America publicly supports India's quest for a permanent
seat at the UNSC, India has to be mindful of this idea too; it
played out in the 2017 contest at the International Court of
Justice. The post-COVID, post-Trump America may be more
inclined to align with India, but that is to be seen.

With the naming of China and Russia as revisionist powers
in the NSS and the assertion that 'great power rivalry is back'
in the Nuclear Posture Review (NPR) announced by the
Pentagon in February 2018, professional strategists are now
trying to make sense of America's role in the world, far from
Krauthammer's notion of a world in concentric circles around
the US. Their attempt is to establish some clarity in thinking
on the question of 'Who is our enemy?', the confusion over
which is part of the political turmoil in the country.

From an American perspective, questions regarding the
challenges to a world order led by it are not confined to China.
They apply to India as well, though to a lesser extent. This
is how Hillary Clinton spoke of some of the questions that
confronted her, including China and India, when she became
the secretary of state in 2009:

> Everyone knew that it was a time of dizzying changes, but
> no one could agree on what they all meant. Would the
> economic crisis bring new forms of cooperation or a return
> to protectionism and discord? Would new technologies do
> more to help citizens hold leaders accountable or to help
> dictators keep tabs on dissidents? Would rising powers such
> as China, India and Brazil become global problem-solvers
> or global spoilers?[28]

All these questions have become only starker in the years that followed. In multiple ways, India and China are equivalent in the American view, as both seek to expand their strategic space. For the Obama–Biden administration, both were difficult partners in climate negotiations. Obama, as well as Hillary Clinton during her campaign trail in 2016, touted the success in winning them over as a key achievement of his presidency and her leadership at the state department. For Trump, India and China are two countries that managed to pull a fast one on America in climate negotiations. He mentioned multiple times that both countries were beneficiaries of American stupidity and violators of American intellectual property rights. So, from the perspective of Washington, India and China are either 'problem-solvers' or 'global spoilers', depending on the issue at hand and the president who is talking.

On 20 May 2020, the White House published a document titled 'United States Strategic Approach to the People's Republic of China'.[29] The characterization of China in this document is instructive for understanding how it could square with US views of India. From the strategic perspective, India finds two mentions in this paper—India's Security and Growth for All in the Region policy as a potential point of convergence, and the border tensions with China as a sign of the latter's aggression. It identifies One Belt One Road (OBOR) as a design to reshape international norms, standards and networks to advance Beijing's global interests and vision, an 'expansion of bad practices around the world'.

The Xi doctrine is clear that there is an ongoing battle between two competing ideas of human organization and development. The Trump administration was the first one to acknowledge this view of China, and agreed that there indeed is a competition of two world views in the conflict with China, ' . . . Beijing is clear that it sees itself as engaged in an ideological competition with the West. In 2013, General Secretary Xi called on the CCP to prepare for a "long-term period of cooperation and conflict" between two competing systems and declared that "capitalism is bound to die out and socialism is bound to win". From the same documents, the issues that the US considers problematic or in conflict with the values of the US are "(1) an anticorruption campaign that has purged political opposition; (2) unjust prosecutions of bloggers, activists, and lawyers; (3) algorithmically determined arrests of ethnic and religious minorities; (4) stringent controls over and censorship of information, media, universities, businesses, and non-governmental organizations; (5) surveillance and social credit scoring of citizens, corporations, and organizations; and (6) arbitrary detention, torture, and abuse of people perceived to be dissidents. In a stark example of domestic conformity, local officials publicized a book-burning event at a community library to demonstrate their ideological alignment to 'Xi Jinping Thought"'.'

On several of these points there are Indian parallels, though there can be disputes regarding intensity and scale. The document mentions Chinese policies in Xinjiang province and Chinese interference in other countries, the UK for instance. Comparably, a senior functionary of the RSS had boasted about its ability to sway election outcomes in both the UK and the US. As we discuss elsewhere in this book, the Hindutva Strategic Doctrine is upfront about its desire to recruit the diaspora as an instrument of advancing national interest. The report terms as 'discriminatory' the Chinese National Cyber Security Law, which requires localization of Chinese data by global companies, and government access to foreign data. A similar law of data protection by the Modi government remains a bone of contention between India and the US. Not only that, India is moving further ahead with the nationalization of the digital economy. 'The United States holds the PRC government to the same standards and principles that apply to all nations.'

In the global disorder that George W. Bush proactively created between 2001 and 2009, and bequeathed to his successor Obama, America's new-found relations with India could not have been a stand-alone component. The Obama–Biden administration acquired two intractable wars, in Iraq and Afghanistan, and an economy in free fall. 'We are dealing with a different America after 2008,' a senior Indian minister told me in 2010. The US had to substantially recalibrate its dealings with China to manage its own economy, and India was less of a priority.

After coming into office, the Obama–Biden administration launched the US–China Strategic and Economic Dialogue to combine both tracks into one stream, primarily to deal with the economic meltdown of 2008. The Obama–Hu joint statement mentioned above that caused heartburn in New Delhi even included a commitment by the US to manage its economy well and keep deficit under check, for it was China that was buying up US treasury bonds and contributing to stabilizing it. As the nature of American ties with China changed post 2008, India too had to recalibrate its terms with both countries.

While an Indian perspective naturally focuses on the unmistakable and inevitable rivalry between America and China, 'there is a long tradition of American political leaders going batty over Beijing,' pointed out John Pomfret, a former *Washington Post* bureau chief in Beijing and the author of *The Beautiful Country and the Middle Kingdom: America and China, 1776 to the Present*.[30] Clinton had promised not to 'coddle the butchers of Beijing', but was quick to drop any link between human rights and ties with China. 'Following the bloody crackdown on pro-democracy protests around Tiananmen Square in June 1989, President George H.W. Bush vowed in a letter to Deng to keep the relationship on track, almost as if the United States, not China, was responsible for damaging ties,' writes Pomfret.[31] George W. Bush had repeatedly criticized Clinton for failing to recognize that China was 'a competitor, not a strategic partner', and he acted upon that vision to some extent.

To understand what makes Trump different from his predecessors, we could consider what the Obama–Biden administration's ambassador to Beijing said after he left office on 20 January 2016, the day Trump assumed charge. Max Baucus said he was frustrated with the Obama–Biden administration by the time he left office.

> The Washington foreign-policy establishment tends to put China on another shelf, to deal with it later [. . .] We're much too ad hoc. We don't seem to have a long-term strategy, and that's very much to our disadvantage [. . .] It was very frustrating [. . .] The White House would make a decision, and we'd roll our eyeballs, and say, 'This isn't going to work, partly because we're backing off, we're being weak. What's the strategy going forward?'[32]

The Obama–Biden administration did stand up to the Chinese practice of using cyber spies to steal US trade secrets, but on Chinese protectionism, it could not get the country around. 'China has a long-term strategy to build up its own champion industries, for its own benefit and to the detriment of other countries,' the former ambassador said.[33]

What the rise of China entails for the American dominance of the world remained a lingering concern through multiple administrations. Both sides have tried to capture it in pithy phrases over recent years. The George W. Bush administration used the 'responsible stakeholder' approach; in 2009, Zoellick's successor at the state department sought 'strategic reassurance' from China, more or less meaning the same thing. In a reflection of this concern, the Obama–Hu joint statement in November 2009 said, 'China welcomes the United States as an Asia–Pacific nation that contributes to peace, stability, and prosperity in the region.'[34]

The Obama–Biden administration, in 2011–12, carried out a comprehensive review of the American strategy towards China.

This review produced the now-famous 'pivot to Asia' policy. The review entailed a detailed assessment of where America's interests should be concentrated, going forward. Historically, America placed first priority on Europe, second on the Middle East, and third on Asia. But the 2011 strategic review resulted in a new formulation—Asia was now America's highest priority. (Asia in US parlance, usually refers to Asia–Pacific.)

There are three questions that guide US–China relations.[35] The first two are: can America contain China and can China push America out of the Asia–Pacific? The answers to both questions being no, the third question is, 'How do China and America establish a working relationship with each other that accommodates the legitimate interests of other Asian states?'[36]

'That [Pivot to Asia] is not to take on China, that's to say that there is a large group of countries that have a shared interest in there being freedom of navigation and peaceful resolution of dispute,' Obama's adviser Ben Rhodes said during his final briefing for foreign journalists in 2016.

There are five points that are discernible from statements regarding China originating from American officials, congressional discussions and scholars over several years. The first is, America wants its trade with China to be 'free and fair'. The second is that it wants the sea and air routes around China open to uninterrupted and uninterruptible communication. Three, the US wants to ensure that the latter does not threaten the interests of its allies in the region, a threat that emerges from China's military build-up. When we speak of allies in this context, it is specifically about three treaty allies of the US in the Asia–Pacific. The fourth concern is a subset of the first one, 'free and fair' trade. China's aggressive push in high technology industries has led to a business model that a large section of American and European companies finds alarming. China forces Western companies to share advanced technologies, a practice that some American critics call 'innovation mercantilism'. The fifth is North Korea and its nuclear ambition, which has been on the agenda of US–China ties for decades.

In these five points, Trump had opinions that were different from his predecessors and career officials, many of whom represent the long-evolving American views on all the above issues. Beyond these specific ones, as a guiding principle, the US does not want an Asia dominated by any one country. 'The United States has long been wary of any single power within Asia attempting to establish a hegemonic position as Japan briefly did in the first part of the 20th century. These historic American strategic priorities persist in the 21st century, and help to explain much of the complexity in U.S.–China relations today.'[37]

America has achieved this objective primarily by throwing its weight behind the right partner at the right time. China was a partner against the Soviet Union, and Japan and South Korea have been partners against China. India is increasingly being advocated for this role in the dynamic. Japan, South Korea and China have shown different models of engagement with the US. India is trying to figure out its own model.

On most of the American concerns about China, and the overall concept that Asia cannot be a theatre of Chinese hegemony, India and the US are in alignment. The idea of 'free and fair' trade has different connotations for India and America, with the latter accusing the former of not being 'free and fair' enough. On Chinese military expansionism, its ambitions for domination and the question of freedom of navigation, Modi's strategic doctrine can be called traditional Indian positions on steroids.

Any chances of a military threat to the American mainland from China have always appeared distant. Economic ties are no guarantee against conflict, strategic commentators have argued, citing pre-World War trade links among European countries. But the US–China economic links are qualitatively of a different nature. American companies fume about unfair state interventions and IPR losses in China, but the Chinese market and manufacturing plants are essential for their global operations. For the American state, China, as a threat, comes in the category of 'important, but not urgent'. Moreover, it finds in China a valuable partner in dealing with some more urgent questions. During the Obama years, these were climate change and North Korea. For Trump, it has primarily been the latter. All American discussions on Islamist terrorism or Afghanistan count China as a partner.

'For fifty years, our policy was to fence in the Soviet Union while its own internal contradictions undermined it. For thirty years, our policy has been to draw out the People's Republic of China,' said Zoellick in 2005.[38] Obama adviser Ben Rhodes's analysis of US–China relations was not very dissimilar at the end of the Obama–Biden administration. China has been successful in reading the American mind and has drawn from the lessons of the Soviet Union's collapse. It is practically nobody's first threat anywhere in the world. In a Pew Global Attitude Survey released in August 2017, Chinese power and influence are considered the least of the eight threats listed before respondents from thirty-eight countries. Russian power and influence are also among the least of the threats. American power and influence were considered a slightly higher threat, while ISIS and climate change were much greater threats. The COVID-19 pandemic and the persistent politics of the Trump administration turned global public opinion against China by the end of 2020 on the one hand, and on the other, its ability to withstand the fallout of the pandemic too was noted. On its part, China has increasingly taken a view that it is not affected by global opinion. 'Responding to global criticism (of its measures in Hong Kong), the head of China's Hong Kong and Macau Affairs Office affirmed the new CCP approach, replying, "The era when the Chinese cared what others thought and looked up to others is in the past, never to return."'[39] The Hindutva Strategic Doctrine is not too distant on this question. Jaishankar points out that, as a rising power, India would not be constrained by international opinion about it.

China was an overwhelming threat in only two countries in 2017—Vietnam and South Korea—in that survey. In India, the Chinese threat came in third, after ISIS and climate change.

So, a Chinese challenge to global order and the international system might seem pressing to professional strategic affairs specialists, but was not essentially a critical emergency for a large part of the world's public perception.[40] This may have likely changed in 2020. One cannot gloss over the fact that China is the biggest trading partner for 120 countries, including the US and India. The Chinese GDP stands at $10 trillion and it is responsible for a quarter of the world's growth. This was reflected in the relative neglect of China as a threat in US mainstream media discussions, compared to the hysteria around Russia. The latter, claiming the Orthodox Christian nationalist mantle under Vladimir Putin, is a rival in America's Eurocentric imagination—though the same feature makes it an ally in the Christian nationalist civilizational imagination that Trump draws from. It is not that American scholars or commentators are unaware of the Chinese threat, but it does not arouse the same kind of urgency or alarm as the relatively lesser threat posed by Russia.

Trade Woes

Trade deficit with China is a key concern for India and the US, and under Modi and Trump, this became an even more salient issue in their domestic constituencies. America's trade deficit with China constitutes around 60 per cent of the total deficit of the country—$310 billion of $500.6 billion in 2016, goods and services combined. For goods alone, in 2016, it was $347 billion; for 2019, it was only marginally lower at $345 billion; after the Trump administration initiated a tariff war, which it said would reduce the gap.[41] India had a trade deficit of $52.69 billion in the financial year 2015–16, rising from $48.48 billion the previous financial year. In 2018–19, it was \$53.56 billion; in 2019–2020, it stood at \$48.64 billion. In 2003–04, the deficit was only \$1.1 billion. Roughly 45 per cent of India's trade deficit is accounted for by China. The BJP and RSS-affiliated Hindu nationalist groups are agitated over this issue. The Modi government says it has 'consistently taken steps to balance trade with China by increasing exports and reducing India's dependence on imports'.

During Diwali in 2016, the RSS chief, Mohan Bhagwat, exhorted people not to buy idols of Hindu gods and goddesses made in China only because they were cheaper. The RSS-affiliated economic outfit, Swadeshi Jagran Manch, launched a campaign to boycott Chinese products in 2018.[42] The Chinese embassy in New Delhi responded with a veiled warning that trade with China was responsible for giving Indians access to affordable goods, whereas exports to India accounted for only 2 per cent of China's global goods exports that was worth \$2276.5 billion in 2015. The statement also warned that 'the boycott will negatively affect Chinese enterprises to invest in India and the bilateral cooperation, which both Chinese and Indian people are not willing to see'.[43]

A significant aspect of Modi's strategic vision is attracting investment to India. Trump also wants Chinese investment in the US, but those meant to take over American technology companies have become a major source of conflict between Beijing and Washington. Chinese investment in India was \$870 million in 2015, ascending by six times in one year.[44] Investments from China and Hong Kong into India declined 72 per cent to \$952 million in 2020, from \$3.4 billion in 2019 after New Delhi imposed new regulations to restrict Chinese investments.[45] US investments in China and Chinese investments in the US continued to rise through the trade war under Trump.[46] The Indian fascination for Chinese goods is not something that fits in with the nationalist paradigm. It was reported that half a million Chinese-made Xiaomi mobiles were sold in India around Diwali in 2016.[47] Trump tried to restrict the entry of Chinese goods into America and added more national security regulations for Chinese investments in the US and vice versa.

In the US, Chinese trade has allowed Americans to buy cheap consumer goods and clothes—a study by the US–China Business Council in 2017 calculated that every American family saves $850 because of cheap goods from China coming into their country. The same logic applied to India. According to Jaishankar, 'The intensive competitive nature of the Indian market that puts such premium on price points saw a natural value in imports from China. This applied in the case of infrastructure building, especially in power generation and telecommunications, where it was also supported by attractive financing.'[48]

'America First' nationalism and Hindutva nationalism began to review this scenario from the perspective of national capacity and job creation. Peter Navarro, head of the National Trade Council at the Trump White House, had earlier calculated that 57,000 American factories had shuttered since China joined the WTO. His documentary on the issue is titled *Death By China*.

Trade with China may have contributed directly to the rise of nationalism in the US. The social and economic dislocation caused by it has been a key driver of Americans' resentment of globalism. Over one quarter of the decline in American manufacturing jobs between 1990 and 2007 was due to Chinese imports, according to one study.[49] The authors argued that while dislocation due to technological advancement is spread across the country, the impact of trade with China is concentrated in certain pockets—in cities such as Detroit in Michigan that would go on to vote for Trump in November 2016.

Not only did people lose their jobs, trade with China impacted their love lives too, apparently! Scholars argue that a decline in manufacturing has contributed to two developments: a reduction in the number of marriages as men with less stable incomes are less desirable partners for women, and a sharp rise in the number of children born out of wedlock or living in single-parent families. The study notes:

> Between 1979 and 2008, the share of U.S. women between the ages of 25 and 39 who were currently married fell by 10 percentage points among the college-educated, by 15 percentage points among those with some college but no degree, and by fully 20 percentage points among women with high-school education or less. [. . .] The fraction of U.S. children born to unmarried mothers more than doubled between 1980 and 2013, rising from 18 to 41 percent.

The authors propose that 'manufacturing jobs are a fulcrum on which traditional work and family arrangements rest' and the decline in manufacturing due to trade has affected young men in multiple ways, causing a cascading effect on family formation. The authors add the caveat that a decline in manufacturing is not the prime driver of either of these trends, which are caused by multiple other factors too.[50] All this contributed to the emergence of 'America First' politics. The exit of Trump from the White House has by no means drawn curtains on it.

Low Intensity Coercion

On the economic front, while the Chinese have penetrated deep into America and India, their military build-up is seen differently by New Delhi and Washington, though both agree that it is destabilizing in nature. For India, it is an immediate and present threat, while for America it is always below the threshold that calls for urgent action. In 2017, the Pentagon termed it 'low intensity coercion'. China continues to exercise low intensity coercion to advance its claims in the East and South China Seas.[51]

In other words, China is trying to expand its global military presence and its influence in a manner that avoids direct conflict with other countries. It most likely will seek to establish additional military bases in countries with which it has a long-standing friendly relationship and similar strategic interests, such as Pakistan, and in which there is a precedent for hosting foreign militaries, according to the Pentagon. 'China is expanding its access to foreign ports to pre-position the necessary logistics support to regularize and sustain deployments in the "far seas", waters as distant as the Indian Ocean, Mediterranean Sea, and Atlantic Ocean,' the Pentagon report said, noting the construction of a Chinese military base in Djibouti, a first. The peculiarity of this is that it does not amount to a military crisis as had happened between the US and the erstwhile USSR during the Cuban missile crisis. China has termed the assessment 'irresponsible'. The Pentagon classifies repeated skirmishes on the India–China border also in the category of 'low intensity coercion'.[52]

Much like Modi and Trump who have a strategic vision driven by their domestic experiences and a nationalistic view of the world, Chinese premier Xi too has a nationalistic vision of China's future. Modi has an 'India First' approach—'My politics is India First', he declared at numerous rallies during the 2014 election campaign—as also his 'Make in India' programme. US politics, under Trump and after, is hinged on 'America First' and a promise to revive its manufacturing sector. Xi's aim is a 'great rejuvenation of the Chinese nation'.

Commentaries on US–China ties now increasingly account for the nationalistic fervour created by the politics of Xi and Trump in their respective countries. This point equally applies to the domestic politics in India championed by Modi, and his interactions with the US–China compact. Despite being a self-declared communist country—Ronald Reagan famously called the Chinese 'so-called Communists'—Xi's tools of national rejuvenation include Buddhist religious nationalism as also age-old Confucian wisdom, a trait he shares with Hindutva and America First. Religion is not central to Xi's politics, but the idea of a religious nation-building project is attractive to him. 'He [Xi] helped rebuild several famous temples, but ordered that 1,500 crosses be pulled off the steeples of churches while he was chief of Zhejiang province between 2002 and 2007. The Chinese state interferes in the running of the Catholic Church in the country, and the Vatican has conceded this. This became a point of friction between the Trump administration and the Vatican in 2020.'[53]

In Xi's assertion of Chinese nationalism, there lies a strong suspicion of Muslims and their patriotism, akin to Hindutva and 'America First'. In May 2018, the Chinese government directed that all mosques should raise the national flag to 'promote a spirit of patriotism' among Muslims. This will 'further strengthen the understanding of national and civic ideals, and promote a spirit of patriotism among Muslims of all ethnic groups', said the order.[54] Christians and Buddhists are also recruited for patriotic education. China has been taking advantage of the 9/11 moment of suspicion against Muslims everywhere, and targeting them in Xinjiang, which is crucial to the BRI.

The Chinese premier's notion of a Buddhist globalization is another cause of conflict between his and Modi's ambitions for Asia. Buddhism, with its roots in several Asian countries, has been a calling card of Modi's Hindutva Strategic Doctrine. Hindutva considers Buddhism, Sikhism and Jainism to be part of its cultural fold which, unlike Islam and Christianity, are not 'foreign'.

Made in China 2025

The Made in China 2025 strategy is focused on high technology because Xi is aware that Chinese dominance in low-cost, low-value manufacturing will not ensure its growth to the next level. American corporations were at the forefront of knocking out human rights, democracy and other political issues from the US–China bilateral agenda starting in the 1990s. But in the 2000s, multiple views began to emerge among American capitalists on what Washington should push vis-à-vis Beijing.

A loudly heard recent complaint in the US is about Xi's Made in China 2025 push. In May 2017, Premier Li Keqiang said the focus would be on 'developing strategic emerging industries'. 'We will accelerate R&D on and commercialization of new materials, new energy, artificial intelligence, integrated circuits, bio-pharmacy, 5G mobile communications and other technologies, and develop industrial clusters in these fields.'

The plan also covers the manufacturing of aircraft, robots, electric cars, rail equipment, ships and agricultural machinery, which will enable China to free itself from the domination of companies like Boeing, Airbus, General Electric,

Siemens, Nissan, Renault, Samsung and Intel.[55] The Trump administration brought this question to the front and centre of US–China relations. This will continue to influence Biden's policies too.

If China is allowed to succeed in its attempt to overturn the global trade order, it may act as a model for 'other nations, such as Indonesia, Malaysia, Vietnam, and even India, whose policymakers believe they have no choice but to keep up with China and to emulate its unfair trade practices', according to an American view.[56] Now, the way China has leveraged its market strength and labour force to bargain with America is indeed a model that Modi does want to emulate. In his first address to a gathering of US policy wonks in September 2014, at the Council on Foreign Relations in New York, Modi said:

> One benefit that comes from India is that we have three things that the world does not have. In no country in the world, no country has all these three things together. One may have one or second or the third, but not all. One is democracy. The other is demographic dividend. And the third is demand.[57]

India is a democracy that China is not, Modi appeared to be telling the Americans. India has never been comfortable with the American habit of unilaterally raising human rights, internal democracy, minority rights and civil society issues concerning India. Under Hindutva, such concerns have gained a new sharpness. Modi has been immensely successful in the attempt, going by the mute American reaction, for instance, to the crackdown on protestors in the Kashmir Valley since he came to power and the ending of the special constitutional status of Jammu and Kashmir in 2019. The Trump administration did not bother to emphasize on human rights, governance and other domestic issues of a partner country on the agenda of bilateral ties; regardless of the Democrat rhetoric on these questions, the Biden administration's ability or inclination to be any different in its approach towards India is suspect. By proposing the 3D framework of 'democracy', 'demography' and 'demand', Modi is trying to reset the contours of ties with the US on terms that would be more favourable to India.

The American political elite, while in favour of the India–US axis as pushback against China, is nervous about India's own calculations. India's calibrated opening of its market is what tests the patience of American leaders. Republican lawmaker Matt Salmon said at a congressional hearing, 'Let's start doing a better job in getting our products over there [to India]. China has really taken great advantage of us [. . .] and we don't want to make the same mistakes with India.'[58]

The American foreign policy establishment cannot conclude with any certainty whether China will play by the rules Washington sets for the global order or not. According to Ben Rhodes, most of the signature foreign policy initiatives of the Obama–Biden administration were built in part on US–China cooperation. 'There is no Paris climate agreement without the U.S. and China leading that effort with the agreement we reached in Beijing. There's no Iran deal without Chinese cooperation on sanctions and then diplomacy with Iran.' There's no way to deal with the global economic crisis and return the global economy to a pathway to growth without the US and China cooperating. Rhodes said that the US must push back against China on issues such as its aggressive moves in the South China Sea, but 'there's just much more to be gained from pursuing cooperation when we can with China rather than seeing it as an adversary'. 'I think that'd be very dangerous for the whole world, frankly,' he had said about Trump's plan to confront China head-on. Even then, there was a constituency in the Beltway that understood that the US could not cooperate with China without the latter also trying to undermine the US political system and democracies everywhere; that the Chinese were both mercantilist and zero-sum in their political calculations. People like Matt Pottinger—who served as Trump's deputy NSA—worked with this reality in mind and simply used the Trump moment to craft a more sensible China policy.

The Obama–Biden administration had tried to push back China by attempting to build a new order for world trade through the TPP agreement, which was presented as a platform for America to make rules in the twenty-first century.

In one of the first measures he took as President, Trump withdrew the US from the TPP. All the achievements that Rhodes mentions were immaterial in Trump's world view and the new order that he wanted to create. He also withdrew the US from the Iran nuclear deal, not to mention the Paris Agreement. The Iran nuclear deal and the end of secondary sanctions placed by America under Obama had opened immense strategic and commercial opportunities for India. The Paris treaty was a point of agreement too between India, America and China. Biden has echoed the same view about competing with China on making rules for the twenty-first century. 'America First' nationalism has, however, changed the fundamentals of America's approach to trade and trade deals.

'I would not rejoin the TPP as it was initially put forward. I would insist that we renegotiate. Either China's going to write the rules of the road for the 21st century on trade or we are. We have to join with the 40 percent of the world that we had with us and this time make sure that there's no one sitting at that table doing the deal unless environmentalists are there and labor is there,' said Biden.[59] Trump had set the tone when he renegotiated the NAFTA, which is now the United States–

Mexico–Canada Agreement (USMCA), by making labour and wages part of its core. The new deal 'uses trade rules to drive higher wages by requiring that 40–45 percent of auto content be made by workers earning at least $16 per hour'. In effect, this upends the globalization logic that takes work to places where workers can be paid less.[60]

While, in principle, both India and China would swear to protect the 'world order', there are some issues on which both Asian countries would like to bend the rules as written by the Western winners of the world wars and the Cold War. According to Jaishankar, 'questioning the 1945 order is important, but a task to be handled with considerable delicacy.' 'For all the talk of a more contemporary world order, it is evident that the entrenched powers will not readily give up their privileges, even if it means a more dysfunctional international system,'[61] Jaishankar points out. India and China both question the intellectual property regime as it exists today. Modi or Xi would not directly confront America on this issue, but the former made his disagreement apparent in a humorous way during his address to the US Congress in 2016. Pointing out that India's ancient heritage of yoga has over 30 million practitioners in the US, Modi said, 'It is estimated that more Americans bend for yoga than to throw a curve ball. And, no Mr Speaker, we have not yet claimed intellectual property right on Yoga.'[62] China might join hands with India in questioning some parts of the world order, but it would not want India to be a permanent member of the UNSC.

A New Dis-Order

China has been lobbying America for a 'New Type of Great Power Relations', a grand bargain between Beijing and Washington, DC. American presidents over the years have been swayed by this promise, as we noticed in the joint statements that have a direct bearing on India earlier in this chapter, but the complexities involved did not allow for anything conclusive to take shape. The Chinese suggestion of G-2 relations is based on the idea of both countries respecting each other's 'core interests'. The US believes that its pre-eminence will be better maintained by being the sole superpower while maintaining a plurality of robust bilateral ties with all countries in the world, with several new great powers—Japan, India and Germany—among them. This is not enough for China.

China's flagship project—the BRI—is often described by Chinese scholars as being part of 'Globalization Version 2.0'. The Trump–Modi joint statement in June 2017 indicated a complete acceptance of the Indian position on the BRI. Only a few weeks earlier, America had accepted the Chinese position on the BRI, as part of a deal in which both countries took measures to increase market access for one another. Trump also sent a high-level American delegation to the BRI forum meeting in Beijing. This vacillation in the US on the BRI has given way to more clarity during the later years of the Trump regime.

Both India and America, while wary of China's rise, also want to identify that Islamism and terrorism are evils that can be fought with Chinese cooperation. For one, increasing Chinese expansion is good for the anti-terrorism fight around the world, according to one American view. In June 2018, ahead of the US–China Diplomatic and Security Dialogue in Washington, DC, Susan Thornton, the US acting assistant secretary of state for East Asia, said the US wanted China to be more involved in global counterterrorism measures. 'We believe that China is increasingly affected by the growing global challenge of terrorism,' she said, referring to the two

Chinese citizens who were taken hostage and killed by terrorists in Pakistan in February 2018.[63]

India expressed similar sentiments in 2017 about working with China in Afghanistan. China is beginning to feel the heat of terrorism emanating from the Af–Pak region, but how much it will cooperate with India on this remains an open question. During S. Jaishankar's visit to Beijing in February 2017 as foreign secretary, 'Officials reportedly even discussed the possibility of "joint development projects" that could be undertaken despite economic rivalries between the two countries in other parts of the subcontinent.'[64] Considering the double standards of China on the question of terrorism, it is a futile exercise to seek cooperation with it on this issue, scholars have said.[65]

For India, finding common ground with China on terrorism is an uphill task, given Beijing's persistent support to Pakistan, which is the major sponsor of Islamist terrorism around the world. China stonewalled India's efforts to designate Pakistan-based Jaish-e-Mohammed founder Masood Azhar a global terrorist at the UN for several years before finally lifting its opposition in 2020. The question of Azhar—who was among the terrorists released by India following the hijack of IC 814 in 1999—came to the foreground after India held him responsible for the 2 January 2016 Pathankot airbase attack. India accuses Azhar of masterminding the 13 December 2001 attack on Parliament as well.[66]

Being involved in the US–China rivalry is tricky for Asian neighbours of the latter. South Korea is a stark example. In May 2017, three months after Trump assumed office, South Korean President Moon Jae-in was elected to office, promising a reconciliatory position towards China and talks with North Korea. Moon had also promised during his campaign to review the deployment of THAAD (Terminal High Altitude Area Defense), an American-made missile defence system, on its soil, which was being staunchly opposed by Beijing. But in the run-up to the election, the US managed to deploy the first two THAAD systems, in a golf course owned by Lotte, a South Korean–Japanese conglomerate.

Moon was reportedly furious with the turn of events that tied his hands and ordered that further deployment would be allowed only after an environmental assessment that could take more than a year.[67] But continuing missile tests by North Korea and the heightening nuclear tension left him with no option but to erect more systems, which he ordered in July 2017. Meanwhile, China retaliated against Lotte, on whose golf course the THAAD systems were deployed. Nearly two dozen Lotte stores on the mainland were shuttered, its website was brought down by a denial-of-service (DoS) attack originating from Chinese Internet addresses, and a number of Chinese e-commerce sites halted the sale of Lotte goods.[68]

South Korea's exports to China in 2016 were over $120 billion, a quarter of the country's total exports, which puts the country under pressure from China.

Trump's meeting with North Korean leader Kim Jong-un in June 2018 marked a significant step in rolling back American presence in the Indo–Pacific and upended the decades-old wisdom of American strategic policy. Trump declared that US–South Korea joint military exercises would stop immediately. He also announced that he wanted to withdraw American soldiers from the Korean peninsula. 'I want to get our soldiers out. I want to bring our soldiers back home. We have right now 32,000 soldiers in South Korea,' he said, and added, 'That's not part of the [North Korea] equation right now. At some point, I hope it will be.'[69] For South Korea, which has been a front of America's Asia presence for several decades, any thaw in America's relations with North Korea is both opportunity and risk. South Korean President Moon Jae-in was the key catalyst in the breakthrough, and he called the Trump–Kim summit a 'huge step forward' towards peace that 'helped break down the last remaining Cold War legacy on Earth'.[70] But the dilemma of the America ally is that it has a limited or little role in determining its own relations with North Korea. However, in Trump's overall approach towards the North, considerations about South Korea were not central. Trump was under attack by American strategists for conceding to the North Korean demand of stopping military exercises, which had also been a Chinese demand for years. Withdrawing American troops is not something American professional strategists will easily concede. But Trump's Korean policy was exactly what China wanted, according to a section of American opinion makers.[71] Trump considered American military presence in the peninsula a favour to South Korea and, as mentioned earlier, had publicly grudged that the latter was not paying enough for it. It is possible that the Biden administration would have a different approach to dealing with the North, and the South would again be a mere recipient of wisdom from Washington. The Trump administration was, however, emphatic about using the term Indo–Pacific, which was an encouraging signal for India and an irritant for China. Biden has appointed a coordinator for the Indo-Pacific at the White House, creating a new post, which is a sign of a continuity from Trump.

The idea that allies of the US would get lenient trade deals and military protection has been reopened by 'America First' nationalism. Biden has been categorical that he will deal with the China challenge by marshalling all American allies around the world. Assuming that Biden does indeed manage to reset US relations with Asian partners to a pre-Trump mould, they would still face the uncertainty of a potential new deal between China and the US.

Shifting Partners

While India and America appear to form one side of the war of nerves with China, it is not entirely true in all situations. The triangular relationship has other permutations as well. Trump clubbed India and China together in the announcement of his decision to leave the Paris Agreement.

> . . . under the agreement, China will be able to increase these emissions by a staggering number of years—13. They can do whatever they want for 13 years. Not us. India makes its participation contingent on receiving billions and billions and billions of dollars in foreign aid from developed countries.[72]

According to Trump, the Paris Agreement would lead to a redistribution of American wealth to other countries and the transfer of American jobs abroad.[73] The Obama-Biden administration had argued that by promoting a global climate regime, the US would create wealth and jobs at home. It had showcased the Indian and Chinese endorsement of the Paris accord as a key diplomatic success. Under Biden, the US has returned to the Paris treaty and climate change will be top of his global agenda.

India and China have, over the years, protested against America's effort to undermine their national sovereignty on multiple issues. 'America First' has turned that debate on its head, with the argument that global treaties are an infringement of American sovereignty.

So, where are US–China relations headed and how is India placed in this evolving power game? Graham Allison's 2017 book, *Destined for War: Can America and China Escape Thucydides's Trap?*, probed the possibility of a war between China and America. 'Over the past five hundred years, in sixteen cases a major rising power has threatened to displace a ruling power. In twelve of those, the result was war. The four cases that avoided this outcome did so only because of huge, painful adjustments in attitudes and actions on the part of challenger and challenged alike,' he told me in an interview.

The US and China are seeking to make that adjustment. Whether they manage to arrive at that or not, there will be implications for India.

A sharpened China–US conflict would put the country in a difficult spot, literally. Obama and George W. Bush appreciated the sensitivities of India, since it shares a border with China. Such appreciation of a partner's difficulties was not part of Trump's 'America First' politics. While India appears keen to be an American partner in the region at one level, it also wants to be in control of the pace and range of that relationship. There is a streak of irony also in the situation. India, during Modi's initial years, tried to pull its neighbours, particularly Bangladesh, Nepal, Bhutan and Sri Lanka, closer to it, possibly disturbing the fine balancing act these countries have been doing between India and China. These dynamics contributed to the difficulties that have accumulated for India in its neighbourhood.

A conventional strategic autonomy approach or a Nehruvian neoliberal approach for New Delhi has been to *balance* its ties with China and America. That is the 'balancing power' approach pursued by previous governments, but sought to be discontinued by Modi in the initial years. The 'leading power' strategic principle that the Modi government has announced with the 'Act East' policy could be read, at least by China, as a willingness to lead an alliance in Asia with help from America in terms of arms and muscle. India's fine balancing act as it moved closer to the US involved simultaneously improving its ties with China. The latter is inclined to view India's closeness with the US as willingness to act as an American outpost in Asia, while America wants to see it as India's readiness to act as its frontline against China. According to Stanly Johny, 'China doesn't see India as a "swing state" any more. It sees India as an ally-in-progress of the U.S. Its actions were not reckless, taken at the risk of losing India strategically. Its actions in Ladakh in 2020 are a result of the strategic loss that has already happened.'[74]

Chinese Whispers

Trump took China head-on, without any restraint, challenging its power and ambition like no other American president ever before. The US presidents in the past have tried to coax and appease China to a great extent, but Trump was different. A challenged China, its low intensity coercion suddenly disrupted by an American president, perhaps tried to humour India. Xi's willingness to grab Modi's extended hand in 2018 within months of the Doklam standoff had something to do with his difficulties with Trump. Some scholars argue that China had given up on India by 2020, and wanted to express its hostility by its aggression in Ladakh. The ties between China and India could also undergo a qualitative change if China emerges from a confrontation with America bruised, militarily or otherwise. But the flip side of the same situation is that India could become a direct party to any US–China hostility. If India, partly of its own volition and partly because of circumstances, indeed does end up being at the frontline of such a conflict, it will have consequences.

What is curious about the American strategic priorities as outlined in the NSS, NPR and NDS (National Defense Strategy), all published in the first year of the Trump presidency, is that they club Russia and China together as America's rivals. The sustainability of such an approach is doubtful. Naming China, Russia, North Korea, Iran and stateless extremist organizations as threats to America does not clarify thinking. Nor does it resolve the internal crisis of strategic clarity that has afflicted America since the end of the Cold War. The real challenge to American power comes from a China that is growing, has patience and is endowed with all the tools it needs to stake a claim to the status of a superpower. An American response to China would have been robust and strategic in the event of an improvement of its ties with Russia. But the current political situation in America leaves little scope for that. During the Obama years, he and Secretary John Kerry faced immense difficulties in forging a partnership with Russia on Syria and Iran, as interest groups within the US establishment created roadblocks at each turn. With the alleged interference of Russia in the 2016 US presidential election, there has been a further slide in US–Russia relations all the way. 'Just as Richard Nixon's opening to China during the Cold War expanded America's leverage with the Soviet Union, closer relations with Russia may help counterbalance a more powerful and assertive China,'[75] feels Allison, but that is a distant possibility.

The American military posture is primarily anti-Russia, though China is counted as a threat.

So, Asian countries including India will have to deal with this rivalry between the incumbent superpower and the challenger. How will they do it? 'I suspect each country will grapple with this challenge differently,' Allison said, and went on to add a more serious concern—an Asian rivalry or crisis pushing America and China into a war that they do not want. This happened once at the time of the Korean War (25 June 1950–27 July 1953). Another situation that could have escalated happened in 2010, when North Korea sank the South Korean warship *Cheonan*, killing forty-six sailors.

Making a grand G-2 bargain that accommodates the multifaceted interests of both countries and several partners of the US in the region, many with fluid loyalties like Pakistan and the Philippines, may turn out to be challenging. China and the US could continue in a state of low intensity conflict for a prolonged period. India would need to patiently and painstakingly work to protect its own interests.

The US and China might try and manage their divergences in Asia by regular and enhanced engagement. What makes such engagement challenging is the rising tide of nationalism in both countries. When we insert India into that equation, we are talking of two countries where regimes are currently thriving on a resurgence of national pride and with the objective of reclaiming perceived or actual lost historical pre-eminence. The US under Biden will try to disown the toxic rhetoric of the Trump era, but it cannot obliterate the nationalist sentiment in the country.

One can identify several defining changes on the American, Chinese and Indian sides in recent years that suggest that a fundamental revision of their relations and respective roles in the world is underway. The American restraint in dealing with China for the last three decades has been inspired by the interests of its corporations and consumers, given the organization of its political economy. Since Trump's 'America First' nationalism altered the very architecture of America's political economy the voice of American labour has become an important factor in the country's decisions. Trade relations between the two countries that many hoped would be a soothing factor in strategic rivalry have become a focal point of tension.

Meanwhile, Xi believes the Chinese path to progress could be a model for the rest of the world. At the 19th Congress of the Communist Party in 2017, he said the 'Chinese model' offered a 'brand new option' for countries that 'want to develop economically while preserving their independence'. The Chinese president is also offering 'Chinese wisdom' and 'Chinese approach' to dealing with the challenges of our times. All this comes with a concerted effort by Chinese scholars to formulate an entire compact of scholarship that they call the 'Chinese School'. Effectively, China under Xi is challenging the neoliberal world order that America under Trump also challenged. The rise of Trump signified the crisis of liberalism that has not ended with his fall. Xi is offering an alternative development model. According to China scholar Jabin T. Jacob, 'Chinese foreign policy activism [. . .] might be best described as a new form of *tianxia*—or 'all under heaven'— [. . .] a framework used by successive Chinese imperial rulers to refer to China's overlordship, including cultural and economic superiority, over neighbouring kingdoms and its prominent role in arbitrating disputes and conflicts between them.'[76] 'Xi has dramatically restructured the Party-state apparatus, giving the Party a greater say in running the country, and breaking down the walls between the Party set-up and the state machinery [. . .] The Party is turning to nationalism as an important source of legitimacy and unity, having come to one key realization: economic growth cannot forever remain the source of its legitimacy.'[77] 'The General Secretary of the Chinese Communist Party, Xi Jinping [. . .] now speaks openly of China moving closer to the center stage, building a socialism that is superior to capitalism, and replacing the American dream with the Chinese solution,' according to William Barr, attorney general in the Trump administration.[78]

Trump officials had argued that, in the tariff war, America would win because it imports more than it exports to China. In 2021, it is clear that things did not turn out that way. But one trend is evident—American corporations that depended on cheap Chinese labour for their bottom lines could be increasingly forced by the country's political factors to look for a new model. The big opportunity for them could come from automation.

The Messy Decoupling

We have discussed the role of American global companies in undermining American state power. These companies, however, do the opposite in China, by reinforcing and reiterating Chinese state power. Cisco helped the CCP build the Great Firewall of China, which is considered the most sophisticated surveillance and censorship system in the world now. 'America First' nationalists have brought the role of US corporations into sharp focus on this question since 2016. 'Over the years, corporations such as Google, Microsoft, Yahoo, and Apple have shown themselves all too willing to collaborate with the CCP,' according to William Barr. Apple removed the news app Quartz from its app store in China, following Chinese government complaints about its coverage of the Hong Kong protests. It removed apps for virtual private networks, which had allowed users to bypass the Great Firewall. Apple also announced that it would locate iCloud data servers in China, making them susceptible to surveillance. But for the US government, it has a different approach regarding protection of privacy of its clients and consumers. 'That's the double standard that has been emerging among American tech companies.'[79]

American companies are under pressure from its politics to hold the country above profits, but the logic of capitalism is not helpful here. China has sensed the danger on the horizon, and there are responses already underway. It is creating its own strengths in frontier areas of technology. For instance, 'while America spent the past decade upgrading its bank based magnetic striped cards with chips, China experienced a retail payment revolution. Leapfrogging the card-based system, two new payment systems have come to dominate person-to-person, retail, and many business transactions. China's new system is built on digital wallets, QR codes, and runs through their own big tech firms: Alipay running through Alibaba (China's version of Amazon) and WeChat Pay running through Tencent (China's version of Facebook).'[80]

The Chinese state enforces strong control over the country's financial market, for the obvious reason of staying firmly in control of its capitalism—guided as it is. Foreign credit card companies were denied entry into the Chinese market for years, while local incumbent UnionPay maintained a monopoly on card networks. American Express was finally granted a licence in November 2018 and approved to start operations in June 2020. By this time, Alipay and WeChat Pay had grown to displace card network transactions, claiming more than 90 per cent of the $27 trillion mobile payments market in 2018. These platforms have begun to threaten Chinese banks and the government is now trying to keep them in check.

By the end of 2019, when the Trump trade war with China was playing out, only about 3 per cent of US companies in China said they were relocating to the US because of tariffs. Under 7 per cent said they were leaving China. 'China has comparatively weak labor protections on one hand, and a diverse pool of talent on the other—from stitch-and-sew factory workers to scientists and other high tech, advanced machine tool operators are all at the ready. There are hundreds of thousands of them. No country has this.' In 2019, *Newsweek* ran a cover story titled 'How America's Biggest Companies Made China Great Again'. American corporations were the biggest votaries of China's admission into the WTO. In 2020, the pandemic raised new questions about US dependency on China, along with calls for creating new supply chains with the support of American partners. The US might even want to encourage companies to relocate to India. 'India can quickly become a favourable jurisdiction for more of the industrial activities that are happening currently in China,' Thomas Vajda, assistant secretary of state for South Asia in the US Department of State, is learnt to have told Indian business representatives.[81] However, in a comparison of India and China on corporate tax rates, political stability, crime rates, environment and pollution, energy costs, port infrastructure, China has the upper hand. 'Where is the company that has stopped doing business with China because of human rights matters?'[82]

US companies are not delinking from China in a hurry. In November 2020, Nike and Coca-Cola, and the US Chamber of Commerce were among companies and business groups lobbying the US Congress to water down the provisions of a proposed law that could ban imported goods made with forced labour in China's Xinjiang region. The business did not support forced labour of course, but feared that the requirements of the new law could 'wreak havoc on supply chains that are deeply embedded in China.'[83]

According to the US–China Business Council (USCBC) annual survey, a quarter of its member companies have reduced or stopped planned investment in China in 2020, 'a historic high for this survey'. 'The top reasons for reducing or stopping investment in China are increased costs or uncertainties from US–China tensions and uncertainty stemming from COVID-19.'[84] However, 'despite years of trade friction and swelling calls for economic disengagement by hawks in the United States and China, both our data as well as conversations with member companies indicate that American companies remain committed to the China market over the long term. Eighty-three percent of companies counted China as either the top or among the top five priorities for their company's global strategy. Projections about the five-year business outlook in China are similarly sanguine, with nearly 70 percent expressing that they are optimistic about the commercial prospects of the market.' These companies are worried over restrictive measures of China such as different technical standards, and IPR issues. 'The percentage of companies that are somewhat or very concerned about China's information flow and technology security policies increased this year to 84 percent from 76 percent in 2019.' As part of the Phase One trade deal with China negotiated by the Trump administration, it promised to not force companies to transfer technology, but companies remained unsure of how trustworthy this would be.

China's Battle for the American Mind

The Trump administration and its nationalist allies forced a new narrative about China on reluctant listeners in the US business world. It may not have become the default America position yet, but the view that the 'CCP envisions itself atop a new hierarchical global order in which the world acquiesces to China's worldview while supplying it with markets, capital, resources, and talent,' is influential and will remain so in the coming years.[85] US policy influencers also took note of the 'cumulative effect of China's influence in UN organizations, after the World Health Organization (WHO) DG publicly praised Beijing's handling of the COVID-19 outbreak', the push for [. . .] a 'parallel order of alternative China-centric organizations, including the Belt and Road Initiative (BRI)' and 'leadership in international standardization bodies and export Chinese technical standards'.

Trump focused his 2020 re-election campaign on China, and the template set by him and his associates such as Mike Pompeo will continue to resonate in American thinking. Cumulatively, American nationalists believe that the country had a very good relationship with pre-Communist China, and focuses on the transgressions of the CCP. Trump said the 'world needs answers on the virus' from China. NSA Robert C. O'Brien said the miscalculation about China was the 'greatest failure of American foreign policy since the 1930s'. 'We closed our ears and our eyes.'[86] He said China was using social media platforms such as TikTok that had 40 million users in the US, to control individual American minds.

FBI Director Christopher Wray said in July 2020 that 50,000 counter-intelligence cases were underway regarding Chinese infiltration of the US system. Attorney General William Barr said American companies had 'succumbed to China', and called attention to the US's dependency on China for medical devices and active pharmaceutical ingredients.

China is using its economic clout to push back against the unfavourable attention that it gets, and here again, it finds allies in Western companies. In 2013, Xi told his colleagues to 'tell China's story well, and properly disseminate China's voice.'[87] This approach had its effect. For instance, in 2019, ESPN televised a map that showed Taiwan as part of China and appeared to endorse Chinese claims in the South China Sea.[88]

'Under pressure from the Chinese Communist Party, American, Delta, and United Airlines all removed references to Taiwan from their corporate websites [. . .] Mercedes Benz even apologized for posting an inspirational quote from the Dalai Lama on social media . . .'[89] American companies that have ties with China have so 'internalized Beijing's demands', they intuitively push positive views of China and suppress negative ones.[90] 'I've bought copies of this book for my colleagues as well. I want them to understand socialism with Chinese characteristics,' Mark Zuckerberg, Founder & CEO, Facebook, endorsed what is described on the Amazon site as 'the first published work by a sitting Chinese President'—Xi Jinping's *The Governance of China*, which 'offers a unique look inside the Communist Party of China and its vision for the future'. While the market-driven, capitalist media enterprises around the world are scaling back on operations and firing journalists, the Chinese state media has an abundant supply of journalists around the world. In 2018, *The Guardian* reported that almost 6,000 people were applying for ninety jobs of 'reporting the news from a Chinese perspective' from London. 'For western journalists, demoralised by endless budget cuts, China Global Television Network presents an enticing prospect, offering competitive salaries.'[91] The Trump administration asked the Chinese state media to register under the Foreign Agents Registration Act (FARA), and not operate as media platforms. The Chinese diaspora, particularly students, have come under increasing scrutiny following rising American concerns about influence operations. There are 150 branches of the Chinese Students and Scholars Association across America's campuses for students of Chinese origin. In 2019, there were 3,60,000 Chinese students in the US generating annual economic activity of about $14 billion. In a crackdown, the Trump administration announced in September 2020 that it had revoked student visas of 1000 Chinese nationals on account of suspected links with the Chinese military.[92]

Scepticism regarding China trade in both India and the US is driven by national security concerns, but it is also a strand of the economic nationalism that is holding sway in both countries. Trade scepticism of the Modi government took a dramatic form when India decided to walk out of the RCEP negotiations in 2019. A bloc of fifteen countries, including the ten ASEAN members, China, Japan, South Korea, Australia and New Zealand, signed the partnership on 15 November 2020. Two members of the Quad, Japan and Australia, are part of RCEP along with China. Several members of the grouping have border disputes with China. The US is facing a dilemma here. 'As most U.S. companies have no choice but to participate in the Asia–Pacific market, an RCEP without the U.S. means these companies will have to relocate more of their operations to RCEP countries to take advantage of the lower tariffs within the bloc.'[93]

Conclusion

'Both China and India aspire for the same goals in the same geographical region; hence they will, at any given time, be more competitors than friends,' according to RSS ideologue Ram Madhav.[94] Sardar Patel had said Chinese Communism was nothing but nationalism with a facade. India was the first country to oppose BRI—a point that Jaishankar underlines in his book. American nationalists have been pushing for a new bipolarity of the world, between western liberalism and Chinese communism. But there are forces that work against the emergence of such a scenario. By the end of 2020, Huawei was announcing manufacturing facilities in France, and Germany had said the Chinese giant could have a foothold in the country's 5G layout.[95]

Even at the height of Trump's campaign against China on all fronts, the administration was 'badly fractured intellectually' between '"panda huggers" like Treasury Secretary Steven Mnuchin; confirmed free-traders like National Economic Council Director Larry Kudlow; and China hawks like Commerce Secretary Wilbur Ross, lead trade negotiator Robert Lighthizer and White House trade adviser Peter Navarro,' according to John Bolton, who was briefly Trump's NSA. Biden had close contacts with the Chinese establishment and during 2020, there were even allegations of wrongful association.[96] Biden's China policy is unlikely to remove tariffs rolled out by Trump and the general tone of his politics,[97] but NSA Jake Sullivan is for 'managed coexistence with China'. India's China challenge has a Pakistan angle that is even more complicated. Tanvi Madan argues that India–US partnership to tackle a China challenge is 'neither inevitable nor impossible'. 'The two countries have come together against China, but only when certain conditions are in place (i.e., when they have agreed not just on the nature and urgency of the threat, but also on how to deal with it).'[98]

To assume that the US would make democracy or human rights the central point of its relations with either China or India would be too simplistic. The history of the US foreign policy is proof enough that these are not the critical determinants of its action, though they are at times the explanation. So, there is no reason to assume that human rights or domestic issues of India or even China would be consequential. What is consequential, however, is market access. That is the precise point that will keep India and the US at loggerheads in the coming days. The US's experience with China will shadow its dealings with India. 'India's rise will inevitably be compared to that of China,' according to Jaishankar. 'There is this assumption that the Indian market is so huge that people have to come to India on our terms. But that [. . .] is a fairly optimistic assessment,' according to Shyam Saran.[99]

We must recall here that the last big break in US–China relations, in 1972 between Nixon and Mao, came against the backdrop of an Asian war that America was entangled in—Vietnam. Afghanistan is America's new Vietnam. China, meanwhile, has travelled long. We shall discuss US entanglement in Af–Pak in the next chapter. Proponents of the Hindutva Strategic Doctrine can claim that they were right on China and Pakistan; and on Communism and Islamism.

5

Pakistan—Frenemy in a Forever War

' . . . we've been fighting wars together: first Soviet invasion of Afghanistan, Pakistan was a frontline state, allied to the U.S. And then again the War on Terror, which was after 9/11.'

—Pakistan Prime Minister Imran Khan, at a joint media briefing with President Trump, 22 July 2019, at the White House[1]

The rise of Islamist terrorism has been a backdrop to the rise of cultural nationalism in both the US and India in recent years. Nationalists in both countries promise a more muscular national response to it. The election of a member of a minority community as the chief executive, Barack Obama and Manmohan Singh, respectively in the US and India, was used by the proponents of cultural nationalism to advance their cause. These leaders were accused of being soft towards Islamism, and even their patriotism was questioned. The rhetoric on Islamist terrorism often includes questioning the patriotism of Muslim citizens too, in both India and the US. While India has bitter memories of its encounter with Islamist politics and terrorism for the last several decades, America's association with jihad has a more curious recent history. For the US, it was a strategic tool to begin with, before it turned into the ideology of the other and the assassins landed at their doorstep. And the epicentre of America's affair with the jihadis, first as partners, now as rivals, has been in India's backyard—the Afghanistan–Pakistan region, or Af–Pak as the Americans have named it.

In the last seven decades of America's strategy in South Asia, there has been one constant, and that is Pakistan and its military—as a partner in propping up jihadis, then fighting them and now being found out as playing both sides. Also noteworthy is the fact that the US's entanglement with Pakistan and China are inseparable from one another. Pakistan had aided US–China ties in the 1970s; and today, Pakistan does not fight shy of its loyalty and admiration for China. In January 2021, Pakistan PM Imran Khan said the Chinese model of development was something that his country would want to emulate. 'I think Pakistan is going to help us out to extricate ourselves (from Afghanistan),' Trump said in July 2019.[2] In January 2018, he had said, 'They have given us nothing but lies & deceit, thinking of our leaders as fools.'[3] Trump's contradictory, strident remarks are unusual for a president, but these are instructive. General Lloyd Austin, appointed defense secretary by Biden, said during his confirmation hearing that Pakistan had taken 'constructive steps' in the Afghanistan peace process.[4]

For all the strategic clarity that the US is supposed to possess, it cannot decide for sure whether Pakistan is an ally or an enemy. Much in the same manner as its ties with China, its relationship with Pakistan remains an unsettled question in

Washington, DC. Pakistan, due to its linkages with Islamist terrorism, also becomes a component of the US approach to the larger Islamic world. Trump and 'America First' nationalists have tried to restructure the country's ties with the Islamic world by ratcheting up tensions with Iran on the one hand and reinforcing the relationship with the UAE and Saudi Arabia on the other. For India's Hindutva nationalists, Pakistan is an intimate enemy. Hindutva defines itself often in terms of Pakistan. The strength and resolve of India are tested in opposition to Pakistan.

'I want to find out why we've been there for 17 years,' Trump had demanded in one review meeting on Afghanistan in early 2017.[5] However, Trump signed the order to extend America's Afghan war for an indefinite period of time—against his own instincts, he said publicly, going by the opinion of professional strategists after a review. But he would change track soon enough and return to his instincts, which is to disengage from the mess in Afghanistan and withdraw US troops from there. The US will have to make a choice with regard to dealing with Islamism. Should it try to reorganize the societies that foster Islamism or should it focus its attention strictly to securing the homeland from any threat from non-state actors? For 'America First' nationalists, the choice has already been made—Islamism is a threat to the whole world, and the US has no particular responsibility to tackle it. In fact, countries that are directly threatened by it should be dealing with it. US strategy should focus on protecting itself. Biden would insist that he would not confine the US to a policy of looking after itself alone, and profess the good of championing a world order.

The reality on the ground makes such ambitions very costly, and prohibitively so in the changed landscape of

American politics that is overwhelmed by nationalism. The endless nature of the wars launched by the US in the first decades of the twenty-first century was among the reasons for the popularity of Trump's 'America First' nationalism. America's approach to Af–Pak has a direct bearing on India's calculations.

'America First' politics sees Afghanistan as a mess created by American elites. America has a second Vietnam in Afghanistan, Steve Bannon declared in October 2017. 'The geniuses in the foreign policy elite, what they left on President Trump, is essentially the Bay of Pigs in Venezuela, the Cuban missile crisis in Korea, and the Vietnam War in Afghanistan, all at one time [. . .] This is the geniuses of both political parties.'[6] The Trump phenomenon would so change the vocabulary of American politics that Biden, a champion of US establishment all his life, would promise to end the 'forever wars'. Whether he would be able to deliver on this promise is a different question, however. Trump had made a similar promise, but four years later, US military is fighting in Afghanistan, Iraq, Somalia, Syria, Yemen and other places.

The Obama–Biden administration had walked a similar path as Trump on Afghanistan soon after taking over in 2009— an eagerness to quit the war, a review, announcement of a new strategy and continuation of troops until the end of term. They wanted to end the war in Iraq also. The wars stretched on and Obama left the next review to his successor; and the baton has now come back to Biden. Afghanistan is today the longest war that America has fought in its entire history.

Trump's strategy differed from Obama's on two significant points. First, he committed American troops in Afghanistan for an indefinite period. Second, he made India a central part of his Afghan strategy—or at least announced that it would be so.

India welcomed the statement. Trump and Modi had spoken about expanding India's role in Afghanistan during the latter's visit to Washington, DC in June 2017. 'Another critical part of the South Asia strategy for America is to further develop its strategic partnership with India, the world's largest democracy and a key security and economic partner of the United States,' Trump had said.[7] Neither of these differences counted for much during his term in office as the Indian role remained limited; and Trump laid out an exit plan for the US from Afghanistan, regardless of the outcome. Trump had only reluctantly agreed to stay on in Afghanistan and overruled his advisers who sought another troop surge. In general, he was averse to wars. 'I am especially proud to be the first president in decades who has started no new wars,' he said in his exit speech in 2021.[8]

In June 2019, advisers urged him to strike Iran after it shot down a US surveillance drone. '"Too many body bags," said Trump,' according to John Bolton, who fell out with him after a brief stint as NSA, ' . . . which he was not willing to risk for an unmanned drone [. . .] "Not proportionate," he said again. In my government experience, this was the most irrational thing I ever witnessed any President do,' Bolton writes. 'Trump had behaved bizarrely.' That was the kind of ire that Trump evoked among the professional strategists of Washington, DC.[9]

He failed to pull out all American soldiers from Afghanistan, but he kicked off talks with the Taliban, with the aim of complete withdrawal by May 2021. He accepted the fact that the US could not think of stability in Afghanistan without involving the Taliban in governance.

In 2016, when Trump took over as President, the Afghan war was in the sixteenth year; in 2021, when Biden came to power, it was in the twentieth year, and Taliban presence had grown. Biden might consider keeping a small presence of US troops in Afghanistan, but the realization that wiping off the Taliban or the larger family of Islamists is not a worthwhile pursuit is increasingly mainstream in the US. With a majority of Americans opposed to military involvement in Afghanistan, militarists have been tamed to a certain extent.[10] Biden has been a core member of the establishment for more than four decades, and giving up his own legacy of militarism may not come easily to him, however.

The Afghan war is not merely about Afghanistan. Effectively, it is a global war, against an amorphous enemy that surfaces at places of its choosing around the world, at irregular intervals—what we use the blanket term 'Islamist terrorism' for. To understand what this entails for India, we need to take a step back and take a closer look at how we got where we are.

Afghan Jihad and Millennial Terror

America woke up to the first day of the new millennium with the relief that the Y2K bug did not wreak any large-scale havoc— lights did not go off, the party went on as long as it needed to. The fear of Y2K had opened American shores to a new wave of Indians who came in large numbers to fix that problem and would soon increase their wealth and influence in their host country. As for India, it woke up to the millennium with the new reality of Islamist terrorism. It would be another two years before the rest of the world came to take serious note of it.

A few hours to the turn of the millennium, the passengers of IC 814, an Indian Airlines plane that was hijacked on 24 December 1999, returned to New Delhi from Kandahar, Afghanistan, where 190 people were held on the thin edge between life and death for seven days. India exchanged three

Kashmiri separatists held in Indian prisons for the release of the aircraft and its passengers. The Taliban, which was then ruling Afghanistan, allowed the hijackers and the three released militants ten hours to leave Afghanistan. It was clear to anyone who bothered to look where they went. The Af–Pak region had become a haven of Islamist terrorism. It would turn uglier in the years that followed.

The hijack had a brief prehistory. In July 1999, US President Bill Clinton had forced Pakistan prime minister Nawaz Sharif's hand to order the withdrawal of Pakistan's military from Kargil in Jammu and Kashmir, which America considers disputed territory between the two countries. Pakistan's then Army chief Pervez Musharraf, who ordered the capture of Indian-controlled territory, was furious at the civilian leadership for succumbing to American pressure. He considered it a betrayal of the country by its politicians and took over power in a coup in October 1999. The hijack happened in December.

The three prisoners released by India would soon become key players in the global jihadi network; among them Omar Saeed Sheikh, the mastermind behind the killing of *WSJ*'s Daniel Pearl, who continues to enjoy the protection of the Pakistani establishment. But the Western media was unable to see the looming danger. Juanita Phillips, a CNN interviewer, asked the then Indian NSA Brajesh Mishra, 'Well, you're talking about terrorism. I presume you're talking about the recent hijacking crisis. India has accused Pakistan of being behind that crisis but has not come with any firm evidence. What proof do you have?'[11] Brian Nelson, another anchor of CNN, asked Mishra:

This leaves your two countries and the whole region in a state of a stalemate. So the question I want to ask you now is what is your government prepared to do to try to break that stalemate? Is there any gesture that India can make, and is it willing to perhaps initiate a plebiscite in Kashmir, as the Pakistanis are demanding?[12]

The jihadi assembly line in South Asia was started by Pakistan to carry out a war outsourced by America—against the Soviet Union. The American objective was to make Afghanistan into a 'Russian Vietnam', says Bruce Riedel, a key Central Intelligence Agency (CIA) official who has since then written a series of books on South Asia, and who describes the Afghan jihad as the most cost-effective 'federal programme'. 'WE WON', CIA's Islamabad station chief cabled his bosses 'in 1989, when the Soviets crossed the border to go home after the most successful covert intelligence operation in U.S. history,' writes Riedel.[13] Soviet troops had entered Afghanistan in 1979 to support its friendly regime in Kabul. The fall of Afghanistan quickened the collapse of the Soviet Union. Riedel notes that it was the cheapest war ever—the total cost for the entire decade from 1979–89 was about $3 billion, compared to the Vietnam War that cost over $300 billion. And the Iraq War that would drain over $1 trillion. 'From a taxpayer's perspective, there may be no other federal program in history that produced so much historic change in world politics at such a small price.'[14] But the US has spent a trillion dollars in trying to tame the Taliban and Islamists elsewhere since 9/11. If China believes that its hybrid of communism and capitalism would outlive and outsmart American liberal capitalism and democracy, the Taliban believe that they can defeat the current super power, as they defeated the Soviet Union. The Islamists are disrupters of the liberal world, but they too have an alternative vision of organizing humanity. For the state of Pakistan, terrorism targeting India is a tool of asymmetric warfare, but for the global jihadi movement, the ambitions are grander. 'Victory against the Soviets in Afghanistan remains al Qaeda's crown jewel, proving that the mujahideen can defeat a superpower,' Katherine Zimmerman, an expert on Islamist terrorism, told a US congressional hearing in July 2017.[15] Al-Qaeda was primary among the jihadi groups that fought the Soviets in Afghanistan. They believe that America can be defeated, just like the Soviets.

Riedel rejects the argument that American actions in Afghanistan contributed to the rise of global jihadism in any way. On the contrary, he argues that it was the Soviet invasion of Afghanistan that led to the rise of religious soldiers in Afghanistan and American support to them was immaterial to the trajectory of events in South Asia and the world.[16] What is not a matter of debate is that today, jihad continues to be 'cost-effective'—a few thousand men hiding in caves, riding horses or camels and driving pick-up trucks, who keep highly armed, modern armies of states across the world on their toes, claiming innocent lives and creating terror. Not a single American life was lost in its campaign against the Soviet Union, but the jihad that has since spread around the world has already claimed hundreds of thousands of lives, including American ones.

India was among the first targets of the jihadi overflow from Afghanistan. The money that America sent to jihadis in Afghanistan went through Pakistan's spy agency, the Inter-Services Intelligence (ISI). The Saudi government matched the contribution as part of a pact with the US, and discreetly sent more to jihadi groups in Afghanistan. Private donations from wealthy Sunnis were added to this. Holy warriors from around the world assembled in South Asia in the fight against communism, aided by the military-mullah compact of Pakistan.[17]

After the Soviets left, the Taliban took control of Afghanistan. Pakistan, Saudi Arabia and the UAE were quick to recognize the Islamist regime that took over power in 1997. It was the success of the jihad in Afghanistan that encouraged Pakistan to think that this form of unconventional warfare could be an optimal strategy against its enemy, India. Hussain Haqqani believes that Pakistan's calculation was that India would leave Kashmir like the Soviets did in Afghanistan, as the cost outweighs the benefits of holding on to the territory.[18]

In 2009, Obama appointed a committee headed by Riedel to review America's Afghan war—which by then was in its eighth year—which concluded, 'Pakistan, the birthplace of global Islamic jihad and now its epicenter, had become a crucible of terror and was the most dangerous country in the world. Clearly, it held the key to destroying both al Qaeda and the larger syndicate.'[19]

By the end of 2015, the Republican lawmaker and then chairman of the house committee on foreign affairs, Congressman Ed Royce, summed up the US–Pakistan relations thus:

Pakistani Governments have come and gone, but its northwestern frontier [on the border with Afghanistan] has remained a terrorist haven, with its security services supporting what it considers to be 'good' Islamist terrorist groups. These 'good' groups—under Pakistan's calculus—destabilize Afghanistan and threaten neighboring India while the government simultaneously opposes what it considers the bad Islamist groups.[20]

There is no easy way to tackle this. In response to Royce, Richard Olson, then the US special representative for Afghanistan and Pakistan, said: 'While we do not always see eye to eye on every issue, our relationship with Pakistan is vital to the national security of the United States.'[21] This has remained a key consideration of the US. Though Trump questioned this premise, there are compulsions that prevent the US from pushing Pakistan to a breaking point. When the Trump administration proposed cuts in assistance to Pakistan in the US budget for FY2018, the state department opposed it. The department's views are reflective of the establishment's take on the issue.

> Pakistan plays a key role in the US counterterrorism strategy, the peace process in Afghanistan, nuclear non-proliferation efforts, and stability and economic integration in South and Central Asia. It is also a large and growing economy offering profitability for US businesses.[22]

Trump and some of his key advisers thought that Pakistan could be pressured to take more action against the terrorist groups that it nourished. In February 2018, the Trump administration moved the Financial Action Task Force (FATF), a watchdog that monitors terrorist financing, which led to Pakistan being placed on a 'grey list' for enhanced monitoring. The designation disrupts investments into the country. Pakistan had been there earlier—in 2008, and from 2012 to 2015. The pressure has had its impact. Pakistan put some restrictions on Lashkar-e-Taiba (LeT) and sentenced its leader Hafiz Saeed, to eleven years in prison. Pakistan wants to get off the grey list; at a minimum, it wants to avoid being on the blacklist.

Though the CIA ran its fight against communism the world over, its ties with Pakistan's ISI and its military forged during that period turned out to be strong and enduring. Till date, despite all the noise and acrimony that surrounds US–Pakistan relations, the Pentagon, the American military generals and a large segment of their strategic thinkers want to keep Pakistan close, at least for tactical reasons. Pakistan has always used this American dilemma to its own advantage against India, and 'could always divert covert funds from the Afghan insurgency toward fomenting insurgencies against the source of its perceived principal threat—India'.[23] From India's perspective, the American indulgence in dealing with jihadis was the most egregious in the case of David Coleman Headley, the American intelligence operative who aided the planning of the Mumbai terror attacks of 2008 for the LeT.

9/11 and Beyond

After the collapse of the Soviet Union, America had lapsed into a self-congratulatory lassitude, with the assurance that its model of market economy and democracy was the future of mankind. The disintegration of the Soviet Union happened partly due to a very cost-effective 'federal programme' called the jihad, but all jihadis had not attained martyrdom; thousands of them survived to fight the next battle. For Pakistan, extending this jihadi programme was not only cost-effective, but also profitable. Soon enough, disaster would visit the American mainland on 11 September 2001.

After the collapse of the Soviet Union, America took note of Pakistan's nuclear build-up—which it had ignored during the Afghan jihad—and George H.W. Bush's administration stopped aid to Islamabad in 1990, citing the Pressler

Amendment. The story of the campaign against Pakistan's nuclear recklessness is narrated in a book by former senator Larry Pressler.[24] America partially disengaged from Pakistan in the 1990s. Meanwhile, 9/11 was planned and launched against it from Afghan soil. The terrorist attack put Pakistan right back at the centre of Washington's calculations for the region, as the US launched its 'war on terror' against Al-Qaeda and its Taliban protectors.

That war has spread across all continents today and has fundamentally changed the functioning of American democracy and its ideals of free society. The US Congress, which has the sole authority to declare war, authorized the president of the US, in September 2001, to launch war against unspecified targets and countries.[25]

Bush, Obama and Trump used this authorization to attack targets around the world in the last twenty years, though there has been resistance within the US to such a sweeping interpretation of the congressional authorization. Since then, until Trump became president, America had paid Pakistan $33.3 billion under various accounts, related to the war on terror. Soon after 9/11, the Pressler Amendment a distant memory, the George W. Bush administration had given Pakistan $230 million from counterterrorism programmes to upgrade its F-16 fighter planes.

Even after American special forces found and killed Osama Bin Laden in Pakistan in 2011, the Obama–Biden administration campaigned hard to give eight more F-16s to it. It had to give up the effort in the face of strong opposition from the US Congress. Pakistan was using F-16s to fight terrorists, administration officials argued before the Congress. A formidable lobby within the American system till today believes that America's disengagement from Pakistan through the late 1980s and 1990s led to the developments that culminated in 9/11. Richard Olson said:

> We can draw on the lessons of history there, especially the period in the 1990s and late 1980s, when we did somewhat disengage from the region, and we paid, I think, a significant price as a country for that at the beginning of the last decade. I think that with all of the challenges of the relationship, I think it is most important for the U.S. to be engaged and to build a partnership with Pakistan.[26]

'Pakistan is an essential partner in any peace process in Afghanistan,' Secretary Austin said in January 2021.[27]

Pakistan's has been a story of colossal failure in terms of stability and progress, but it has been extraordinarily successful in extracting rent from America. In a way, the two are linked. Pakistan's rulers have for decades convinced—or threatened—America that its military and ruling establishment are what prevented the communist takeover of South Asia, and later, an Islamist apocalypse. Americans have bought into this narrative partly as strategy and partly out of ignorance. When the Clinton administration pressed Musharraf on issues of democracy, he 'warned that a presidential snub would "strengthen the hands of the extremists", essentially the same argument that Nawaz Sharif had repeatedly used with me in seeking American leniency before and after the Pakistani nuclear test,' writes Strobe Talbott, Clinton's key interlocutor for South Asia.[28]

Even Prime Minister Indira Gandhi fell for this, as she showed Pakistan leniency in 1972 at the Shimla conference, after its thorough defeat in the Bangladesh War. India could have easily imposed a harsh agreement on Pakistan. But that was not to be.

Bhutto told Indira Gandhi that Pakistan's domestic political situation did not allow him to sign a treaty settling the argument over Kashmir forever and the Pakistani military would not accept, even in defeat, an explicit no-war pact. Radical opinions would gain popularity in Pakistan, he argued, that would accuse him of losing Kashmir in addition to East Pakistan. Bhutto pleaded for the middle ground suggesting that de-escalation of tensions take place in stages.[29]

When Talbott tried to convince Sharif that Pakistan must not conduct a nuclear test in 1998, even after India's test, he was told that if he heeded his advice, next time Talbott would 'be meeting a mullah with a long beard' sitting in the prime minister's chair. The idea that Pakistan could be taken over by an Islamist group was scary for the Americans. Though politicians and the military in Pakistan generously incite religious passion to retain their hold over the country, they have extracted a good bargain by holding out the prospect of a jihadi takeover of the country. This has takers in the American capital. Trump's NSA John Bolton viewed this as a fundamental concern in dealing with Pakistan, despite his hawkish militarism.

Supplying ever-increasing numbers of conventional weapons to Islamabad was the American way of reinforcing the self-proclaimed, 'lesser' Islamist leaders of Pakistan, allowing them to project strength internally. Pakistan has seventy F-16s supplied by the US. The Obama–Biden administration wanted to give eight more F-16s to Pakistan under the US Foreign Military Financing (FMF) programme. FMF involves the US giving money to a foreign country to buy arms manufactured by the US, in other words, paid for by American taxpayers.

Between 1983 and 1987, Pakistan received forty F-16s that it modified for delivery of nuclear bombs. The Obama administration's move to replenish Pakistan's F-16 fleet was stalled by Indian diplomacy that harnessed the strength of Indian–American political participation in the US. Demands by Indian–American voters to Congress members led to a legislative intervention that stalled the supply of these planes. With the US tightening the screws on Pakistan, it is reportedly trying to turn to Chinese-supplied JF-17 fighters. Pakistan is today the biggest importer of Chinese arms.[30] America's complicated role in India–Pakistan ties was tested again after a 14 February 2019 terrorist attack in Kashmir by Pakistan-based Jaish-e-Mohammed that killed forty Indian soldiers. The Hindutva Strategic Doctrine adheres to a principle of conventional military response to Pakistan's proxy war tactics and India launched an airstrike in Pakistan-controlled territories in retaliation. India said it shot down an F-16 fighter of the Pakistan Air Force in the dogfight that ensued, but US defence officials said all F-16s were accounted for.[31] The US tracks and keeps a tab on all military equipment it has given to other countries. Reports also suggested that Trump intervened to secure the release of an Indian air force pilot who had baled out in Pakistani territory.

For decades, America has tried to pay Pakistan for good behaviour, but that has not been successful. As the jihadi factories expanded beyond the control of the ISI, relations began to sour, but Pakistani generals would still offer sufficient cooperation to the American counterparts to be counted as an ally. Joshua White, a key official in the Obama White House, said:

> Pakistan has in a number [of] important respects, been a meaningful counterterrorism partner of the U.S. for years. It was a partner in decimating Al Qaida's presence, it has been a partner in dealing with a number of security threats.[32]

A Subcontinent Divided

In the recent decades of accelerated cooperation between India and the US, the former has maintained a pet peeve—Washington's relationship with Islamabad and an approach different from India's on dealing with Islamists and the Taliban. Indian policy, over decades, has attempted to convince America of the dangers posed by Pakistan and its shades of Islamism. For India, Islamic nationalism was a bane even during its struggle for independence from British colonialism, and the founding fathers of India were clear that Indian nationalism had to be non-religious. But the dangers posed by religious nationalism were evident as the Muslim League, based on its two-nation theory, argued that Hindus and Muslims were separate nations and could not be part of the same country.

The demand for Pakistan as a separate country for the Muslims was met, as India won independence from the British in 1947. Not only was India divided geographically, Hindu nationalism/political Hinduism or Hindutva set down roots in the process. Mohandas Karamchand Gandhi fell prey to the bullets of a Hindu nationalist, who had a different interpretation of his religion and of India than Gandhi. The millions of Hindus who had to flee Pakistan and the millions of Muslims who fled to Pakistan from India in the aftermath of Partition carried stories of horror and violence, which became the foundational memories of the two neighbours, whose relations slid progressively over the seventy-plus years of their existence. Barring a few interim points when normalization of relations seemed possible, the two have been locked in a spiral of endless hostilities. They have fought four wars and continue to constitute a dangerous global nuclear flashpoint.

The Islamist terrorism that India faces today was preceded by militarism and conventional wars inspired by Islamic nationalism promoted by Pakistan's generals and populist leaders who believed that India was a Hindu country that it could never be friends with. The Islamist state of Pakistan turned out to be a closer ally of America than secular India. The US–Pakistan alliance was initially based on a shared interest in resisting communism. Being at the frontline of the war against communism, on behalf of the free world, Pakistan went down the abyss that the limited vision of its leaders had forced upon its population.

The rise of separatism in Kashmir in the early 1990s, which later got enmeshed with jihadi terrorism that was institutionalized as a legitimate form of war in Afghanistan against the Soviets, added a new phase of Islamist militarism in India. Sikh separatism, and the terrorism associated with it, also received material and logistical support from Pakistan through the 1980s and 1990s.

While it was extracting rent from America, devoid of a strong economic base of its own, Pakistan wanted to be in a race for parity with India, which contributed to its current turmoil, argues Haqqani. Ideas of parity and competition often dominate discussions on the rectangular relationship involving Pakistan, India, China and America. When hypernationalism is added to such discussions, they become toxic and self-defeating. Pakistan imagined for itself the position of leader of the Islamic world and embarked upon a military build-up which led it to invest in the 'Islamic bomb', and currently involves spending 3.6 per cent of its GDP on defence.

An elementary comparison of the four countries would be perceptive in this context. India's GDP is eight times that of Pakistan and its per capita GDP at purchasing power parity (PPP) is 23 per cent more; China's GDP is five times more and its per capita GDP at PPP is double that of India's. In turn,

America's GDP is 88 per cent more than China's and its per capita GDP is six times that of the latter.[33] 'If Indians hope to match China's GDP, they will have to wait for many [more] years than they might expect—until 2075.'[34] Any discussion on Indian strategy today must account for this factor, particularly when we discuss military modernization.

The Hindutva segment of Indian strategic thought tried to seek an alliance with the US by offering to do what Pakistan had been doing for America—be at the frontline of America's war on terror. Days after 9/11, during a phone conversation between Vajpayee and Bush, India offered three air bases and unspecified port facilities on the Arabian Sea, as well as logistical support for the US forces to launch its operation against Taliban and al Qaeda in Afghanistan.[35] On 19 September, Musharraf offered Pakistan's readiness to be at the frontline in the war on terror, like it had been at the frontline in the war against communism. Pakistani rulers on the one hand fanned the flames of anti-Americanism as part of their Islamist agenda, but justified their alliance with the US as a bulwark against India.

On 19 September 2001, Musharraf told his country, 'They [India] have readily offered all their bases, facilities, and logistic support to the United States. They want the United States to side with them and to declare Pakistan a terrorist state. They also want our strategic assets and our Kashmir cause to be harmed.' Pakistan's alliance with the US was therefore necessary to 'save Islam', he said, adding that India planned to install an anti-Pakistan government in Afghanistan.[36]

The idea that India must join America's war on Islamic terror would not disappear from Hindutva thought—when America invaded Iraq, a considerable section within the BJP government argued for the deployment of Indian troops in Iraq. The move was nipped in the bud by Vajpayee. 'In the summer of 2003, senior ministers like L.K. Advani and a number of Indian strategic commentators kept up a steady drumbeat calling for the country to send troops to help the Americans. But Vajpayee kept his cool and refused,' writes journalist Devirupa Mitra.[37]

The American understanding of India often fails to appreciate its complexities, leading to a stunted and one-dimensional perspective of the country. For the purpose of this discussion, we need to take into account the essentialization of India as Hindu and, later, the conflation of Hinduism and Hindutva, a topic that has already been discussed earlier in the book. John Dulles, the US secretary of state from 1953–59 under President Dwight Eisenhower, and a promoter of a coalition with Pakistan, said, 'In India, Soviet communism exercises a strong influence through the interim Hindu government,' which was led by Nehru![38] On the other hand, America's military, its commentators and the system in general had little problem dealing with the military and intelligence agencies of Pakistan.

With the war in Bangladesh looming in the beginning of the 1970s, the US's own diplomats on the ground in Dhaka wrote to their bosses in Washington, DC that America was 'bending over backwards to placate the West Pakistan-dominated government'.[39] Kissinger and Nixon thought that the crisis in Bangladesh was not the result of Pakistan's refusal to accept the democratic decision of the majority, but the result of Hindu–Muslim hatred.[40] This is a policy implication of the strong American tendency to essentialize India as Hindu. At other times, inversely, American agencies thought democracy was too messy to deal with. After the Obama administration made moves to promote civilian authority in Pakistan, the CIA complained that it was making decision-making slower and the war in Afghanistan more difficult to handle.

Emerging from a colonial yoke, India was guarded in its dealings with America. It did seek partnership with the US, realizing that its potential for development could be tapped with American help. But Indian officials could never match the Pakistani playbook in dealing with Americans. American scholar C. Christine Fair, who has extensive experience in dealing with officials on both sides, thinks India should have copied some of Pakistan's tactics of winning over Americans. Indian officials used to meet only their own counterparts on the American side, while Pakistan's attitude was so welcoming of the Americans that 'even a junior analyst at think tanks can meet virtually anyone,' she says. 'U.S. Congressional delegates are particularly delighted when they get to meet the army chief [. . .] In contrast to Indian officials who are often stiff, hectoring, disinterested, and often seem bored, the (much higher ranked) Pakistani official is engaging, jocular, (seemingly) forthcoming, self-effacing, humorous and charming,' she writes. 'This gives rise to the chattering among diplomats, journalists, scholars and think-tank analysts who visit both countries who are wont to observe, "The Pakistanis may lie like rugs and kill our troops, but they sure are accommodating."'[41]

While Pakistan was peddling its 'shared values and interests' with America—as Ayub Khan put it—India was seeking cooperation from both the Soviet Union and the US and trying to maintain a fine balance with both. This balancing act and the expression of self-respect and autonomy by India's bureaucratic and political elite did not earn it any favour with the US.

American interlocutors have generally been impatient with the slow nature of Indian bureaucratic and legislative processes, even though as a democracy, America's own processes are often slow and entangled. Its lawmaking processes are at least as troublesome and long-winded as India's, and often extended due to the increasing fragmentation and polarization of political opinions and constituencies. India and America were and should have been in a better position to appreciate each other's democracies. But that is not how it turned out to be, as American opinion makers and decision makers instinctively gravitated towards the 'decisiveness' and 'stability' that came with authoritarianism and dictatorship.

Pakistan's relationship with the US is primarily military and governmental, with less civilian and people-to-people contact, compared to its relationship with India. Also, Pakistan has, as part of deliberate state policy, encouraged public opinion against America to fester, which is not the case in India. Even American presidents least liked domestically are admired in India. Former prime minister Manmohan Singh said, Indians 'loved' President Bush. India and Israel are among the countries where Trump was most popular. Public perception in America and Pakistan about each other is extremely hostile. In Pakistan, for years, only around 20 per cent of people had a favourable image of America.[42] In America, only 10 per cent of people thought Pakistan could be trusted.[43] Meanwhile, India is the eighth-most liked country for Americans,[44] and in India, 56 per cent of the people had a favourable view of America in 2016, though it went down to 49 per cent in 2017 under Trump.[45]

American policymakers continue to hold on to the hope—though considerably weakened in recent times—that it could facilitate a grand deal involving both India and Pakistan. On various occasions, including in 2015, it toyed with the idea of offering Pakistan a nuclear deal along the lines of the India–US civil nuclear deal. As secretary of state, Hillary Clinton suggested that if Pakistan wanted a nuclear deal like India and Israel, the only way to achieve it was by stopping proliferation. Her point of concern was the risk of fissile materials falling into terrorist hands. Just as the Obama administration was taking over in 2009, the vice president-elect, Joe Biden, offered Asif Ali Zardari a South Asia deal that included an American initiative to foster a new India–Pakistan relationship.[46] Trump offered several times to mediate between India and Pakistan. 'And I think maybe if we can help intercede and do whatever we have to do,' he said, Imran Khan by his side, at the White House in July 2019.[47]

While American policymakers are increasingly convinced that Pakistan played them, Pakistani leaders have come to accuse America of being a fair-weather friend that used them for its interests and abandoned them when it did not suit them. Pakistan's former NSA Nasir Khan Janjua has said it was only because of Pakistan's support that America could claim to be a superpower and defeat the Soviets in Afghanistan. A day after his meeting with Obama in Washington, DC in October 2015, Sharif hinted that the US was making unreasonable demands of Islamabad. Pakistan could not bring the Taliban to the negotiating table 'and be asked to kill them at the same time', he said at a public event at the US Institute of Peace.[48]

American policymakers do not appreciate India's attempts to raise Washington's dealings with Pakistan in bilateral talks. This changed considerably under the Trump presidency, but did not go away completely. I have heard the same argument from officials of both Trump and Obama–Biden administrations. 'I want to make the point here that US relationships with India and Pakistan really stand on their own merits and terms. We don't see a zero-sum relationship when it comes to the US relationship with Pakistan and the US relationship with India [. . .] We're certainly eager to deepen the strategic partnership with India,' an official of the Trump White House said days before the first Modi–Trump meeting. 'We are also interested in continuing our co-operation with Pakistan,' the official said, adding that the US is concerned about tensions between India and Pakistan.[49]

A senior official of the Obama White House stated the same idea, in almost the same words, in June 2016 after Modi's visit:

> America is a global power that has interests in all parts of the world. So, what it does in one place should not be a concern to others [. . .] We believe it's in both countries' interests.[50]

Trump disowned the nation-building project in Afghanistan that had become part of the US strategy. That the US must not nurture grand ambitions in its anti-terrorism war is not a Trump policy so much. There is remarkable continuity here from the Obama years. Obama's White Paper on Afghan policy in 2009 reached the same conclusions. 'All of the president's [Obama's] advisers agreed that the primary goal in the region should be narrow—taking aim at Al Qaeda as opposed to the vast attempt at nation-building the Bush administration had sought in Iraq. The question was how to get there'.[51] 'As President, my greatest responsibility is to protect the American people. We are not in Afghanistan to control that country or to dictate its future,' said Obama.[52] These attitudes are part of the Trump doctrine on Islamist terrorism, though his administration and many commentators try to portray it as a fresh beginning, and a *new* South Asia policy. At the end of this tenure, the tangible outcomes of Trump's South Asia policy are a near certain disengagement from Afghanistan and a near total end of American aid to Pakistan. Biden's willingness and ability to return to the earlier format of the US approach to Pakistan may be limited, though he was himself the architect of that to a great extent and might want to restore ties with Islamabad to its earlier glory.

The US could decide to ignore governance and stability in Afghanistan, but the stability of Pakistan is in a different category. It has been a concern for all US administrations, and this has not changed even after Washington realized and acknowledged that its long-term ally may not be, well, an ally. The ability of a potential India–Pakistan conflict to destabilize South Asia has always bothered American policymakers, including Trump. 'To lessen tensions between two nuclear-armed nations that too often teeter on the edge of escalation and confrontation, we must pursue constructive diplomacy with both India and Pakistan,' Obama had said in 2009.[53]

'For its part, Pakistan often gives safe haven to agents of chaos, violence, and terror. The threat is worse because Pakistan and India are two nuclear-armed states whose tense relations threaten to spiral into conflict. And that could happen,' Trump said in his 2017 South Asia policy speech.[54] John Bolton, before being appointed Trump's NSA, analysed the South Asia policy of the administration as follows, 'The Bush and Obama administrations also criticized Pakistan's support for terrorists, without effect. Putting too much pressure on Pakistan risks further destabilizing the already volatile country, tipping it into the hands of domestic radical Islamicists, who grow stronger by the day.'[55]

An ultimate deal with the Taliban is also at the core of the American strategy to deal with Islamism and bring the Afghan conflict to a close somehow, a position that has not been palatable to India for long. The Obama–Biden administration went on to push for a congressional authorization of $1.5 billion per year to Pakistan, to aid its social programmes and enhance its anti-terrorism capabilities. Obama made a distinction between the 'uncompromising core of the Taliban' that 'must be met with force, and must be defeated' with 'those who've taken up arms because of coercion, or simply for a price. These Afghans must have the option to choose a different course,' he said, in a differentiation that India views with scepticism.[56]

Ever since the war began in Afghanistan, America has been reimbursing Pakistan for the logistical and operational support given to US-led military operations, which is technically not billed as 'foreign assistance'. This accounted for roughly 20 per cent of Pakistan military's expenses for many years. In the current war against the jihadis, as opposed to the previous one alongside them, America paid $14.5 billion to Pakistan as reimbursement. In recent years, it has cut back on payment to Pakistan under what is called the Coalition Support Fund (CSF), primarily due to laws passed by Congress. For 2015, the US Congress authorized up to $1 billion in CSF to Pakistan, but a new rider ensured that $300 million of that money was subject to a certification by the US defence secretary that Pakistan had taken sufficient measures to disrupt the infamous Haqqani network.

The requirement for this certification could not be waived citing national security concerns, which the US state department routinely used to do for the rest of the money. In 2016, the amount ineligible for waiver was raised to $350 million of the total $900 million; and following the National Defense Authorization Act for Fiscal Year 2017, of the total $900 million, $400 million was ineligible for waiver.

The administration did not issue certifications for FY2015–FY2018.[57] This need for a certification from the US secretary of state for aid was established by the Kerry-Lugar-Berman Bill, which was an attempt to pump in more money to stabilize and develop Pakistan. The secretary of state never certified that Pakistan met these criteria, but gave repeated waivers citing national interest for the rest of the money. The Trump administration tightened the screws further. Trump's first Twitter post on New Year's Day 2018 was a blistering attack on Pakistan. 'The United States has foolishly given Pakistan more than 33 billion dollars in aid over the last 15 years, and they have given us nothing but lies & deceit, thinking of our leaders as fools. They give safe haven to the terrorists we hunt in Afghanistan, with little help. No more!' Trump wrote. Within days, his administration announced that it was freezing assistance worth $2 billion for Pakistan. Altogether, the Trump administration calculated that aid worth $1.3 billion for Pakistan was suspended by 2018. Musharraf had publicly admitted that the Pakistani military diverted a major portion of the assistance it received from America for war preparation against India. But the same administration was willing to give this to Pakistan provided it played along on Afghanistan. 'To be honest, I think we have a better relationship with Pakistan right now than we did when we were paying that money. But all of that can come back, depending on what we work out,' Trump said, during his joint media appearance with Khan cited above.

American nationalists see Islamism as a problem of the entire world.

There are some issues in the world that are America's problems. There are some issues in the world that are the world's problems, and they're as much Canada's problems as they're America's problems as they're Germany's problems [. . .] At the end of the day, we have to have a thoughtful discussion about how we go about doing it. But what I do know about the president's view is that America should not be bearing the entire burden for everyone's security around the world.[58]

Trump saw Afghanistan or Islamism as a problem for the whole world and he has constantly refuted the idea that it is America's responsibility to fix it.

America always indicated to India, at least prior to about 2012 or 2013, that greater engagement on security issues in Afghanistan could be problematic. After 2012–13, the US sent signals that India should make its own choices in this regard. 'I think New Delhi recognized economic assistance and political engagement was highly productive, and security assistance only limited to providing some equipment and training in India, was reasonable. I think New Delhi has been anxious and unwilling to go beyond that,' said White.[59] The US had not asked India to expand its role in Afghanistan in any particular fashion, officials said after Trump's speech on his new South Asia strategy.

While the larger fight against Islamism remains, America needs an end to the war in Afghanistan. 'The United States can address Afghanistan only with a political initiative. The ultimate answer to the Pakistan conundrum is to start a diplomatic initiative to bring peace to Afghanistan by opening talks with the Taliban,' says Richard Olson.[60] A political solution was meant to be pursued with the Taliban once it was militarily weakened. The way it turned out by the end of 2020 was the opposite as the Taliban entrenched itself further militarily.

Ending his blame game with Pakistan, Trump wrote a letter to Khan seeking his support for talks with the Taliban and intra-Afghan negotiations, in December 2018.[61] 'Pakistan produced Mullah Baradar, the deputy leader of the Taliban who had been in Pakistani custody. His release helped jump-start the peace process, and Baradar became the Taliban's chief negotiator. In many ways, Pakistan was uniquely positioned to help, enjoying leverage with the Taliban and a working relationship with the United States.'[62] US Special Representative for Afghanistan Reconciliation Ambassador Zalmay Khalilzad, appointed by Trump, visited Islamabad at least fifteen times by the end of 2020.

India has been strident in its opposition to any deal with the Taliban since it believes there cannot be a distinction between 'good' and 'bad' Taliban—the distinction Obama made in his 2009 speech.

India and the US under the Obama administration were not on the same page as far as Afghanistan was concerned, White recalls:

We didn't always see eye to eye, we appreciated our Indian counterparts' anxieties about engaging with the Taliban, anxieties about the future of Afghanistan and what it would mean for India. We had candid conversations on that. Our dialogue on Pakistan was more definitely more stilted—India came to expect that whatever the U.S. said about Pakistan probably would make a difference in Pakistan's behavior. Within the U.S. government also there was a reluctance to talk to India about Pakistan. So those conversations were somewhat less productive. But every country has its own individual perspective and I am proud that we were able to deepen the relationship with India, and had candid conversations on all Indian concerns and openly talked about our disagreements and moved the relationship forward. In South East Asia there is convergence not only in strategic objectives but also of tactics, whereas Pakistan was a topic of more complicated conversations.[63]

A Nuclear Flashpoint

While the argument for sterner measures against Pakistan is a strong one, the fact that it is an unstable nuclear state weighs on the minds of American strategists, apart from the tactical factor that its support is crucial for operations in Afghanistan. A series of American presidents so far have viewed South Asia as a nuclear flashpoint. Pakistan's nuclear stockpile is estimated to be 130–140 warheads and is estimated to grow to 220–250 warheads by 2025, making it the world's fifth-largest nuclear weapons state. What is of particular alarm and lingering concern in the US capital is Pakistan's deployment of short-range 'tactical nuclear weapons'.[64]

Pakistan has been open about the possibility of countering India's conventional military advantage with a nuclear first strike. It has sought to justify its continuous lowering of the nuclear strike threshold by pointing towards India's Cold Start doctrine, which envisages quick, sharp and conventional military retaliation against Pakistan in the event of another Mumbai-style terrorist attack. The Cold Start doctrine apparently involves 'launching quick strikes into Pakistan within two to four days with eight to nine brigades simultaneously'.[65] This could be India's way of dealing with Pakistan's nuclear deterrence and finding space for a conventional war. The latter has publicly stated that it will 'not hesitate to use those weapons for our defense', bringing the threshold to a new low. India under Modi has a new policy of 'surgical strikes' against Pakistan in retaliation of terrorist strikes in India. Some observers have argued that his policy has called Islamabad's nuclear bluff.

For India, a tactical nuclear attack on its forces would constitute nuclear first strike, leaving it free to retaliate as per its 'no first use' nuclear doctrine. Overall, another massive terrorist strike in India has the potential to snowball into a nuclear war in the subcontinent, according to predominant American thinking on the issue. That is a concern the Trump administration had inherited from Obama and predictably, the Biden administration—which could be a continuation of the Obama administration in many ways. 'The threat that al Qaeda poses to the United States and our allies in Pakistan—including the possibility of extremists obtaining fissile material—is all too real. Without more effective action against these groups in Pakistan, Afghanistan will face continuing instability.'[66]

> Pakistan's pursuit of tactical nuclear weapons potentially lowers the threshold for their use. Early deployment during a crisis of smaller, more mobile nuclear weapons would increase the amount of time that systems would be outside the relative security of a storage site, increasing the risk that a coordinated attack by non-state actors might succeed in capturing a complete nuclear weapon.[67]

Pakistan-based terrorist groups will present a sustained threat to US interests in the region and continue to plan and conduct attacks in India and Afghanistan, according to a senior US official. 'The threat to the United States and the West from Pakistan-based terrorist groups will be persistent but diffuse. Plotting against the U.S. homeland will be conducted on a more opportunistic basis or driven by individual members within these groups,' he said. 'The emerging China Pakistan Economic Corridor will probably offer militants and terrorists additional targets,' he added.[68] A Trump White House official, speaking in the background, said China would want stability in Af–Pak for this reason—to ensure the safety of the Belt and Road Initiative.

The Road through Kashmir

Pakistan's constant refrain has been that the route to 'peace in Afghanistan is through Kashmir', the argument being that unless America forces India to make concessions in Kashmir, no progress was possible in Afghanistan—making both Kashmir and Afghanistan part of the same continuum of transnational Islamist politics. American presidents until Obama were sympathetic to this position, though nobody stated it in obvious terms. The Obama–Biden administration too tiptoed around this difficult topic with India. According to White:

> The Obama administration was careful [to] take a line that Kashmir is a dispute to be resolved between India and Pakistan. There was always one view in the Obama administration for closer interlinking between the Kashmir problem and the problem in Afghanistan arguing that if Pakistan feels more secure in its dealing with India, it will behave more responsibly. That was not a dominant view.[69]

Rex Tillerson, who was the first secretary of state under Trump, had said that India had a role to play in changing Pakistan's behaviour. Though American officials have continued to raise the need for engaging Pakistan with India, the Trump administration has been much less forceful than Obama on this issue. The Modi government believes that surgical strikes, and not talks, are the means to change Pakistan's behaviour. That would be an approach that career diplomats in the US and conventional policymakers detest.

The Trump approach of force and more force to deal with terrorism was in alignment with Hindutva's strong-arm approach not only towards Pakistan, but also within Jammu and Kashmir. As was evident, the Trump administration's response to the Modi's government's decision to revoke the special constitutional status of Kashmir in August 2019 was muted.

India's resistance to the American view of seeing Kashmir and Afghanistan as components of the same puzzle predates Modi's Hindutva doctrine. India strongly resisted the American attempt to include Kashmir in the mandate of America's special envoy for Afghanistan and Pakistan. While opposing any link between Kashmir and Afghanistan, the prime ministers before Modi were willing to separately engage with Kashmiri separatists and Pakistan on the issue. Since 2014, the country's position has become more strident and combative.

If Pakistan actually pulls back its official support to separatism in Kashmir and denies safe havens to groups that attack Afghanistan, what could be the impact and would it end the crisis? At any rate, it will have a positive impact on the situation in Kashmir. The indigenous part of the resistance might be amenable to political negotiation. If Pakistan puts a stop to its operations, it would majorly reduce violence in the region.

During the campaigns for the Kashmir assembly elections in 2014, which Modi participated in as prime minister, the BJP attacked the two democratic parties that wanted the state to stay with India—the National Conference and the People's Democratic Party (PDP). The delegitimization of mainstream parties in the eyes of the Kashmiri public was heightened when the BJP and the PDP joined hands to form the government. So, we have a situation wherein the political parties that do participate in the electoral process are at the lowest ebb of their credibility. The ruling PDP had little political space to engage with the disenchanted population of the state. This is a remarkable departure from the Vajpayee era, when the Centre engaged separatist leaders and even allowed them to travel to Pakistan for talks with leaders on the other side. The BJP and the PDP had a common minimum programme that left negotiations with the separatists solely with the PDP and in Srinagar, and the central government showed little interest in addressing insurgency in the state other than by military force. In late 2017, the Modi government appointed Dineshwar Sharma as interlocutor for Kashmir, whose failure was foretold, as discussed in chapter 2. In June 2018, the BJP ended its alliance with the PDP, and in August 2019, the special constitutional status of Jammu and Kashmir was rescinded, it was stripped of its statehood and divided into two union territories directly under the administrative control of the Centre.

Dealings with Jammu and Kashmir have indeed acquired a symbolic value for India, but unfortunately not the way Naeem Akhtar, senior leader of the PDP, described it to me during the 2014 assembly election campaign. 'India should have been celebrating us as a success of its democracy, but unfortunately, we are being treated like a troublesome mofussil,' Akhtar said. 'When Jammu and Kashmir became a part of India in 1947, that was the first time in the 1400-year-old history of Islam that a Muslim nation became part of a secular, democratic country.'[70] Akhtar was among those who were jailed following the crackdown on all politics in Jammu and Kashmir after its special status was stripped.

Though the Congress and the BJP have both used the state to demonstrate their strength, the 'complete integration' of Jammu and Kashmir has been a fundamental political agenda of the Jana Sangh, the BJP's forebear, and the Hindutva Strategic Doctrine. *'Ek desh mein do vidhan, do pradhan aur do nishan, nahi chalega'* (In one country, there cannot be two Constitutions, two heads and two flags) became its slogan against the special constitutional status granted to the state. Unlike Vajpayee, Modi began taking decisive steps towards this 'complete integration', among other things, by rejecting talks between the Centre and the separatists. Mirwaiz Umar Farooq told me in an interview, 'Vajpayee did not offer us azadi [freedom] but acknowledged that there is a problem that needs to be addressed.'[71]

Vajpayee's approach comprised three components: empower regional mainstream parties, engage the separatists and involve Pakistan. On all these fronts, Modi has followed a different path. He has shut Pakistan out of the equation, disengaged with separatist groups and weakened and delegitimized both the National Conference and the PDP.

Jammu and Kashmir is one of the most vexed problems that all prime ministers of India have had to face. At this juncture, there are three possibilities for Jammu and Kashmir. The first—the most desirable, but the most fraught—is the region's emergence as the crown of a secular, progressive India, where diversity and democracy are celebrated. The second—and the most aggressive approach right now—is to visualize Kashmir as the final frontier of a Hindu India, to be conquered and controlled. The third—which could be violent and beyond the control of actors in New Delhi—is the dim possibility of the state becoming a theatre for the clash of civilizations, where global jihadis pursuing dreams of Islamist hegemony clash with the pursuit of a Hindu nation.

The Trump administration's decision to declare Hizbul Mujahideen (HM) a global terrorist organization marked a shift in the US policy on Kashmir, and the Modi government was quick to point out the clear American slant in its favour in this matter. HM is a group of indigenous militants, and its leader, Syed Salahuddin, has been asking his cadres to keep away from international outfits, including Al-Qaeda and ISIS. Such distinctions, between indigenous militants and transnational terrorist groups, have become immaterial with the global spread of Islamism.[72] This allows the Modi government's 'take no prisoners' approach in an all-out sweep against the Kashmiri movement. Trump had no patience for self-determination debates or civil rights movements anywhere in the world. Biden proffers a different approach that includes the assertion of US leadership on human rights and democracy questions around the world.

While Pakistan has been pleading with America to be more interventionist in Kashmir, India has resisted all such moves. When Obama decided to appoint a special representative for the Af–Pak region, the original idea also involved having Kashmir as part of the new ambassador's brief. During a meeting with US Ambassador David Mulford on 9 January 2009, the then foreign affairs minister and later President, Pranab Mukherjee, is reported to have said the move 'smacks of interference and would be unacceptable [to India]'.

'Mukherjee was deeply concerned about any move toward an envoy with a broad regional mandate that could be interpreted to include Kashmir. Such a broad mandate would be viewed by India as risky and unpredictable, exposing issues of vital concern to India to the discretion of the individual appointed.'[73] India was also concerned about the possibility of a US–Pakistan deal in which India's interests were sidelined and excluded. Shivshankar Menon, who was then foreign secretary, is said to have conveyed this in a meeting with US under secretary Bill Burns. A US diplomatic cable released by WikiLeaks subsequently cites Menon as telling him that India is concerned about the possibility of a narrow deal in which it would tell Pakistan the Mumbai terrorist attacks will not 'stick on you' as long as 'you keep fighting in the West [against militants in the western region of Pakistan]'.[74]

Subsequently, Kashmir has been a point of nationalist assertion under the Hindutva doctrine and the Modi government has moved its practices closer to it than Vajpayee could or would have wanted to. A highly regarded security expert, and the former head of India's Border Security Force (BSF), E.N. Rammohan is a strong proponent of retaliation against Pakistan for cross-border acts of aggression, but is clear that Muslim citizens of India should be treated with compassion. Narrating one such incident during his stint as the inspector general of BSF in Kashmir between 1993 and 1995, he says:

> Once, two of our soldiers were beheaded by the Pakistani forces on the Line of Control. To avenge their deaths, two of our Naga soldiers beheaded three Pakistani soldiers. For the next two years, Pakistani forces didn't bother us much. This is the only answer to their brutality. That's exactly what we should do even now.

However, if you project religious nationalism into Kashmir, it will lead to ugly outcomes, he said. 'The anti-Muslim and

Hindutva approach of BJP in Kashmir is damaging [. . .] You have to tell the public of Kashmir that you [the government] are above all religion. Once you give the feeling that you are pro-Hindu, you cannot operate in that place.'[75]

Trump's South Asia Policy

Trump had been vocal about his views on Islam and Muslims and has accused the Democrats of trying to 'appease' them. His ideas about the world were defined by commercial, transactional aspects on the one hand and civilizational, cultural notions on the other. The ideological component comes from his ideas of Western civilization and how it compares with the rest.

> We are [. . .] the greatest community. We write symphonies. We pursue innovation. We celebrate our ancient heroes, embrace our timeless traditions and customs [. . .] We strive for excellence, and cherish inspiring works of art that honor God. We treasure the rule of law and protect the right to free speech and free expression [. . .] We are fighting hard against radical Islamic terrorism, and we will prevail. We cannot accept those who reject our values and who use hatred to justify violence against the innocent,' he said in Poland in July 2017.[76]

Trump clearly looked at the ongoing conflict as a civilizational one, and his idea of Western, nay Christian, exceptionalism is unmistakable. On the other hand, he thought America could be friends with the Sunni monarchs in West Asia. He has also outlined the terms of engagement between America and the part of the Muslim world he is willing to be partners with.

Addressing the leaders of fifty Muslim countries in Riyadh, Trump did not push his audience on their generally poor human rights records, which many analysts think contribute to terrorism and which Obama had taken up with the Muslim partners of America. 'We are not here to lecture,' said Trump. 'We are not here to tell other people [. . .] what to do. [. . .] The nations of the Middle East cannot wait for American power to crush this enemy for them. [. . .] A better future is only possible if your nations drive out the terrorists and extremists.' 'Drive them out,' he repeated five times, reported *The Economist*. 'To that end, Mr Trump announced the sale of "beautiful" weapons worth $110 billion to Saudi Arabia, the opening of the Global Center for Combating Extremist Ideology in Riyadh and the creation of a Terrorist Financing Targeting Center.'[77] So, a major component of Trump's anti-Islamist strategy was to prod countries facing terrorism to buy American weapons and crush them. In India, the notion of Islamist terrorism is closely linked to Pakistan, and the separatism in Kashmir. Hindu nationalists in India also make the perfunctory differentiation between good Muslims and terrorism, but by constantly raising Pakistan in domestic election campaigns, the underlying notion of civilizational conflict is never allowed to subside.

An ignorance of complexities also contributes to America's disabilities in this war. As American strategists historically find it convenient to essentialize India as a 'Hindu' country, they also tend to operate on some essentialized notions of Islam and Muslims, the discerning among them offering to differentiate between 'good' and 'evil'. The 2009 Obama document spoke about a new strategic communication approach, including addressing questions of US reliability 'as a long-term partner' in both Afghanistan and Pakistan[78]—given the history of

America's abrupt withdrawal and disinterest in the region after the collapse of the Soviet Union.

The Obama approach was based on the assessment that America's interactions with the Muslim world were not well informed. In September 2017, the US military dropped pamphlets in Afghanistan that turned out to be deeply insulting of Islam, leading to an apology within hours. The leaflets dropped in the Parwan province showed the Shahada, the Muslim profession of faith, painted on the image of a dog, an animal that many Muslims view as unclean. 'Get your freedom from these terrorist dogs. Help the coalition forces find these terrorists and eliminate them,' the text read in Pashto, depicting the dog as the Taliban. The Taliban uses Shahada or the recitation 'There is no god but God, and Muhammad is his prophet' on its flag, but it is a creed common to all Islam.[79]

Trump was not the first American president who has said there must be a 'regional' strategy to deal with Afghanistan. Obama also called it a regional strategy in which India, China, Russia, etc., will play a role along with Pakistan.[80] The components of Obama's regional strategy had included some stated and some unstated components, such as stability in Afghanistan, securing the Pakistani nuclear arsenal from terrorists and stabilizing Pakistan by integrating it with the regional economy. It was from this perspective that the Obama administration continuously pressured India to engage Pakistan. The Trump administration's South Asia strategy was touted as a 'regional' approach, but there was nothing much other than desperately seeking an end to the Afghanistan stalemate with the support of Pakistan. Biden is at it again. 'I will encourage a regional approach that garners support from neighbours like Pakistan, while also deterring regional actors, from serving as spoilers to the Afghanistan peace process,'

Secretary Austin told the Senate confirmation hearing. [81] This regional approach needs the cooperation of several countries.

Isaacson of the American Jewish Committee spoke about the prospect of a trilateral India–Israel–US relationship. Israel has been generous when it comes to high technology trade for India—something that America is still very tight-fisted and choosy about. On the other hand, Israel's dogged attempts to gut the Iran nuclear deal did not help India. Israel, and its prime minister Benjamin Netanyahu, was on the same page as Trump that the Iran nuclear deal had to be dismantled. The deal was a breakthrough in the US policy for West and South Asia as it opened new strategic opportunities in multiple ways. The improvement in US–Russia ties was an additional advantage, but a thaw in US–Iran relationships would have helped the situation in Syria, Iraq and Afghanistan. But the Trump administration, despite its avowed commitment to a 'regional' approach, is acting out of line with it, adding to the instability in the region. Biden's ability to reset the Iran nuclear deal will be severely constrained by the influence that Israel and Arab monarchies have in the US.

Russia is no longer a partner in any American project in Asia. As a result, it seeks to undermine US reputation in Afghanistan and South Asia. 'The main emphasis in the new strategy [. . .] is settlement through use of force,' Russian Foreign Minister Sergey Lavrov said days after Trump announced his new South Asia strategy.[82] A US official said Russians are trying to undermine the American position in Afghanistan thus.[83] US–Russia tensions might go up under Biden.

Trump personally pursued a confrontational view with regard to Iran that the US security establishment tried to restrain. And he had a reconciliatory view on Russia that the establishment would not allow him to pursue. The US now accuses Russia and Iran of supporting the Taliban. Both countries had supported the overthrow of the Afghanistan Taliban regime in 2001. They maintain that their contact with the Taliban is only diplomatic in nature, with the purpose of seeking a solution.[84] America does not accept Russia's position and it seems that the die is cast with regard to Afghanistan turning into a zone of rivalry that includes America and its allies on the one side and Russia and Iran on the other, as has been the case in Syria for the last several years.[85] In June 2020, *NYT* reported, based on anonymous intelligence sources, that Russia was offering bounties to Afghan militants for killing soldiers of the US and its allies.[86]

While the US is convinced that Russia is out to undermine America in Afghanistan and South Asia, it has a different view on China. It believes that China will be interested in stability in these two regions. According to the Pentagon's assessment:

> China's low but increasing levels of military, economic, and political engagement in Afghanistan are driven both by domestic security concerns that violent extremism will spread across the Afghan border into China and, increasingly, a desire to protect regional economic investments [. . .] China is a member of the Quadrilateral Coordination Group (QCG) seeking to support Afghan and Taliban peace and reconciliation efforts, and Afghanistan continues to seek Chinese pressure on Pakistan to assist reconciliation efforts and eliminate insurgent sanctuaries.[87]

'I think we see China is interested in seeing stability in this region. They have their One Belt and One Road (OBOR) project that they are seeking to build. So, they are looking for stability in the region,'[88] a White House official said. This sounds theoretically true, but China may not care who is in power in Afghanistan as long as they do not stir up any trouble inside China. Given its antipathy to elections and Western-style democracy, China also doesn't care much specifically for electoral democracy in Afghanistan. We discussed the fluctuating positions of the US on the Chinese BRI project, also called OBOR.

Trump and the American establishment undermined each other on relations with Russia and Iran, cumulatively weakening America's position in Afghanistan. And with these confrontations, America's strategy in Afghanistan had become anything but 'regional'. During the Obama administration, an overall easing of tensions with Iran and Russia had allowed it to bring some pressure to bear on Pakistan. The Trump administration spoiled that balance. While Trump blew the Iran relations by imposing new sanctions and dismantling the nuclear deal against the advice of professional diplomats, Trump's attempted embrace with Russia created a massive retaliation from American intelligence agencies, media and most commentators who have not yet recovered from the memories of the Cold War.

Given American pressure on Pakistan even before Trump came to power, the Taliban is reportedly trying to reduce its dependence on Pakistan and build connections with Russia and Iran.[89] Months before 9/11, in July 2001, Putin had warned President Bush at the G-8 Summit that it was only a matter of time before the Pakistan–Taliban–Al-Qaeda axis resulted in a major catastrophe.[90] That was then. Given the toxic pit that the Russia–US relations have fallen into now, Russia has no incentive to allow the stabilization of Afghanistan. It is now suspected of joining hands with the same Taliban to turn the tables on America. It was America that wanted Afghanistan to be the Soviet Union's 'Vietnam'. But it has turned out to be a long nightmare for Washington, a second Vietnam for itself.

'. . . the United States is stumbling its way into another decade of war in the greater Middle East. And this next decade of conflict might prove to be even more destabilizing than the last one,'[91] according to one view.

As it happens, the war on Islamism is not America's to stop. America's ability to negotiate any settlement in Afghanistan is also limited by its knowledge of the situation and its vulnerability to be played by multiple actors in the conflict. It now appears that the killing of Taliban chief Akhtar Mohammad Mansour by an American drone strike in 2016 might have been a strategic blunder. The Taliban leader was trying to assert his autonomy from Pakistani intelligence, and was trying to open talks with the Americans and Afghanistan. The Pakistani intelligence did not like this. The fact that they reported his travel from Iran, where he had reached from Dubai, to Pakistan suggests that the Pakistani agencies were tracking him. They then tipped off the Americans. American strategists have since then been debating whether his killing was a setback to the peace process.[92]

This is a long war and America must stop thinking of Afghanistan and Islamist terrorism as a year-on-year project, according to David Petraeus, who commanded the US forces in Afghanistan and Iraq. It is a 'generational endeavor', he believes. 'We have to see this as similar to the situation of Korea—where we have thousands of troops for sixty-plus years.'[93] The example of Korea is particularly telling and ominous. It was in the Korean peninsula that the American forces first began fighting communism, before Afghanistan. South Korea, which became an American ally, attained a level of prosperity the people in the North cannot dream of, but the regional conflict that festered has crystallized into an existential threat to humanity today. The Korean peninsula today is emblematic of the limits of a superpower. When Petraeus talks of South Asia as the next Korean peninsula, it does not bode well for India, given its proximity to both Afghanistan and Pakistan.

Pakistan honoured Biden in 2008 with the second highest civilian honour, Hilal-e-Pakistan; the new president has deep relations with the country. Biden was chairman of the Senate Foreign Relations Committee for many years, and held the view that US aid was essential to stabilize Pakistani state and society. As an establishment politician, he possibly concurred with the notion of Kashmir as a nuclear flashpoint. During the 2020 presidential campaign, Biden was critical of the Modi government's Kashmir policy and changes in India's citizenship law.

A document titled 'Joe Biden's agenda for Muslim American community' said the CAA and the National Register of Citizens were inconsistent with the country's long tradition of secularism and with sustaining a multi-ethnic and multi-religious democracy.

The paper clubbed together Kashmir and Assam in India with the forced detention of over a million Uyghur Muslims in western China, and discrimination and atrocities against Myanmar's Rohingya Muslim minority. On Kashmir, it asked the Indian government to restore rights of all the people. 'Restrictions on dissent, such as preventing peaceful protests or shutting or slowing down the internet, weakens democracy,' and Biden was 'disappointed by the measures that the government of India has taken with the implementation and aftermath of the National Register of Citizens (NRC) in Assam and the passage of the Citizenship (Amendment) Act into law,' the policy paper said.[94] Pakistan has relentlessly sought US intervention on Kashmir. Whenever it felt that Kashmir was not getting American attention, it escalated tensions on the border with India and inside Kashmir through its proxies. But Biden is returning to power constrained by new realities. 'Biden is unlikely to have much bandwidth left for Kashmir as he copes with a range of domestic and foreign policy challenges,' thinks C. Raja Mohan.[95] Meanwhile, Pakistan has reinforced its ties with China to a new level. 'Pakistan's closeness with a rising China has offset some of Pakistan's existential angst about its relationship with the United States.'[96]

Trump outlined his terms of engagement for allies in Saudi Arabia—buy American arms and drive out the terrorists. He also sharpened the division between the Sunni and Shia groups within the global Islamic community. But this promotion of divisions across the region will, far from tackling terrorism, exacerbate it. 'Rising sectarianism, not just between Sunni and Shi'a, but between Muslims and non-Muslims, will polarize populations. Of concern are the reflections today in places such as India, where far-right Hindu groups are attacking Muslims for eating cow,' American terrorism expert Katherine Zimmerman told a US congressional hearing in July 2017.[97] A.Q. Khan, notorious nuclear proliferator and father of Pakistan's Islamic bomb, had said, 'We are Muslims, they are Hindus. We eat cows. They worship cows. That we lived on the same land and spoke the same language does not make us the same people.'[98]

The idea of Pakistan is rooted in the notion that Hindus and Muslims are different nations. Pakistan has been struggling to achieve this objective given the fact that there are nearly as many Muslims in India as there are in Pakistan. 'Denying the "Indianness" of Pakistan's identity meant emphasising the "Hinduness" of India and reinforcing the "Islamic" nature of Pakistan,' points out Aparna Pande, a scholar on Pakistan.[99] Ironically, the Hindutva Strategic Doctrine is in agreement with that.

Acknowledgements

A word of gratitude is due to several people who stood by me. From 2015–2018, I worked in the United States as *The Hindu*'s representative. Dr. Malini Parthasarathy gave me this opportunity, and I am indebted to her for that. My three-year stint in the US has formed the foundation of this book, and enabled me to be in the thick of things as the country went through a rupture in its politics. I travelled extensively in the US and sensed, from very close range, the feelings that were driving massive political changes in the country. To N. Ravi and N. Ram, I am grateful for their generosity and guidance. Suresh Nambath, editor of *The Hindu*, a tough taskmaster, has been an understanding and patient boss, too. This book has evolved through my writings in *The Hindu* since 2015, reporting and commentaries. For the ease of presentation, I have not referenced my own prior writings individually in most cases in this book. This must serve as a collective attribution to my own pieces in *The Hindu* over the years.

I have been blessed with wonderful colleagues, mentors and friends, each of whom have had a unique contribution in shaping my work. Shekhar Gupta, Mukund Padmanabhan, Srinivasan Ramani, Pranay Lal, P. Jacob, Amit Baruah, Suhasini Haidar, Mini Kapoor, Suresh Sheshadri, G. Ananthakrishnan, Souresh Roy, Narayan Lakshman, Vikas Pathak, Nistula Hebbar, Namita Kohli, Puja Mehra, Smita Sharma, Maya Mirchandani, Ashok Malik, Unni Rajen Shanker, Raj Kamal Jha, Indrani Bagchi, Pramit Pal Chaudhuri, Ginu Zachariah, Appu Esthose Suresh, Yamini Aiyar, Samir Saran, K.M. Gopakumar, S. Prasannarajan, Manish Tewari, Manish Tiwari, Swati Chopra, Sabin Iqbal, Madhumita Chakraborty, Vaishna Roy, Leena Mariam, Sudipta Dutta, Chandan Yadav, M.K. Venu, George Joseph, Biju Kumar, Abhirami, Sriram Lakshman and Sam Koshy—they have all been there for me.

I recall fondly my travels with Lalit Jha who made our several trips across the US that much more enjoyable. Asif Ismail and Aziz Haniffa went out of their way to be of help many times during my stay in Washington, DC.

Special thanks to Jayanth Jacob, Seema Sirohi, Stanly Johny, Jabin T. Jacob who took out time to read the manuscript and offered their valuable suggestions. Amitabh Mattoo, Bobby John and Shajahan Madampat have been intensely loyal friends and intellectual companions for me for long. At Penguin Random House, Elizabeth Kuruvilla and Milee Ashwarya put their trust in me and the book, which is now into its second, revised edition. Vandana Seth supported with research; and Kanishka Gupta has been a persistent literary agent. Saloni Mital and Ralph Rebello did the copyediting. I am grateful to all.

A special word of thanks to Sanay, Ayana and Melvi for being on the front lines of suffering because of my lifelong obsession with politics. My parents, George and Alice, and sister Margaret, and parents-in-law, Kurian and Annammma, remain a perennial source of energy for me. A special word of thanks to them.

Notes

Foreword

1. Bruce Reidel, *JFK's Forgotten Crisis: Tibet, the CIA, and the Sino-Indian Wars*, HarperCollins India, 2015.
2. Gary J. Bass, 'The Terrible Cost of Presidential Racism', *New York Times* (2020), https://www.nytimes.com/2020/09/03/opinion/nixon-racism-india.html

Introduction

3. https://www.ted.com/talks/bill_gates_the_next_outbreak_we_re_not_ready?language=en

Chapter 1: 'America First': From Trump to Biden

1. 'Remarks by President Trump in Press Conference', *Official Website of The White House* (2017), https://www.whitehouse.gov/briefings-statements/remarks-president-trump-press-conference/.
2. Lalit K. Jha, 'Success is going to bring US Together: Trump; Biden says Country's Character on Ballot', *Outlook* (2020), https://www.outlookindia.com/newsscroll/success-is-going-to-bring-us-together-trump-biden-says-countrys-character-on-ballot/1960678.

3. 'Bill Clinton Presidential Campaign Announcement', C-Span video (1991), https://www.c-span.org/video/?21803-1/governor-bill-clinton-dar-presidential-campaign-announcement.

4. Laura Vozzella, 'White Nationalist Richard Spencer Leads Torch-Bearing Protesters Defending Lee Statue', *The Washington Post* (2017), https://www.washingtonpost.com/local/virginiapolitics/alt-rights-richard-spencer-leads-torch-bearing-protesters-defending-lee-statue/2017/05/14/766aaa56-38ac-11e7-9e48-c4f199710b69_story.html?utm_term=.e12900dbb949.

5. 'Nuclear Posture Review' (2018), https://media.defense.gov/2018/Feb/02/2001872886/-1/-1/1/2018-NUCLEAR-POSTURE-REVIEW-FINAL-REPORT.PDF.

6. 'China will build String of Military Bases around World, says Pentagon', *The Guardian* (2019), https://www.theguardian.com/world/2019/may/03/china-will-build-string-of-military-bases-around-world-says-pentagon.

7. Shivshankar Menon, *Choices: Inside the Making of India's Foreign Policy* (Gurugram: Penguin Random House India, 2016), p. 34.

8. Strobe Talbott, *Engaging India: Diplomacy, Democracy and the Bomb* (Washington, D.C.: Brookings Institution, 2004), p. 52.

9. Ronald Reagan, 'Tear Down this Wall', *The History Place: Great Speeches Collection* (1987), http://www.historyplace.com/speeches/reagan-tear-down.htm.

10. '"BUILD THAT WALL!" Donald Trump Chants After Major Endorsement', YouTube video, posted by FOX 10 Phoenix, 2016, https://www.youtube.com/watch?v=ZGSAhNZnisk.

11. David E. Sanger, 'The End of "America First": How Biden Says He Will Re-engage With the World', *The New York Times* (2020), https://www.nytimes.com/2020/11/09/us/politics/biden-foreign-policy.html.

12. James Traub, 'Biden Is Getting Ready to Bury Neoliberalism', *Foreign Policy* (2020), https://foreignpolicy.com/2020/08/27/biden-is-getting-ready-to-bury-neoliberalism/.

13. https://www.washingtonpost.com/news/book-party/wp/2017/07/18/samuel-huntington-a-prophet-for-the-trump-era/

14. Neta C. Crawford and Catherine Lutz, 'Costs of War', *Watson Institute* (2019), https://watson.brown.edu/costsofwar/figures.

15. Andrew Exum, 'The Fight Against the Islamic State Just Got Harder', *The Atlantic* (2017). https://www.theatlantic.com/international/archive/2017/04/trump-syria-strike/522258/.

16. Charles Krauthammer, 'Universal Dominion: Toward a Unipolar World', *The National Interest* 90 (1989): p. 46.

17. Ibid.

18. Gideon Rachman, 'Easternization: Asia's Rise and America's Decline' (New York: Other Press, 2017), p. 93.

19. CNN, 'You Are Either with Us or Against Us' (2001), http://edition.cnn.com/2001/US/11/06/gen.attack.on.terror/.

20. Varghese K. George, 'A Tale of Two Americas', *The Hindu* (2016), http://www.thehindu.com/opinion/lead/A-tale-of-two-Americas/article16091019.ece.

21. 'Remarks by President Trump', *Official Website of The White House*.

22. Gideon Rachman, 'Easternization: Asia's Rise and America's Decline', (New York: Other Press, 2017), p. 153.

23. Fareed Zakaria, 'The Rise of the Rest', *Newsweek*, (2008), https://fareedzakaria.com/columns/2008/05/12/the-rise-of-the-rest

24. Peter B. Bach, 'Trump's Drug-Pricing Ideas Would Cost Taxpayers a Bundle', *Bloomberg* (2020), https://www.bloomberg.com/opinion/articles/2020-09-29/trump-s-drug-pricing-ideas-would-cost-taxpayers-benefit-pharma.

25. Jeffrey Goldberg, 'The Obama Doctrine', *The Atlantic* (2016), https://www.theatlantic.com/magazine/archive/2016/04/the-obama-doctrine/471525/.

26. Jeffrey Goldberg, 'Hillary Clinton: "Failure" to Help Syrian Rebels Led to the Rise of ISIS', *The Atlantic* (2014), https://www.theatlantic.com/international/archive/2014/08/hillary-clinton-failure-to-help-syrian-rebels-led-to-the-rise-of-isis/375832/.

27. W. Gardner Selby, 'Ted Cruz Says Obama Made "A Worldwide Apology Tour"', PolitiFact (2012), http://www.politifact.com/texas/statements/2012/jan/20/ted-cruz/ted-cruz-says-obama-made-worldwide-apology-tour/.

28. Jeffrey Goldberg, 'The Obama Doctrine', *The Atlantic* (2016), https://www.theatlantic.com/magazine/archive/2016/04/the-obama-doctrine/471525/.

29.   Melissa Quinn, 'Trump Reiterates Commitment to "America First" in Weekly Address', *Washington Examiner* (2017), https://www.washingtonexaminer.com/trump-reiterates-commitment-to-america-first-in-weekly-address.

30.   'Ronald Reagan: Farewell Address to the Nation, 11 January 1989', https://www.reaganlibrary.gov/archives/speech/farewell-address-nation

31.   'Remarks by President Trump to the 72nd Session of the United Nations General Assembly', *Official Website of The White House* (2017), https://www.whitehouse.gov/briefings-statements/remarks-president-trump-72nd-session-united-nations-general-assembly/.

32.   Scott Morris, 'Trump's Treasury Delivers at the World Bank: More Capital for Climate, Solid Policy Framework', *Center for Global Development* (2018), https://www.cgdev.org/blog/trumps-treasury-delivers-at-the-world-bank.

33.   Felicia Escobar, 'Celebrating Hispanic Heritage Month: "Immigrants Are the American Character"', *Official Website of The White House—President Barack Obama* (2016), https://obamawhitehouse.archives.gov/blog/2016/09/16/immigrants-are-american-character.

34.   Yale News, 'Ambassador Samantha Power's 2016 Class Day Address' (2016), https://news.yale.edu/2016/05/22/ambassador-samantha-powers-2016-class-day-address.

35.   https://www.splcenter.org/fighting-hate/intelligence-report/2013/year-hate-and-extremism

36.   https://thehill.com/blogs/blog-briefing-room/news/253515-poll-43-percent-of-republicans-believe-obama-is-a-muslim

37.   https://ifstudies.org/blog/the-us-divorce-rate-has-hit-a-50-year-low

38.   https://www.cdc.gov/nchs/products/databriefs/db362.htm

39.   Asma Khalid, 'How Joe Biden's Faith Shapes His Politics', *NPR* (2020), https://www.npr.org/2020/09/20/913667325/how-joe-bidens-faith-shapes-his-politics.

40.   'Remarks by President Trump to the People of Poland', *Official Website of The White House* (2017), https://www.whitehouse.

gov/the-press-office/2017/07/06/remarks-president-trump-people-poland-july-6-2017.

41. https://www.theguardian.com/us-news/2020/sep/30/trump-white-supremacy-extremist-rhetoric

42. Jeffrey Goldberg, 'The Obama Doctrine', *The Atlantic* (2016), https://www.theatlantic.com/magazine/archive/2016/04/the-obama-doctrine/471525/.

43. Peter Müller, 'The Germans Are Bad, Very Bad', *Spiegel International* (2017), http://www.spiegel.de/international/world/trump-in-brussels-the-germans-are-bad-very-bad-a-1149330.html.

44. Reality Check team, 'Trump: What does the US contribute to Nato in Europe?', *BBC* (2020), https://www.bbc.com/news/world-44717074.

45. Barbara McQuade and Joyce White Vance, 'These 11 Mueller Report Myths Just Won't Die. Here's Why They're Wrong', *TIME* (2019), https://time.com/5610317/mueller-report-myths-breakdown/.

46. Eric Randall, 'Russia Is Mitt Romney's "Number One Foe"', *The Atlantic* (2012), https://www.theatlantic.com/international/archive/2012/03/russia-mitt-romneys-number-one-foe/330108/.

47. Radina Gigova, 'Putin Congratulates Trump, Not Obama, in New Year's Statement', *CNN* (2016), https://edition.cnn.com/2016/12/31/europe/russia-putin-trump-obama-greetings/index.html.

48. George, Varghese K., 'Playing the Angles with Russia', https://www.thehindu.com/opinion/lead/Playing-the-angles-with-Russia/article16974248.ece.

49. Donald J. Trump, Twitter, 21 July 2011, 1:40 a.m., https://twitter.com/realdonaldtrump/status/93774719052029953?lang=en.

50. Ronald Brownstein, 'Putin and the Populists', *Atlantic* (2017), https://www.theatlantic.com/international/archive/2017/01/putin-trump-le-pen-hungary-france-populist-bannon/512303/.

51. Jon Stone, 'Italy Breaks with European Allies and Voices Support for Russia after Populist Party Takes Power', *Independent* (2018),

https://www.independent.co.uk/news/world/europe/italy-prime-minister-giuseppe-conte-russia-sanctions-end-populist-five-star-vladimir-putin-crimea-a8385626.html.

52. Jordan Fabian, 'Trump Calls for Russia to Be Reinstated into G-7', *The Hill* (2018), http://thehill.com/homenews/administration/391321-trump-calls-for-russia-to-be-reinstated-into-g7.

53. L. Rafael Reif, 'How to Maintain America's Edge', *Foreign Affairs* (2017), https://www.foreignaffairs.com/articles/united-states/2017-03-23/how-maintain-america-s-edge.

54. Jeffrey Mervis, 'Trump has Shown Little Respect for U.S. Science. So Why are Some Parts Thriving?', *Science* (2020), https://www.sciencemag.org/news/2020/10/trump-has-shown-little-respect-us-science-so-why-are-some-parts-thriving.

55. Misha Ketchell, 'Biden's Pivot to Science is Welcome—Trump Only Listened to Experts When it Suited Him', *The Conversation* (2020), https://theconversation.com/bidens-pivot-to-science-is-welcome-trump-only-listened-to-experts-when-it-suited-him-149734.

56. Jeffrey Goldberg, 'The Obama Doctrine', *The Atlantic* (2016), https://www.theatlantic.com/magazine/archive/2016/04/the-obama-doctrine/471525/.

57. Matthew Nussbaum and Andrew Restuccia, 'Kelly Furious over Putin "Do Not Congratulate" Leak', *Politico* (2018), https://www.politico.eu/article/john-kelly-furious-do-not-congratulate-leak-trump-putin/.

58. Rosa Brooks, *How Everything Became War and the Military Became Everything* (New York: Simon & Schuster, 2016).

59. Ronan Farrow, *War on Peace: The End of Diplomacy and the Decline of American Influence* (New York: W.W. Norton & Company, 2018).

60. Micah Zenko, 'America's Military Is Nostalgic for World Wars', *Foreign Policy* (2018), https://foreignpolicy.com/2018/03/13/americas-military-is-nostalgic-for-great-power-wars/.

61. James Joyner, 'How Perpetual War Became U.S. Ideology', *The Atlantic* (2011), https://www.theatlantic.com/

international/archive/2011/05/how-perpetual-war-became-us-ideology/238600/.

62. Jeffrey Goldberg, 'The Obama Doctrine', *The Atlantic* (2016), https://www.theatlantic.com/magazine/archive/2016/04/the-obama-doctrine/471525/.

63. Author's interview with a former Bush adviser.

64. Varghese K. George, 'Kissinger, an Idea that Lives On', *The Hindu* (2017), http://www.thehindu.com/news/international/kissinger-an-idea-that-lives-on/article18446912.ece.

65. Charles Savage and Scott Shane, 'US Reveals Death Toll from Airstrikes Outside War Zones', *The New York Times* (2016), https://www.nytimes.com/2016/07/02/world/us-reveals-death-toll-from-airstrikes-outside-of-war-zones.html.

66. David J. Lynch and Damian Paletta, 'Trumps Fluid Approach to National and Economic Security Is Leaving His Allies Baffled', *The Washington Post* (2018), https://www.washingtonpost.com/business/economy/trumps-fluid-approach-to-national-and-economic-security-is-leaving-his-allies-baffled/2018/05/28/b08c5908-5f95-11e8-9ee3-49d6d4814c4c_story.html

67. https://www.nytimes.com/1989/01/12/news/transcript-of-reagan-s-farewell-address-to-american-people.html

68. https://www.nytimes.com/2020/06/03/opinion/tom-cotton-protests-military.html

69. https://www.hrw.org/report/2020/07/31/revoked/how-probation-and-parole-feed-mass-incarceration-united-states

70. https://www.statista.com/statistics/262962/countries-with-the-most-prisoners-per-100-000-inhabitants/

71. https://edition.cnn.com/videos/politics/2020/06/01/houston-police-chief-art-acevedo-trump-mouth-shut-vpx.cnn

72. Michael Beckley, 'Rogue Superpower: Why This Could Be an Illiberal American Century', *Foreign Affairs*, November-December 2020.

73. https://www.cnet.com/news/amazon-apple-google-ban-parler-app-over-violent-content-around-capitol-attack/

74. Walter Russell Mead, 'The End of the Wilsonian Era: Why Liberal Internationalism Failed', Volume 100, Number 1, *Foreign Affairs*, January–February 2021.

75.   Beckley, Michael, 'Rogue Superpower Why This Could Be an Illiberal American Century', Foreign Affairs, November–December 2020

76.   https://thehill.com/homenews/state-watch/529926-texas-gop-chair-appears-to-suggest-secession-after-scotus-rejects.

Chapter 2: Hindutva Strategic Doctrine—A New Way for India?

1.   Ross Colvin and Satarupa Bhattacharjya, 'Special Report–The Remaking of Narendra Modi', Reuters (2013), https://www.reuters.com/article/india-modi-idINL4N0FH3IF20130712.

2.   https://theprint.in/defence/indias-military-retains-4th-spot-in-global-ranking-pakistan-drops-to-17/157782/

3.   George K. Tanham, Indian Strategic Thought: An Interpretative Essay (Santa Monica, CA: Rand Corporation, 1992), p. 50.

4.   Brahma Chellaney, Securing India's Future in New Millennium (New Delhi: Orient Longman Limited, 1999), p. xvii.

5.   https://www.ndtv.com/india-news/at-world-hindu-congress-in-us-soft-and-hard-laddu-boxes-for-guests-1913774

6.   Sandy Gordon, 'Indian Security Policy and the Rise of the Hindu Right', South Asia: Journal of South Asian Studies 17 (1994), p. 197.

7.   Rachell Fell McDermott et al., ed., Sources of Indian Traditions: Modern India, Pakistan, and Bangladesh, vol. II (New York: Columbia University Press, 2014), p. 439.

8.   Jaswant Singh, Defending India (London: Palgrave Macmillan UK, 1999), p. 13.

9.   Jaswant Singh, In Service of Emergent India: A Call to Honor (Bloomington: Indiana University Press, 2007), p. 84.

10. Sreeram S. Chaulia, 'BJP, India's Foreign Policy and the "Realist Alternative" to the Nehruvian Tradition', International Politics 39 (2002), p. 220.

11. 'PM Interacts with Indian Community in Washington DC', Official Website of Narendra Modi (2017), http://www.narendramodi.in/prime-minister-shri-narendra-modi-at-indian-community-event-in-washington-dc-usa-535997.

12. 'Modi Lauds Yogi Adityanath for Breaking Noida Jinx', *The Hindu* (2017), http://www.thehindu.com/news/national/modi-lauds-yogi-adityanath-for-breaking-noida-jinx/article22277976.ece.

13. 'Modi in Ayodhya: Ram Temple will become Modern Symbol of our Traditions, says PM', *The Indian Express* (2020), https://indianexpress.com/article/india/ayodhya-ram-temple-bhoomi-pujan-pm-narendra-modi-6540420/.

14. 'Atal Bihari Vajpayee Speech at Dawn of His Stable Government', YouTube video, posted by 'Hindubhumi', 25 March 2012, https://www.youtube.com/watch?v=WpSyk59TmYo.

15. S. Jaishankar, *The India Way* (New Delhi: HarperCollins India 2020), p. 73.

16. C. Raja Mohan, *Modi's World: Expanding India's Sphere of Influence* (New Delhi: HarperCollins, 2015).

17. Ashley J. Tellis, 'India as a Leading Power', *Carnegie Endowment for International Peace* (2016), http://carnegieendowment.org/2016/04/04/india-as-leading-power-pub-63185.

18. Ashley J. Tellis, 'Some in BJP may stifle Modi's reform agenda', *Business Standard* (2016), https://www.business-standard.com/article/opinion/some-in-bjp-may-stifle-modi-s-reform-agenda-ashley-j-tellis-116040900692_1.html

19. S. Jaishankar, *The India Way* (New Delhi: HarperCollins India 2020), p. 55.

20. This paragraph is a paraphrased summary of RSS chief Mohan Bhagwat's speech on 3 December 2020, available at https://youtu.be/6iYIRlKoUUo.

21. 'Text of Prime Minister's Keynote Address at Shangri La Dialogue', *Press Information Bureau* (2018), http://pib.nic.in/newsite/PrintRelease.aspx?relid=179711.

22. 'A Strong India–U.S. Partnership Can Anchor Peace, Prosperity and Stability across the World: PM Modi', Official Website of Narendra Modi (2016), https://www.narendramodi.in/prime-minister-narendra-modi-addresses-joint-meeting-of-u-s-congress-in-washington-dc-484217.

23. Tanvi Madan, 'Modi's Speech to Congress: Bullish on India, Bullish on the U.S.', *Brookings* (2016), https://www.brookings.

edu/blog/order-from-chaos/2016/06/14/modis-speech-to-congress-bullish-on-india-bullish-on-the-u-s/.

24. IANS, 'Modi Doctrine: "A Mix of Personal Victory and Breaking Old Barriers"' (2016), https://www.business-standard.com/article/news-ians/modi-doctrine-a-mix-of-personal-victory-and-breaking-old-barriers-116061200339_1.html.

25. IANS, 'No Guilty Feeling about Gujarat Riots, Says Modi', *The Hindu* (2016), http://www.thehindu.com/news/national/no-guilty-feeling-about-gujarat-riots-says-modi/article4908704.ece.

26. Kanti Bajpai, 'Indian Strategic Culture', in Michael R. Chambers, ed., *South Asia in 2020: Future Strategic Balances and Alliances* (Carlisle, PA: Strategic Studies Institute, US Army War College, 2002), p. 245.

27. Bharat Karnad, ed., *Future Imperiled: India's Security in the 1990s and Beyond* (New Delhi: Viking, 1994), p. 2.

28. 'Text of Prime Minister Shri Narendra Modi's Reply on "Motion of Thanks" on President's Address in Lok Sabha', Official Website of Narendra Modi (2014), http://www.narendramodi.in/text-of-prime-minister-shri-narendra-modis-reply-on-motion-of-thanks-on-presidents-address-in-lok-sabha-2820.

29. 'Text of Prime Minister Shri Narendra Modi's Address to Indian Community at Madison Square Garden, New York', Official Website of Narendra Modi (2014), http://www.narendramodi.in/text-of-prime-minister-shri-narendra-modi-s-address-to-indian-community-at-madison-square-garden-new-york-292061.

30. BJP Manifesto (2014), https://www.thehindu.com/multimedia/archive/01830/BJP_election_manif_1830927a.pdf.

31. Rodney W. Jones, 'Indian Strategic Culture', Defence Threat Reduction Agency (2006), p. 23.

32. Lalmani Verma, 'If Muslims Are Unwanted, Then There Is No Hindutva: Mohan Bhagwat at RSS event', *The Indian Express*

(2018), https://indianexpress.com/article/india/if-muslims-are-unwanted-then-there-is-no-hindutva-mohan-bhagwat-at-rss-event-5363529/.

33. 'India Doesn't Want Favours from the World, India Wants Equality: PM Modi at Wembley', Official Website of Narendra Modi (2015), http://www.narendramodi.in/india-doesn-t-want-favours-from-the-world-india-wants-equality-pm-modi-at-wembley-375884.

34. McDermott et al., ed., *Sources of Indian Traditions,* p. 486.

35. Vaibhav Purandare, *Savarkar: The True Story of the Father of Hindutva* (New Delhi: Juggernaut, 2019), p. 274.

36. Amberish K. Diwanji, 'We Have Overcome Challenges to Become Close', *Rediff* (2000), http://www.rediff.com/news/2000/sep/17pmus1.htm.

37. Rama Lakshmi, 'India Wants to Turn 25 Million in the Diaspora into Global Ambassadors', *The Washington Post* (2015), https://www.washingtonpost.com/world/asia_pacific/india-wants-to-turn-25-million-in-the-diaspora-into-global-ambassadors/2015/02/17/908ee6ff-a650-42bc-ac58-0a2c91530a26_story.html?utm_term=.f8d338ad6cbd.

38. Ashutosh Varshney, 'Modi's Idea of India–1', *The Indian Express* (2016), http://indianexpress.com/article/opinion/columns/narendra-modi-idea-of-india-republic-day/.

39. PTI, 'Bangladeshi "Infiltrators" Would Have to Go Back', *The Hindu* (2016), http://www.thehindu.com/elections/loksabha2014/bangladeshi-infiltrators-would-have-to-go-back-modi/article5986165.ece.

40. Apurva Thakur, 'Why the Citizenship Amendment Bill Goes Against the Basic Tenets of the Constitution' (2018), *EPW Engage,* https://www.epw.in/engage/article/why-the-citizenship-amendment-goes-against-the-basic-tenets-of-the-constitution.

41. Dhananjay Mahapatra, 'Madhya Pradesh Govt Rehabs Bangla Non-Muslims', *The Times of India* (2014), https://timesofindia.indiatimes.com/india/Madhya-Pradesh-govt-rehabs-Bangla-non-Muslims/articleshow/39326264.cms.

42. 'What is NRC? All you Need to Know About National Register of Citizens', *India Today* (2019), *https://www.indiatoday.*

in/india/story/what-is-nrc-all-you-need-to-know-about-national-register-of-citizens-1629195-2019-12-18.

43. 'India was Better Off under British Rule: Mohan Bhagwat', *The Times of India* (2012), https://timesofindia.indiatimes.com/city/nashik/India-was-better-off-under-British-rule-Mohan-Bhagwat/articleshow/11984492.cms.

44. Phil Klay, 'The Citizen-Soldier: Moral Risk and the Modern Military, *The Brookings Essay* (2016), http://csweb.brookings.edu/content/research/essays/2016/the-citizen-soldier.html.

45. Pradip R. Sagar, 'Centre May Not be in Favour of Compulsory Military Training', *The Week* (2018), https://www.theweek.in/news/india/2018/03/17/centre-may-not-be-in-favour-of-compulsory-military-training.html.

46. Ibid.

47. Ritika Chopra, 'To Instil Discipline, Nationalism: Govt Discusses Military Training Plan for Disciplined 10-lakh "Force of Youth"', *Indian Express* (2018), https://indianexpress.com/article/india/to-instil-discipline-nationalism-government-discusses-military-training-plan-for-disciplined-10-lakh-force-of-youth-5262501/.

48. Vinay Sitapati, *Jugalbandi: The BJP Before Modi* (Gurugram: Penguin Random House, 2020), p. 101.

49. McDermott et al., ed., *Sources of Indian Traditions,* p. 484.

50. Vaibhav Purandare, *Savarkar: The True Story of the Father of Hindutva* (New Delhi: Juggernaut, 2019), p. 254.

51. Ibid., p. 253.

52. Bharatiya Jana Sangh, *Party Documents 1951–1972: Resolutions on Defence and External Affairs*, vol. 3 (New Delhi: Bharatiya Jana Sangh, 1973), p. 6.

53. Lt General H.S. Panag (Retd.), 'Gen Panag Exclusive: "Criticism is Needed in Order to Reform Army', *The Quint* (2017), https://www.thequint.com/voices/opinion/lieutenant-general-hs-panag-on-kashmir-human-shield-video.

54. Suhas Palshikar, 'A General Overstepping', *The Indian Express* (2018), https://indianexpress.com/article/opinion/columns/indian-army-general-bipin-rawat-northeast-immigration-5082088/.

55. 'Bipin Rawat is New Army Chief: All You Need to Know about His Appointment, Career', *Firstpost* (2016), https://www.firstpost.com/india/bipin-rawat-as-the-new-army-chief-all-you-need-to-know-about-his-appointment-and-career-3162536.html.

56. 'PM to Heads of Indian Missions', *Press Information Bureau* (2015), http://pib.nic.in/newsite/PrintRelease.aspx?relid=115241.

57. Vinayak Damodar Savarkar, *Hindutva*, 4th ed. (Pune: S.P. Gokhale, 1949), p. 51.

58. 'IIS Fullerton Lecture by Dr S. Jaishankar, Foreign Secretary in Singapore', Media Centre, Ministry of External Affairs (2015),https://www.mea.gov.in/Speeches-Statements.htm?dtl/25493/iiss+fullerton+lecture+by+dr+s+jaishankar+foreign+secretary+in+singapore

59. Husain Haqqani, *Magnificent Delusions: Pakistan, the United States and an Epic History of Misunderstanding* (New York: Public Affairs, 2013), p. 60.

60. 'P. Chidambaram's Address at K. Subrahmanyam Memorial Lecture', *Press Information Bureau* (2013), http://pib.nic.in/newsite/PrintRelease.aspx?relid=92059.

61. Ibid.

62. 'Text of Prime Minister, Shri Narendra Modi's Address to Indian Community at Allphones Arena, Sydney', *Official Website of Narendra Modi* (2014), http://www.narendramodi.in/text-of-prime-minister-shri-narendra-modis-address-to-indian-community-at-allphones-arena-sydney-2896.

63. McDermott et al., ed., *Sources of Indian Traditions,* p. 146.

64. Ibid., p. 282.

65. 'Yoga Is a Vision for a Harmonious Future for Humanity: PM', *Official Website of Narendra Modi* (2015), http://www.narendramodi.in/text-of-pm-s-remarks-at-international-conference-on-yoga-for-holistic-health-163380.

66. 'Text of the Prime Minister, Shri Narendra Modi's Address at the Ceremony held to Rededicate, Sir H.N. Reliance Foundation Hospital and Research Centre in Mumbai', *Official Website of Narendra Modi* (2014), http://www.narendramodi.in/text-of-the-prime-minister-shri-narendra-modis-address-

at-the-ceremony-held-to-rededicate-sir-h-n-reliance-foundation-hospital-and-research-centre-in-mumbai-6792.

67. Milind Ghatwai, 'Everyone Living in India is Hindu, Says RSS Chief Mohan Bhagwat', *The Indian Express* (2017), http://indianexpress.com/article/india/everyone-living-in-india-is-hindu-says-rss-chief-mohan-bhagwat/.

68. https://indianexpress.com/article/india/politics/if-bjp-loses-crackers-will-go-off-in-pakistan-amit-shah/

69. 'Gujarat CM Narendra Modi in *Aap Ki Adalat* (Full Episode)–India TV', YouTube video, 31:14, 31 March 2014, https://www.youtube.com/watch?v=FDzbReWkwI8.

70. Jaswant Singh, *Jinnah: India, Partition, Independence* (New Delhi: Rupa & Co., 2009), p. 1023.

71. Bharatiya Jana Sangh, *Party Documents*, p. ix.

72. Bharatiya Jana Sangh, *Party Documents*, p. 82.

73. Bharatiya Jana Sangh, *Party Documents*. p. 25.

74. Arun Shourie, '"Please Realise, No War is Won with Minimal Force"', *The Indian Express* (2008), http://archive.indianexpress.com/news/please-realise-no-war-is-won-with-minimal-force/397499/1.

75. For an elaborate discussion on the BJP's Pakistan policy under Vajpayee and L.K. Advani, see Vinay Sitapati, Jugalbandi: The BJP Before Modi (New Delhi: Penguin Random House India, 2020).

76. Ibid.

77. Ibid., p. 240.

78. Bharatiya Jana Sangh, *Party Documents*, pp. 46–47.

79. PTI, 'Govt to Initiate Dialogue with all Stakeholders in J&K: Governor', *The Tribune* (2015), http://www.tribuneindia.com/news/jammu-kashmir/community/govt-to-initiate-dialogue-with-all-stakeholders-in-j-k-governor/55242.html.

80. Smriti Kak Ramachandran, 'Modi Govt Won't Talk to Separatists Who Use Kashmiris as Guinea Pigs: Ram Madhav', *Hindustan Times* (2017), https://www.hindustantimes.com/india-news/modi-govt-won-t-talk-to-separatists-who-use-kashmiris-as-guinea-pigs-ram-madhav/story-tGLyNrWtn5K22kcOoTI39M.html.

81. Kumar Uttam, 'De-Link Kashmir from Indo-Pak Talks, Says BJP's Ram Madhav', *Hindustan Times* (2017), http://www.hindustantimes.com/india-news/de-link-kashmir-from-indo-pak-talks-says-bjp-s-ram-madhav/story-vjbLqNItGmUKlxOivGc4AM.html.

82. https://www.hindustantimes.com/lok-sabha-elections/congress-speaking-pakistan-s-language-pm-modi-at-maharashtra-rally/story-3XdRFOLLc2BGliaOHqMRYL.html

83. https://www.washingtonpost.com/world/2019/08/08/kashmirs-new-status-could-bring-demographic-change-drawing-comparisons-west-bank/

84. Swati Gupta, 'UN Calls for International Inquiry into Human Rights Violations in Kashmir', *CNN* (2018), https://www.cnn.com/2018/06/14/asia/united-nations-india-pakistan-kashmir-intl/index.html.

85. PTI, 'China Should Shed Expansionist Mindset: Modi', *The Hindu* (2016), http://www.thehindu.com/news/national/china-should-shed-expansionist-mindset-modi/article5716591.ece.

86. Vinayak Damodar Savarkar, *Hindutva* (Pune: S.P. Gokhale, 1949), p. 52.

87. Walter K Andersen and Shridhar D Damle, 'The RSS: A View to the Inside' 2018 , p. 156.

88. Walter K Andersen and Shridhar D. Damle, 'The RSS: A View to the Inside', 2018 p. 157.

89. Bharatiya Jana Sangh, *Party Documents 1951–1972: Resolutions on Defence and External Affairs*, vol. 3 (New Delhi: Bharatiya Jana Sangh, 1973), p. 78

90. Varghese K. George, 'Rhetoric, Not Foreign Policy', *The Hindu* (2016), http://www.thehindu.com/opinion/lead/rhetoric-not-foreign-policy/article5801653.ece.

91. Personal conversation with Shyam Saran.

92. S. Jaishankar, *The India Way: Strategies for an Uncertain World* (New Delhi: HarperCollins, 2020), p. 151.

93. 'Text of Remarks by Prime Minister at the India–U.S. Business Summit', *Press Information Bureau* (2015), http://pib.nic.in/newsite/PrintRelease.aspx?relid=114960.

94. 'BJP Election Manifesto 2014', http://www.bjp.org/images/pdf_2014/full_manifesto_english_07.04.2014.pdf.

95. Bharatiya Jana Sangh, *Party Documents*, p. 30.

96. Suhasini Haidar and Vijaita Singh, 'Compassion International to Shut Down India Operations', *The Hindu* (2017), http://www.thehindu.com/news/national/Compassion-International-to-shut-down-India-operations/article17152998.ece.

97. Strobe Talbott, *Engaging India,* p. 134.

98. Ibid.

99. Jaishankar S, The India Way: Strategies for an Uncertain World, 2020 p. 128.

100. Jaishankar S, The India Way: Strategies for an Uncertain World, 2020 p. 119.

101. Jaishankar S, The India Way: Strategies for an Uncertain World, 2020 p. 129.

102. Bharatiya Jana Sangh, *Party Documents,* p.37.

103. Bharatiya Jana Sangh, *Party Documents*, p. 43.

104. 'Full Text: Netanyahu's Address to UN General Assembly', *Haaretz* (2017), https://www.haaretz.com/israel-news/1.813336.

105. M.S. Golwalkar, *We or Our Nationhood Defined* (Nagpur: Bharat Publications,1939), pp. 86–87, https://sanjeev.sabhlokcity.com/Misc/We-or-Our-Nationhood-Defined-Shri-M-S-Golwalkar.pdf.

106. PM's keynote speech at the 41st AGM of US India Business Council (USIBC), https://www.pmindia.gov.in/en/news_updates/prime-ministers-keynote-speech-at-agm-of-us-india-business-council-usibc/

107. Suhasini Haidar, 'A Day after RCEP, Jaishankar Slams Trade Pacts, Globalisation', *The Hindu* (2020), https://www.thehindu.com/business/a-day-after-rcep-jaishankar-slams-trade-pacts-globalisation/article33110309.ece

108. Divyanshu Dutta Roy, 'PM Narendra Modi's Speech at World Economic Forum in Davos: Full Text', *NDTV* (2018), https://www.ndtv.com/india-news/pm-narendra-modis-speech-at-world-economic-forum-in-davos-full-text-1803790.

109. 'Significance of Shri Mohan Bhagwat's Speech at BSE', *Organiser* (2018), http://www.organiser.org/Encyc/2018/4/20/Mohan-Bhagwat-at-BSE.html.

110. Ibid.

111. Varghese K. George, 'Modi in America: "Strategic Autonomy", "Non-Alignment" in his Diplomatic Lexicon', *The Hindu* (2016), http://www.thehindu.com/opinion/Modi-in-America-%E2%80%98Strategic-autonomy%E2%80%99-%E2%80%98non-alignment%E2%80%99-in-his-diplomatic-lexicon/article14386295.ece.

112. AFP, 'Narendra Modi Govt Eases Red Tape but Foreign Firms Still Struggle', *Mint* (2016), http://www.livemint.com/Companies/q6sITXwboDmG14h9Odmv0I/Narendra-Modi-govt-eases-red-tape-but-foreign-firms-still-st.html.

113. Bharatiya Jana Sangh, *Party Documents,* p. xi.

114. Sitapati, p. 115.

115. Varghese K. George, 'Newly Tested in Modi Gujarat Lab: Hindutva 2.0', *The Indian Express* (2007), http://archive.indianexpress.com/news/newly-tested-in-modi-gujarat-lab-hindutva-2.0/253725/0.

116. Milan Vaishnav, 'Modi's Going to Have a Much Tougher 2018 than Anyone's Expecting', *The Print* (2017), https://theprint.in/2017/12/19/get-ready-mr-modi-2018-battles-tough-bruising/.

117. https://swarajyamag.com/videos/watch-amitabh-kant-on-pli-scheme-structural-reforms-and-other-strategic-initiatives-to-operationalise-atmanirbhar-bharat

118. Varghese K. George, 'A Hindutva Variant of Neo-Liberalism', *The Hindu* (2016), http://www.thehindu.com/opinion/lead/a-hindutva-variant-of-neoliberalism/article5868196.ece.

119. Pratap Bhanu Mehta, 'You Have Been Warned', *The Indian Express* (2016), http://indianexpress.com/article/opinion/columns/demonetisation-politics-cashless-economy-you-have-been-warned-4379388/.

120. 'Parallel Journeys? Turkey's Experience of AKP Rule and Its Portents for India under the BJP', *Amitav Ghosh* (blog, 2014), http://amitavghosh.com/blog/?p=6857.

121. Swapan Dasgupta, 'Why Modi Chose Hindi Medium to Pitch India to the World', *The Times of India* (blog, 2018), https://blogs.timesofindia.indiatimes.com/right-and-wrong/why-modi-chose-hindi-medium-to-pitch-india-to-the-world/.

122. Narendra Modi, 'Narendra Modi on M.S. Golwalkar, Translated by Aakar Patel–Part 1', *The Caravan* (2014), http://www.caravanmagazine.in/vantage/modi-golwalkar-part-1.

123. Vinay Sitapati, Jugalbandi: The BJP Before Modi (New Delhi: Penguin Random House India, 2020), p. 14.

124. Yasmeen Serhan, 'Trump Has Raised an Ultra-Nationalist British Group out of Obscurity', *The Atlantic* (2017), https://www.theatlantic.com/international/archive/2017/11/the-ultra-nationalist-british-party-trump-raised-out-of-obscurity/547016/.

125. https://indianexpress.com/article/india/mohan-bhagwats-silence-on-madhav-sadasiva-golwalkar-telling-edits-anti-muslim-remark-5365537/

126. https://www.livemint.com/news/india/no-religious-discrimination-in-development-nobody-to-be-left-behind-pm-modi-at-amu-centenary-11608650739812.html

Chapter 3: India in America

1. Joe Biden, 'A More Prosperous Future for the Indian American Community: Op Ed by Vice President Biden for India-West', *Indiawest* (2020), https://www.indiawest.com/blogs/a-more-prosperous-future-for-the-indian-american-community-op-ed-by-vice-president-biden/article_91434690-143a-11eb-8c0f-d33f2c48d683.html.

2. Recording of Schumer's speech at the 20th Annual Legislative Conference organized by the Indian American Friendship Council (IAFC, 2 November 2017).

3. Swami Vivekananda, *The Complete Works of Swami Vivekananda*, Vol. 1 (Kolkata: Advaita Ashram, 1915), p. 2.

4. Sister Nivedita, *Swamiji and His Message* (Kolkata: Advaita Ashram, 2016), p. 3.

5. Sanjoy Chakravorty, Devesh Kapur and Nirvikar Singh, *The Other One Percent: Indians in America* (New York: Oxford University Press, 2016), p. 10.

6. Ibid.

7. Vijay Prashad, *Karma of the Brown Folk* (Minneapolis: University of Minnesota Press, 2000), p. 88.

8. Chakravorty, *The Other One Percent*, pp. 13–14.

9. Ibid., pp. 137–38.

10. Siddharth Varadarajan, 'MEA's Latest: BJP the "Only Alternative", Only Hindus Are "Spiritual"', *The Wire* (2017), https://thewire.in/external-affairs/mea-bjp-propaganda-hindutva-deendayal-upadhyaya-integral-humanism.

11. 'Integral Humanism', Official Website of Ministry of External Affairs, Government of India (2017), http://mea.gov.in/in-focus-article.htm?28971/Integral+Humanism.

12. Varghese K. George, 'The "Acharya Envoys" Who Propagate Indian Culture', *The Hindu* (2018), http://www.thehindu.com/todays-paper/tp-international/the-acharya-envoys-who-propagate-indian-culture/article23043317.ece.

13. Walter Russel Mead, *Special Providence: American Foreign Policy and How It Changed the World* (Knopf, 2012), p. 146.

14. Samir Kalra, 'US Religious Freedom Commission's "Alternative Facts" Attack Hinduism and India', *Medium* (2017), https://medium.com/@samir_46682/us-religious-freedom-commissions-alternative-facts-attack-hinduism-and-india-55bd5b24ddf0.

15. 'India: Democracy in Diversity', *Hindu American Foundation* (2019), https://www.hinduamerican.org/wp-content/uploads/2020/03/HAF-India-Democracy-Diversity-Brief-Aug2019.pdf.

16. PTI, 'Biden Seeks Restoration of Peoples' Rights in Kashmir; Disappointed with CAA, NRC', *The Hindu* (2020), https://www.thehindu.com/news/international/biden-seeks-restoration-of-peoples-rights-in-kashmir-disappointed-with-caa-nrc/article31921284.ece.

17. https://www.hinduamerican.org/press/india-citizenship-amendment-bill

18. 'India's Citizenship Amendment Act: A First Step Opportunity to Better Address Human Rights in South Asia', *HAF* (2019), https://www.hinduamerican.org/press/india-citizenship-amendment-bill.

19. 'What Is the Ram Janmabhoomi Dispute in Ayodhya about?', *HAF*, https://www.hinduamerican.org/issues/ram-janmabhoomi-ayodhya-faq.

20. PTI, 'Indian-Americans Urge Donald Trump to "Fully Support" India on Jammu & Kashmir', *Mint* (2019), https://www.livemint.com/politics/news/indian-americans-urge-donald-trump-to-fully-support-india-on-jammu-kashmir-1565073200111.html.

21. Varghese K. George, 'Indian American Members of Congress Will Play a Crucial Role', *The Hindu* (2017), http://www.thehindu.com/todays-paper/tp-international/'Indian-American-members-of-Congress-will-play-a-crucial-role'/article16990353.ece.

22. Varghese K. George, 'It Is a Trilateral Partnership of India, U.S. and Israel', *The Hindu* (2017), http://www.thehindu.com/news/international/%E2%80%98It-is-a-trilateral-partnership-of-India-U.S.-and-Israel%E2%80%99/article16979190.ece.

23. Ibid.

24. Ibid.

25. 'Remarks by President Trump and Prime Minister Modi of India in Joint Press Statement', Official Website of The White House (2017), https://www.whitehouse.gov/briefings-statements/remarks-president-trump-prime-minister-modi-india-joint-press-statement/.

26. Kadambini Sharma, 'Biden Calls PM, Both Reiterate Commitment to Strategic India-US Ties', *NDTV* (2020), https://www.ndtv.com/india-news/pm-modi-joe-biden-speak-on-phone-reiterate-firm-commitment-to-strategic-partnership-between-india-and-us-2326560.

27. '2019 Report on International Religious Freedom: India', *U.S. Department of State,* https://www.state.gov/reports/2019-report-on-international-religious-freedom/india/.

28. Tobi Thomas, Adam Gabbatt and Caelainn Barr, 'Nearly 1,000 Instances of Police Brutality Recorded in US Anti-Racism Protests', *The Guardian* (2020), https://www.theguardian.com/us-news/2020/oct/29/us-police-brutality-protest.

29. '985 People have been Shot and Killed by Police in the Past Year', *The Washington Post* (2020), https://www. washingtonpost.com/graphics/investigations/police-shootings-database/.

30. 'Homeland Threat Assessment' (2020), https://www.dhs. gov/sites/default/files/publications/2020_10_06_homeland-threat-assessment.pdf.

31. 'Tragedy Strikes Indians in Kansas', *The Hindu* (2017), http://www.thehindu.com/specials/the-kansas-attack/ article17366192.ece.

32. 'Olathe, Kansas Hate Crime Shooter Pleads Guilty in Federal Court', *Hindu American Foundation* (2018), https://www. hinduamerican.org/press/olathe-kansas-hate-crime-shooter-pleads-guilty-federal-court.

33. https://www.thehindu.com/opinion/lead/amid-a-judicial-slide-a-flicker-of-hope-on-rights/article33127578.ece

34. '"Mixed Response" to India's Services Trade Proposal at WTO', *The Economic Times* (2017), https://economictimes.indiatimes. com/news/economy/foreign-trade/mixed-response-to-indias-services-trade-proposal-at-wto/articleshow/59672764. cms.

35. 'World Migration Report 2020', https://www.un.org/sites/ un2.un.org/files/wmr_2020.pdf.

36. Jeffrey S. Passel and D'Vera Cohn, 'Birth Regions and Nations', *Pew Research Center* (2016), http://www.pewhispanic.org/ 2016/09/20/1-birth-regions-and-nations/.

37. R.J. Hauman, 'S.1720–The Raise Act', Federation for American Immigration Reform (2017), http://fairus.org/ legislation/federal-legislation/s-1720-raise-act.

38. PTI, 'Over 21 Lakh Indians Applied for H-1B Visa in 11 Years', *The Hindu BusinessLine* (2018), https://www. thehindubusinessline.com/info-tech/over-21-lakh-indians-applied-for-h1b-visa-in-11-years/article9797346.ece.

39. Sangay K. Mishra, 'Deepening Fault Lines within the Indian-American Community', *The Wire* (2018), https://thewire. in/diplomacy/fault-lines-within-the-indian-american-community; Patrick French, 'All Come to Look for America',

The Indian Express (2016), http://indianexpress.com/article/lifestyle/books/the-other-one-percent-indians-in-america-book-review-migration-4419534/.

40. Maggie Haberman, 'Donald Trump Says He's a "Big Fan" of Hindus', *The New York Times* (2016), https://www.nytimes.com/2016/10/16/us/politics/trump-modi-indian-americans.html.

41. Carol Kuruvilla, '5 Disturbing Highlights from a Rally for Hindu Supporters of Trump', *HuffPost* (2016), http://www.huffingtonpost.com/entry/5-disturbing-highlights-from-a-rally-for-hindu-supporters-of-trump_us_58051126e4b0162c043d64db.

42. 'The Untold Story of Kashmiri Pandits by Anupam Kher', YouTube video, posted by 'Roots in Kashmir' (2018), https://www.youtube.com/watch?v=HR2Ci4NTAS8.

43. Varghese K. George, 'Trump Campaign Chief Is Virulent Opponent of H-1B', *The Hindu* (2016), http://www.thehindu.com/news/international/Trump-campaign-chief-is-a-virulent-opponent-of-H-1B/article14582357.ece.

44. Nicola Leske and Dhanya Skariachan, 'Wrong Gender, Color, Country'—India-Born Aiyengar, JPMorgan's Rising Star', *Reuters* (2014), https://in.reuters.com/article/jpmorgan-retail-banker-anu-aiyengar/wrong-gender-color-country-india-born-aiyengar-jpmorgans-rising-star-idINDEEA130ET20140204.

45. Shefali Chandan, *Jano*, https://janoed.com.

46. Shefali K. Chandan, 'The History of Discriminatory Immigration Laws that Kept Indians Out of the US for 40 Years', *Swarajya* (2017), https://swarajyamag.com/world/the-history-of-discriminatory-immigration-laws-that-kept-indians-out-of-the-us-for-40-years.

47. Interview with the author, Washington, DC, 9 March 2018.

48. Interview with the author, 25 August 2017.

49. Nitasha Tiku, 'India's Engineers Have Thrived in Silicon Valley. So Has Its Caste System', *The Washington Post* (2020), https://www.washingtonpost.com/technology/2020/10/27/indian-caste-bias-silicon-valley/.

50. Associated Press, 'California Sues Cisco Alleging Discrimination Based on India's Caste System', *Los Angeles Times* (2020), https://www.latimes.com/business/story/2020-07-02/california-sues-cisco-bias-indian-caste-system.

51. Nitasha Tiku, 'India's Engineers have Thrived in Silicon Valley. So has its Caste System', *The Washington Post* (2020), https://www.washingtonpost.com/technology/2020/10/27/indian-caste-bias-silicon-valley/.

52. Sonia Paul, 'When Caste Discrimination Comes to the United States', *NPR* (2018), https://www.npr.org/sections/codeswitch/2018/04/25/605030018/when-caste-discrimination-comes-to-the-united-states.

53. 'Ex-Disney Worker on Humiliation of Training Foreign Replacement', *Conservative Review, The Blaze* (2016), https://www.theblaze.com/conservative-review/disney-worker-breaks-down-when-describing-how-he-trained-his-foreign-guest-worker-replacement.

54. John Miano, 'The Impact of "High-Skilled" Immigration on U.S. Workers', *Center for Immigration Studies* (2016), https://cis.org/Impact-HighSkilled-Immigration-US-Workers.

55. Nikhila Natarajan, 'H-1B Whistleblower Théo Negri on How Lottery, Salaries are Gamed by TCS, Infosys, Cognizant', *Firstpost* (2017), https://www.firstpost.com/world/h-1b-whistleblower-theo-negri-on-how-lottery-salaries-are-gamed-by-tcs-infosys-cognizant-3404384.html.

56. Congressman Ro Khanna, https://khanna.house.gov/issues/immigration.

57. Stuart Anderson, 'Latest Data Show H-1B Visas Being Denied At High Rates', *Forbes* (2019), https://www.forbes.com/sites/stuartanderson/2019/10/28/latest-data-show-h-1b-visas-being-denied-at-high-rates/?sh=32ba7d4354c3.

58. Vignesh Radhakrishnan, Sumant Sen and Naresh Singaravelu, 'Data | U.S. firms Edge Out Indian Companies in H1-B Hirings', *The Hindu* (2020), https://www.thehindu.com/data/data-us-firms-edge-out-indian-companies-in-h1-b-hirings/article32448205.ece.

59. Nitasha Tiku, 'India's Engineers have Thrived in Silicon Valley. So has its Caste System', *The Washington Post* (2020),

https://www.washingtonpost.com/technology/2020/10/27/
indian-caste-bias-silicon-valley/.

60. 'H-1B Authorized-to-Work Population Estimate', *U.S.
     Citizenship and Immigration Services,* https://www.uscis.gov/
     sites/default/files/document/reports/USCIS%20H-1B%20
     Authorized%20to%20Work%20Report.pdf.

61. Vivek Wadhwa, 'The End of the Line for Indian Outsourcers—
     or a New Beginning?', *The Washington Post* (2017),
     https://www.washingtonpost.com/news/innovations/
     wp/2017/05/15/the-end-of-the-line-for-indian-outsourcers-
     or-a-new-beginning/?utm_term=.c3e42121378e.

62. 'Statistics', National Chicken Council, http://www.
     nationalchickencouncil.org/about-the-industry/statistics.

63. Clifford Krauss, 'Chewy Chicken Feet May Quash a Trade
     War', *The New York Times* (2009), http://www.nytimes.
     com/2009/09/16/business/global/16chickens.html.

64. David Pierson, 'When the U.S. and Russia Tussle, American
     Chickens Often Pay', *Los Angeles Times* (2014), http://www.
     latimes.com/business/la-fi-russia-chicken-20140806-story.
     html.

65. Michael Schwirtz, 'Russia Seeks to Cleanse Its Palate of U.S.
     Chicken', *The New York Times* (2010), http://www.nytimes.
     com/2010/01/20/world/europe/20russia.html.

66. 'Russian President Says Sanctions Led to Self-Sufficiency
     in Pork', Poultry, https://www.thepoultrysite.com/
     news/2017/06/russian-president-says-sanctions-led-to-
     selfsufficiency-in-pork-poultry.

67. Gayatri Nayak, 'India's Trade Surplus with US Hits a High',
     The Economic Times (2018), https://economictimes.indiatimes.
     com/news/economy/foreign-trade/indias-trade-surplus-
     with-us-hits-a-high/articleshow/63994337.cms.

68. Interview with the author, anonymous US official.

69. 'The President's 2017 Trade Policy Agenda', Resource
     Centre, *Official Website of the Office of the United States Trade
     Representative,* https://ustr.gov/sites/default/files/files/
     reports/2017/AnnualReport/Chapter%20I%20-%20The%20
     President%27s%20Trade%20Policy%20Agenda.pdf.

70. Varghese K. George, 'U.S. Under Trump Will Be a Difficult Partner for India', *The Hindu,* https://www.thehindu.com/business/Industry/us-under-trump-will-be-a-difficult-partner-for-india-to-work-with/article17448975.ece.

71. PTI, 'India's TFS Proposal Has Imparted Momentum in WTO to Discussion on Services: Nirmala', *The Indian Express* (2017), http://indianexpress.com/article/business/indias-tfs-proposal-has-imparted-momentum-in-wto-to-discussion-on-services-nirmala-4758082/lite/.

72. 'Annual Report', *Reserve Bank of India* (2017), https://m.rbi.org.in//scripts/AnnualReportPublications.aspx?Id=1221.

73. Varghese K. George, 'Suresh Prabhu's Meetings Fail to Resolve India–US Trade Disputes', *The Hindu* (2018), http://www.thehindu.com/news/international/suresh-prabhus-meetings-fail-to-resolve-india-us-trade-disputes/article24156049.ece.

74. Trevor Cloen and Irfan Nooruddin, 'The U.S.–India Trade Deal Fell Through. What Happens Now?', *The Washington Post* (2020), https://www.washingtonpost.com/politics/2020/03/05/us-india-trade-deal-fell-through-what-happens-now/.

75. 'Hydroxychloroquine: India Agrees to Release Drug after Trump Retaliation Threat', *BBC News* (2020), https://www.bbc.com/news/world-asia-india-52196730.

76. 'Joe Biden to Remain Tough on Trade while Re-embracing Partners', *Financial Times,* https://www.ft.com/content/c4e1c0e3-ba5b-46f8-87c7-9a56ca7a0a1a.

77. 'Enhancing Defense and Security Cooperation with India: Joint Report to Congress', *Official Website of the Department of Defense,* https://dod.defense.gov/Portals/1/Documents/pubs/NDAA-India-Joint-Report-FY-July-2017.pdf.

78. Ibid.

79. Ibid.

80. Varghese K. George, 'The Great American Arms Bazaar', *The Hindu* (2018), http://www.thehindu.com/opinion/lead/the-great-american-arms-bazaar/article22486458.ece.

81. 'U.S.–India Relations: Democratic Partners of Economic Opportunity', Official Website of U.S. Govt Publishing Office,

*https://www.govinfo.gov/content/pkg/CHRG-114hhrg99469/
html/CHRG-114hhrg99469.htm.*

82. Molly Samuel, 'How the Dream of America's "Nuclear Renaissance" Fizzled', Heard on 'Weekend Edition Sunday', *National Public Radio* (2017), http://www.npr.org/2017/08/06/541582729/how-the-dream-of-americas-nuclear-renaissance-failed-to-materialize.

83. Ibid, p. 68.

84. Nitasha Tiku, 'India's Engineers Have Thrived in Silicon Valley. So Has Its Caste System', *The Washington Post* (2020), https://www.washingtonpost.com/technology/2020/10/27/indian-caste-bias-silicon-valley/.

85. PTI, 'US Lawmaker Calls for Removal of Country Quota in Green Card', *The Times of India* (2017), https://timesofindia.indiatimes.com/nri/us-canada-news/us-lawmaker-calls-for-removal-of-country-quota-in-green-card/articleshow/59820498.cms.

86. Jeffrey S. Passel and D'vera Cohn, 'Overall Number of U.S. Unauthorized Immigrants Holds Steady Since 2009', *Pew Research Center* (2016), http://www.pewhispanic.org/2016/09/20/overall-number-of-u-s-unauthorized-immigrants-holds-steady-since-2009/.

87. https://edition.cnn.com/2019/07/13/politics/obama-trump-deportations-illegal-immigration/index.html

88. https://www.wsj.com/articles/why-trump-has-deported-fewer-immigrants-than-obama-11564824601

89. Vijay Prashad, *The Karma of the Brown Folk* (Minneapolis: University of Minnesota Press, 2000), p. 140.

90. https://www.hinduamerican.org/hinduism-basics

91. 'U.S.–India Relations: Democratic Partners of Economic Opportunity', Official Website of U.S. Govt Publishing Office, *https://www.govinfo.gov/content/pkg/CHRG-114hhrg99469/html/CHRG-114hhrg99469.htm.*

92. 'Text of Prime Minister Shri Narendra Modi's Address to the Indian Community at Madison Square Garden, New York', *Official Website of Narendra Modi* (2014), http://pib.nic.in/newsite/PrintRelease.aspx?relid=136737.

93. Harish Khare, 'India Not to Send Troops to Iraq', *The Hindu* (2003), http://www.thehindu.com/2003/07/13/stories/2003071305290100.htm.

94. Alyssa Ayres, Charles R. Kaye and Joseph S. Nye Jr, 'A New Indo–US Partnership Model', *The Indian Express* (2015), http://indianexpress.com/article/opinion/columns/a-new-indo-us-partnership-model/.

95. Sushant Singh, 'As US Pushes Defence Intelligence Sharing Pact, India Says "Not Ready Yet"', *The Indian Express* (2016), http://indianexpress.com/article/india/india-news-india/as-us-pushes-defence-intelligence-sharing-pact-india-says-not-ready-yet-2772014/.

96. Shubhajit Roy, Outgoing US Ambassador Lists trade, Russia, Atmanirbhar as Friction Points: 'India Must Choose', The Indian Express, https://indianexpress.com/article/india/us-ambassador-on-india-kenneth-juster-farewell-atmanirbhar-campaigns-7134325/.

97. https://www.hindustantimes.com/nri-news/indian-amercians-in-30-us-cities-hold-anti-caa-protests-on-republic-day/story-E4lLKA9bvReXqHUEoSKr6K.html; https://www.thehindu.com/news/international/seven-us-lawmakers-write-to-pompeo-on-farmers-protest-in-india/article33415283.ece

98. Varghese K. George, '#NotInMyName Echoes in US Cities Too', *The Hindu* (2017), http://www.thehindu.com/news/international/notinmyname-echoes-in-us-cities-too/article19292844.ece.

99. Varghese K. George, 'American Muslims Not Welcome for Trump's Iftar', *The Hindu* (2018), http://www.thehindu.com/news/international/trump-to-host-iftar-american-muslims-not-invited/article24097075.ece.

100. 'The End of the Wilsonian Era: Why Liberal Internationalism Failed in Walter Russell Mead', Volume 100, Number 1, *Foreign Affairs*, January–February 2021.

101. Ibid.

102. Ibid.

Chapter 4: China: The Dragon in the Frame

1. 'Trump On China: Putting America First', https://www.whitehouse.gov/wp-content/uploads/2020/11/Trump-on-China-Putting-America-First.pdf.

2. Adam Edelman, 'Biden's Comments Downplaying China Threat to U.S. Fire up Pols on Both Sides', *NBC News* (2019), https://www.nbcnews.com/politics/2020-election/biden-s-comments-downplaying-china-threat-u-s-fires-pols-n1001236.

3. 'Trump On China: Putting America First', https://www.whitehouse.gov/wp-content/uploads/2020/11/Trump-on-China-Putting-America-First.pdf.

4. Seema Sirohi, 'Beware, Dems Are Coming', *The Economic Times,* https://economictimes.indiatimes.com/blogs/letterfromwashington/beware-dems-are-coming/.

5. Brahma Chellaney, 'Biden Lacks Strategic Clarity on China', *The Japan Times* (2020), https://www.japantimes.co.jp/opinion/2020/12/10/commentary/world-commentary/joe-biden-foreign-policy-china/.

6. PTI, 'Ladakh Standoff: China Gives "Five Differing Explanations" for Deploying Large Forces at LAC, says Jaishankar', *The Hindu* (2020).

7. Ashley J. Tellis, 'Hustling in the Himalayas: The Sino-Indian Border Confrontation', Carneige, https://carnegieendowment.org/2020/06/04/hustling-in-himalayas-sino-indian-border-confrontation-pub-81979.

8. PTI, 'Ladakh Standoff: China Gives "Five Differing Explanations" for Deploying Large Forces at LAC, says Jaishankar', *The Hindu* (2020), https://www.thehindu.com/news/national/ladakh-standoff-china-gives-five-differing-explanations-for-deploying-large-forces-at-lac-says-jaishankar/article33291029.ece.

9. Walter K. Andersen, Shridhar D. Damle, *RSS: A View to the Inside* (New Delhi: Penguin Viking, 2018), p. 149.

10. 'Biden Adviser Says Unrealistic to "Fully Decouple" from China', *Reuters* (2020), https://uk.mobile.reuters.com/article/amp/idUKKCN26D1SC?__twitter_impression=true.

11.   Julian Gewirtz, 'China Thinks America Is Losing—Washington Must Show Beijing It's Wrong', *Foreign Affairs* (2020), https://www.foreignaffairs.com/articles/united-states/2020-10-13/china-thinks-america-losing.

12.   Brahma Chellaney, 'Biden Lacks Strategic Clarity on China', *The Japan Times* (2020), https://www.japantimes.co.jp/opinion/2020/12/10/commentary/world-commentary/joe-biden-foreign-policy-china/.

13.   'Trump On China: Putting America First', https://www.whitehouse.gov/wp-content/uploads/2020/11/Trump-on-China-Putting-America-First.pdf.

14.   'Joint Statement—United States and India: Prosperity through Partnership', *Media Center, Ministry of External Affairs* (2017), http://mea.gov.in/bilateral-documents.htm?dtl/28560/United_States_and_India_Prosperity_Through_Partnership.

15.   https://www.thehindu.com/news/international/high-praise-for-manmohan-singh-in-obamas-new-memoir/article33105425.ece

16.   Brian Montopoli, 'In Full: US–China Joint Statement, *CBS News* (2009). https://www.cbsnews.com/news/in-full-us-china-joint-statement/.

17.   PTI, 'Obama Says No Third Party Involvement in Indo–Pak Talks: PM', *The Hindu* (2016), http://www.thehindu.com/news/national/Obama-says-no-third-party-involvement-in-Indo-Pak-talks-PM/article16894300.ece.

18.   William L. Hosch, *The Korean War and the Vietnam War: People, Politics, and Power* (New York: Britannica Educational Press, 2010), p. 208.

19.   'Joint Statement Following Discussions With Leaders of the People's Republic of China', *Foreign Relations of the United States*, 1969–1976, vol. XVII, China, 1969–1972, *Office of the Historian* (1972), https://history.state.gov/historicaldocuments/frus1969-76v17/d203.

20.   'Joint Statement on South Asia', US Government Publishing Office (1998), https://www.govinfo.gov/content/pkg/PPP-1998-book1/pdf/PPP-1998-book1-doc-pg1077.pdf.

21. 'Government of India's Response to the US–China "Joint Statement on South Asia"', *Embassy of India Archives* (1998), https://www.indianembassyusa.gov.in/ArchivesDetails?id=204.

22. Anton Harder, 'Not at the Cost of China: India and the United Nations Security Council, 1950', *Wilson Center* (2015), https://www.wilsoncenter.org/publication/not-the-cost-china-india-and-the-united-nations-security-council-1950.

23. Ananth Krishnan, 'Post-Poll, China Looking at Business as Usual', *The Hindu* (2016), http://www.thehindu.com/todays-paper/tp-national/postpoll-china-looking-at-business-as-usual/article5877770.ece.

24. C. Raja Mohan, *Crossing the Rubicon* (Viking Press, 2003), p. 110.

25. Robert B. Zoellick, 'Whither China: From Membership to Responsibility? Remarks to National Committee on U.S.–China Relations', *U.S. Department of State Archive* (2005), https://2001-2009.state.gov/s/d/former/zoellick/rem/53682.htm.

26. Ibid.

27. Varghese K. George, '"I Expect Things to Get Worse before They Get Better," Says Historian Niall Ferguson', *The Hindu* (2018), http://www.thehindu.com/opinion/interview/i-expect-things-to-get-worse-before-they-get-better/article22870195.ece.

28. Hillary Rodham Clinton, 'Hillary Clinton Reviews Henry Kissinger's "World Order"', *The Washington Post* (2014), https://www.washingtonpost.com/opinions/hillary-clinton-reviews-henry-kissingers-world-order/2014/09/04/b280c654-31ea-11e4-8f02-03c644b2d7d0_story.html?utm_term=.74986d51ff11.

29. 'United States Strategic Approach to the People's Republic of China', https://www.whitehouse.gov/wp-content/uploads/2020/05/U.S.-Strategic-Approach-to-The-Peoples-Republic-of-China-Report-5.24v1.pdf.

30. John Pomfret, 'Trump's Bromance with China's Leader Makes Him a Typical U.S. President', *The Washington Post* (2017),

https://www.washingtonpost.com/news/global-opinions/wp/2017/05/05/trumps-bromance-with-chinas-leader-makes-him-a-typical-u-s-president/?utm_term=.067e4750132a.

31. Ibid.

32. Simon Denyer, 'Don't Let Beijing Push Us Around, Warns "Frustrated" Former Ambassador to China', *The Washington Post* (2017), https://www.washingtonpost.com/world/dont-let-beijing-push-us-around-warns-frustrated-former-ambassador-to-china/2017/02/24/f1eb41a0-fa71-11e6-9b3e-ed886f4f4825_story.html.

33. Ibid.

34. 'U.S.–China Joint Statement', *Official Website of The White House—President Barack Obama* (2011), https://obamawhitehouse.archives.gov/the-press-office/2011/01/19/us-china-joint-statement.

35. 'Joint US–China Think Tank Project on the Future of US–China Relations: An American Perspective' (2017), https://csis-website-prod.s3.amazonaws.com/s3fs-public/publication/170705_US_Report.pdf?V2dPire5xBHPlSp7nx4df9qrtYbs5F4Y.

36. Zorawar Daulet Singh, 'US and China Will Avoid a "Thucydides Trap"', *Outlook* (2017), https://www.outlookindia.com/website/story/us-and-china-will-avoid-a-thucydides-trap/300734.

37. 'Joint US–China Think Tank Project on the Future of US–China Relations' (2017), https://csis-website-prod.s3.amazonaws.com/s3fs-public/publication/170705_US_Report.pdf?V2dPire5xBHPlSp7nx4df9qrtYbs5F4Y.

38. Robert B. Zoellick, 'Whither China: From Membership to Responsibility? Remarks to National Committee on U.S.–China Relations', *U.S. Department of State Archive* (2005), https://2001-2009.state.gov/s/d/former/zoellick/rem/53682.htm.

39. '2020 Report to Congress of the U.S.-China Economic and Security Review Commission', https://www.uscc.gov/sites/default/files/2020-12/2020_Executive_Summary.pdf.

40.   Jacob Poushter and Dorothy Manevich, 'Globally, People
      Point to ISIS and Climate Change as Leading Security
      Threats', *Pew Research Center* (2017), http://www.pewglobal.
      org/2017/08/01/globally-people-point-to-isis-and-climate-
      change-as-leading-security-threats/.

41.   Demetri Sevastopulo and Aime Williams, 'Why Trump No
      Longer Talks About the Trade Deficit with China', *Financial
      Times*,   https://www.ft.com/content/081e6d25-8d67-4caa-
      918a-2765a66f0052.

42.   https://www.indiatoday.in/india/story/swadeshi-
      jagran-manch-campaign-protection-small-
      enterprises-1162903-2018-02-07

43.   https://www.livemint.com/Politics/aykyxKNL04V
      uI4qDMKWRXI/China-warns-of-impact-on-Indiabound-
      investments-from-boycot.html

44.   K.J.M. Varma, 'Chinese Investments in India Increased to $870
      mn in 2015', *Rediff* (2016), http://www.rediff.com/business/
      report/chinese-investments-in-india-increased-to-870-mn-
      in-2015/20160524.htm.

45.   Ashley Coutinho, 'PE/VC investments into India from China,
      Hong Kong Fall 72% in CY20', *Business Standard* (2020),
      https://www.business-standard.com/article/companies/pe-
      vc-investments-into-india-from-china-hong-kong-fall-72-in-
      cy20-120123000038_1.html.

46.   'The People's Republic of China—U.S.-China Trade Facts',
      Office of the United States Trade Representative, https://ustr.gov/
      countries-regions/china-mongolia-taiwan/peoples-republic-
      china#:~:text=Trade%20Balance,(%2473.7%20billion)%20
      from%202018.

47.   Akshay Kumar, 'Xiaomi Says It Sold Over 1 Million
      Smartphones in 2 Days During the Festive Sales', *91Mobiles*
      (2017), https://hub.91mobiles.com/xiaomi-diwali-with-mi-
      sale-one-million-smartphones-sold/.

48.   S. Jaishankar, *The India Way*, p. 145.

49.   David Autor, David Dorn and Gordon Hanson, 'When Work
      Disappears: Manufacturing Decline and the Falling Marriage-

Market Value of Young Men', https://iwer.mit.edu/wp-content/uploads/2017/02/Autor-Paper-1.pdf.

50. Ibid.

51. 'Annual Report to Congress: Military and Security Developments Involving the People's Republic of China 2017', *Office of the Secretary of Defense*, https://www.defense. gov/Portals/1/Documents/pubs/2017_China_Military_ Power_Report.PDF?ver=2017-06-06-141328-770.

52. Ibid.

53. Nicole Winfield, 'Pompeo, Vatican clash over China after tensions spill out', AP News, 2 October 2020, https://apnews. com/article/beijing-elections-campaigns-rome-china-8e662c 8fc000dbc54b1534144b982900.

54. AFP, 'China Asks Mosques to Raise National Flag', *The Hindu* (2018), http://www.thehindu.com/news/international/china-asks-mosques-to-raise-national-flag/article23952708.ece.

55. Keith Bradsher and Paul Mozur, 'China's Plan to Build Its Own High-Tech Industries Worries Western Businesses', *The New York Times* (2017), https://www.nytimes.com/2017/03/07/ business/china-trade-manufacturing-europe.html.

56. Robert D. Atkinson, Nigel Cory, Stephen Ezell, 'Stopping China's Mercantilism: A Doctrine of Constructive, Alliance-Backed Confrontation', *Information Technology & Innovation Foundation* (2017), https://itif.org/publications/2017/03/16/ stopping-chinas-mercantilism-doctrine-constructive-alliance-backed.

57. 'Indian Prime Minister Narendra Modi on India's Economy and U.S.–India Relations', *Council on Foreign Relations* (2014), https://www.cfr.org/event/indian-prime-minister-narendra-modi-indias-economy-and-us-india-relations-0.

58. 'U.S.–India Relations: Democratic Partners of Economic Opportunity', Document Repository, *Official Website of U.S. House of Representatives*.

59. https://www.politico.com/newsletters/morning-trade/2019/08/01/biden-says-he-would-renegotiate-tpp-464000.

60. 'United States–Mexico–Canada Trade Fact Sheet—Rebalancing Trade to Support Manufacturing', *Office of the United States Trade Representative*, https://ustr.gov/trade-agreements/free-trade-agreements/united-states-mexico-canada-agreement/fact-sheets/rebalancing.

61. S. Jaishankar, *The India Way*, p. 128.

62. 'Text of the Prime Minister's Address to the Joint Session of U.S. Congress', *The Hindu* (2016), http://www.thehindu.com/news/resources/Text-of-the-Prime-Ministers-address-to-the-Joint-Session-of-U.S.-Congress/article14391856.ece.

63. PTI, 'China Should Contribute More to Fight Terror: US', *The Economic Times* (2017), https://economictimes.indiatimes.com/news/defence/china-should-contribute-more-to-fight-terror-us/articleshow/59250731.cms.

64. Suhasini Haidar, 'India, China Seek Common Ground on Afghanistan', *The Hindu* (2017), http://www.thehindu.com/news/national/india-china-seek-common-ground-on-afghanistan/article17379581.ece.

65. Jabin T. Jacob, ,On terrorism India Is Inconsistent with China', Moneycontrol (2019), https://www.moneycontrol.com/news/opinion/opinion-on-terrorism-india-is-inconsistent-with-china-3651111.html.

66. Shishir Gupta, Yashwant Raj and Sutirtho Patranobis, '"Brief the Boss": The Backstory of Masood Azhar's Global Terror Tag', *The Hindustan Times* (2020), https://www.hindustantimes.com/world-news/jaish-e-mohammad-chief-masood-azhar-listed-as-global-terrorist-by-un-after-china-lifts-technical-hold/story-HwLxOxNN6fiuE205kDMi4M.html.

67. Thomas Maresca, 'South Korean President Moon Jae-in Suspends Further THAAD Deployment', *USA Today* (2017), https://www.usatoday.com/story/news/world/2017/06/07/south-korean-president-moon-jae-suspends-thaad-deployment/102582572/.

68. Samantha F. Ravich, 'State-Sponsored Cyberspace Threats: Recent Incidents and U.S. Policy Response', *Official Website of the United States Senate* (2017), https://www.foreign.senate.gov/imo/media/doc/061317_Ravich_Testimony.pdf.

69. Josh Rogin, 'The Biggest Winner of the Trump–Kim Summit Is China', *The Washington Post* (2018), https://www.washingtonpost.com/news/josh-rogin/wp/2018/06/12/the-biggest-winner-of-the-trump-kim-summit-is-china/?utm_term=.43790e623500.

70. Hyung-Jin Kim and Kim Tong-Hyung, 'Trump–Kim Summit Raises New Questions over South Korean Role', *PBS* (2018), https://www.pbs.org/newshour/world/trump-kim-summit-raises-new-questions-over-south-korean-role.

71. Emily Rauhala, 'Ending Military Exercises? Trump's Plan for North Korea was China's Plan First', *The Washington Post* (2018), https://www.washingtonpost.com/news/worldviews/wp/2018/06/12/ending-military-exercises-trumps-plan-for-north-korea-was-chinas-plan-first/?utm_term=.388cf562396e.

72. Ibid.

73. 'Statement by President Trump on the Paris Climate Accord', *Official Website of The White House* (2017), https://www.whitehouse.gov/briefings-statements/statement-president-trump-paris-climate-accord/.

74. Stanly Johny, 'Why China Is Being Aggressive along the LAC', *The Hindu* (2020), https://www.thehindu.com/opinion/lead/why-china-is-being-aggressive-along-the-lac/article31917394.ece.

75. Varghese K. George, 'Trump's Biggest Challenge is to Avoid War with China, Says Graham Allison', *The Hindu* (2017), http://www.thehindu.com/news/international/interview-with-graham-allison-trumps-biggest-challenge-is-to-avoid-war-with-china/article17893640.ece.

76. Jabin T. Jacob, 'China's "New Tianxia" and the Indian Response', *Thinking about China in India* (2015), https://indiandchina.com/2015/05/04/chinas-new-tianxia-and-the-indian-response/.

77. Ananth Krishnan, *India's China Challenge: A Journey through China's Rise and What It Means for India* (New Delhi: HarperCollins India, 2020).

78. 'Trump on China: Putting America First', https://www.whitehouse.gov/wp-content/uploads/2020/11/Trump-on-China-Putting-America-First.pdf.

79. Ibid.

80. Aaron Klein, 'Is China's New Payment System The Future?', *Brookings* (2019), https://www.brookings.edu/research/is-chinas-new-payment-system-the-future/.

81. Gulveen Aulakh, 'US Supports Firms Weighing India as Alternative to China', *The Economic Times* (2020), https://economictimes.indiatimes.com/news/international/business/us-supports-firms-weighing-india-as-alternative-to-china/articleshow/75437352.cms?utm_source=contentofinterest&utm_medium=text&utm_campaign=cppst.

82. Kenneth Rapoza, 'Why American Companies Choose China Over Everyone Else', *Forbes* (2019), https://www.forbes.com/sites/kenrapoza/2019/09/03/why-american-companies-choose-china-over-everyone-else/?sh=5c93154371de.

83. Ana Swanson, 'Nike and Coca-Cola Lobby Against Xinjiang Forced Labor Bill', *The New York Times* (2020), https://www.nytimes.com/2020/11/29/business/economy/nike-coca-cola-xinjiang-forced-labor-bill.html.

84. 'Member Survey US-China Business Council: 2020', https://www.uschina.org/sites/default/files/uscbc_member_survey_2020.pdf.

85. '2020 Report to Congress of the U.S.-China Economic and Security Review Commission', https://www.uscc.gov/sites/default/files/2020-12/2020_Executive_Summary.pdf.

86. https://trumpwhitehouse.archives.gov/wp-content/uploads/2020/11/Trump-on-China-Putting-America-First.pdf

87. David Bandurski, 'The Fable of the Master Storyteller', *China Media Project* (2017), https://chinamediaproject.org/2017/09/29/the-fable-of-the-master-storyteller/.

88. Gabriel Crossley, 'ESPN Criticised over China–NBA Coverage for using 'Nine-Dash Line' Map', *Reuters* (2019), https://www.reuters.com/article/china-basketball-nba-espn/espn-criticised-over-china-nba-coverage-for-using-nine-dash-line-map-idUSL3N26U2HE.

89. 'Trump on China: Putting America First', https://www.whitehouse.gov/wp-content/uploads/2020/11/Trump-on-China-Putting-America-First.pdf.

90. Isaac Stone Fish, 'How China gets American Companies to Parrot its Propaganda', *The Washington Post* (2019), https://www.washingtonpost.com/outlook/how-china-gets-american-companies-to-parrot-its-propaganda/2019/10/11/512f7b8c-eb73-11e9-85c0-85a098e47b37_story.html.

91. Louisa Lim and Julia Bergin, 'Inside China's Audacious Global Propaganda Campaign', *The Guardian* (2018), https://www.theguardian.com/news/2018/dec/07/china-plan-for-global-media-dominance-propaganda-xi-jinping.

92. Humeyra Pamuk, 'U.S. Revokes More Than 1,000 Visas of Chinese Nationals, Citing Military Links', *Reuters* (2020), https://www.reuters.com/article/us-usa-china-visas-students/u-s-revokes-more-than-1000-visas-of-chinese-nationals-citing-military-links-idUSKBN26039D.

93. Ho-fung Hung, 'After RCEP's Launch, the US Urgently Needs to Rejoin the TPP', *The Diplomat* (2020), https://thediplomat.com/2020/11/after-rceps-launch-the-us-urgently-needs-to-rejoin-the-tpp/.

94. Quoted in Wanderson, p. 158.

95. David Hutt, 'EU-China Investment Pact Still a Long Way Off', *Asia Times* (2020), https://asiatimes.com/2020/12/eu-china-investment-pact-still-a-long-way-off/.

96. 'The Bidens and China Business', *WSJ* (2020), https://www.wsj.com/articles/the-bidens-and-china-business-11603236651?mod=hp_opin_pos_1.

97. Jacob M. Schlesinger, 'What's Biden's New China Policy? It Looks a Lot Like Trump's', *The Wall Street Journal* (2020), https://www.wsj.com/articles/whats-bidens-china-policy-it-looks-a-lot-like-trumps-11599759286?mod=article_inline.

98. Tanvi Madan, *Fateful Triangle: How China Shaped U.S.-India Relations During the Cold War* (Brookings Institution, 2019), p. 7.

99. Ananth Krishnan, 'Leaving RCEP was a Short-Sighted Decision, says Former Foreign Secretary Shyam Saran', *The Hindu* (2020), https://www.thehindu.com/news/national/leaving-rcep-was-a-short-sighted-decision-says-former-foreign-secretary-shyam-saran/article33118832.ece.

Chapter 5: Pakistan—Frenemy in a Forever War

1. 'Remarks by President Trump and Prime Minister Khan of the Islamic Republic of Pakistan Before Bilateral Meeting', *Official Website of The White House* (2019), https://trumpwhitehouse. archives.gov/briefings-statements/remarks-president-trump- prime-minister-khan-islamic-republic-pakistan-bilateral- meeting/

2. Ibid.

3. Varghese K. George, 'In New Year Tweet, Trump Threatens to Stop Aid to Pakistan', *The Hindu* (2018), https:// www.thehindu.com/news/international/pakistan-has- given-us-nothing-but-lies-and-deceit-says-donald-trump/ article22346765.ece.

4. Suhasini Haidar, 'India Is a Bipartisan Success Story: Secretary of State-designate Blinken, Signals Continuity in Ties', The Hindu (2021), https://www.thehindu.com/news/ international/india-is-a-bipartisan-success-story-secretary- of-state-designate-blinken-signals-continuity-in-ties/ article33619333.ece.

5. Associated Press, 'Trump Hedges as Military Presents New Afghanistan Strategy', *Fox News* (2017), http://www.foxnews. com/us/2017/08/03/trump-hedges-as-military-presents- new-afghanistan-strategy.html.

6. Andrew Egger, 'Bannon: "Geniuses of Both Political Parties" Created Trump's Foreign Policy Headaches', *Washington Examiner, from the archives of the Weekly Standard* (2017), https:// www.weeklystandard.com/andrew-egger/bannon-geniuses-of- both-political-parties-created-trumps-foreign-policy-headaches.

7. 'Remarks by President Trump on the Strategy in Afghanistan and South Asia', *Official Website of the White House* (2017), https://www.whitehouse.gov/the-press-office/2017/08/21/ remarks-president-trump-strategy-afghanistan-and-south-asia.

8. https://www.washingtonpost.com/politics/2021/01/19/fact- checking-trumps-farewell-address/

9. Alex Ward, 'The 3 Elements of Trump's Foreign Policy Biden Should Keep', *Vox* (2020), https://www.vox.com/21564009/ trump-biden-foreign-policy-china-war-hostages.

10. Bonnie Kristian, 'Op-Ed: Trump was Right to bring Troops Home from Afghanistan. Biden should Finish the Job', *Los Angeles Times* (2020), https://www.latimes.com/opinion/story/2020-12-29/afghanistan-u-s-troops-withdrawal-donald-trump-joe-biden-taliban.

11. 'CNN Insight: The Heavy Baggage Aboard Flight 814', *CNN* (2000), http://edition.cnn.com/TRANSCRIPTS/0001/05/i_ins.00.html.

12. Ibid.

13. Bruce Riedel, *What We Won: America's Secret War in Afghanistan, 1979–89* (Washington D.C.: Brookings Institution Press, 2014), p. 10.

14. Ibid., p. 11.

15. Katherine Zimmerman, 'Testimony: Al Qaeda's Strengthening in the Shadows', *Critical Threats* (2017), https://www.criticalthreats.org/analysis/testimony-al-qaedas-strengthening-in-the-shadows.

16. Ibid., p. 151.

17. Husain Haqqani, *Magnificent Delusions: Pakistan, the United States and an Epic History of Misunderstanding* (New York: Public Affairs, 2013), p. 267.

18. Husain Haqqani, *India vs Pakistan: Why Can't We Just Be Friends?* (New Delhi: Juggernaut, 2016), p. 121.

19. Bruce Riedel, *Deadly Embrace: Pakistan, America, and the Future of the Global Jihad* (Washington D.C.: Brookings Institution Press, 2012), p. 2.

20. 'Opening Statement of the Honorable Ed Royce (R-CA), Chairman, House Foreign Affairs Committee Hearing: The Future of U.S.–Pakistan Relations', *Document Repository, Official Website of U.S. House of Representatives* (2015), https://docs.house.gov/meetings/FA/FA00/20151216/104290/HHRG-114-FA00-20151216-SD002.pdf.

21. 'U.S. Relationship with Pakistan', *Official Website of the U.S. Department of State* (2015), https://2009-2017.state.gov/p/sca/rls/rmks/2015/252318.htm.

22. Varghese K. George, 'Trump Administration Proposes Cut in Aid to Pakistan', *The Hindu* (2017), http://www.thehindu.

com/news/international/trump–administration–proposes–cut–in–aid–to–pakistan/article18567197.ece.

23. Husain Haqqani, *Magnificent Delusions: Pakistan, the United States and an Epic History of Misunderstanding* (New York: Public Affairs, 2013), p. 262.

24. Larry Pressler, *Neighbours in Arms: An American Senator's Quest for Disarmament in a Nuclear Subcontinent* (Gurugram: Penguin Random House India, 2017).

25. 'Public Law 107–40, 107th Congress, Joint Resolution', *Authenticated U.S. Government Information* (2001), https://www.congress.gov/107/plaws/publ40/PLAW-107publ40.pdf.

26. 'The Future of U.S.–Pakistan Relations', *Document Repository, Official Website of U.S. House of Representatives* (2015), https://docs.house.gov/meetings/FA/FA00/20151216/104290/HHRG-114-FA00-Transcript-20151216.pdf.

27. Anwar Iqbal, 'Biden Administration to Revive Military-to-military Ties with Pakistan', Dawn (2021), https://www.dawn.com/news/1602541.

28. Strobe Talbott, *Engaging India: Diplomacy, Democracy and the Bomb* (Washington D.C.: Brookings Institution Press, 2004), p. 192.

29. Husain Haqqani, *India vs Pakistan: Why Can't We Just Be Friends?* (New Delhi: Juggernaut, 2016), p. 37.

30. Hans M. Kristensen and Robert S. Norris, 'Pakistani Nuclear Forces, 2016', *Bulletin of the Atomic Scientists* (2016), Vol. 72, No. 6, 368–376, http://www.tandfonline.com/doi/pdf/10.1080/00963402.2016.1241520?needAccess=true.

31. Sameer Lalwani and Emily Tallo, 'Did India Shoot Down a Pakistani F-16 in February? This Just Became a Big Deal', *The Washington Post* (2019), https://www.washingtonpost.com/politics/2019/04/17/did-india-shoot-down-pakistani-f-back-february-this-just-became-big-deal/.

32. Varghese K. George, '"The U.S has Leverage with Pakistan, But Not Without Risks"', *The Hindu* (2017), http://www.thehindu.com/opinion/interview/joshua-t-white-interview/article19661508.ece.

33. http://www.nationmaster.com/au.

34. Mridula Chari, 'India Might Grow Faster than China in 2016. But Guess How Soon It Will Match Beijing's GDP', *Scroll.in* (2015), https://scroll.in/article/701709/india-might-grow-faster-than-china-in-2016-but-guess-how-soon-it-will-match-beijings-gdp.

35. 'India's Help Carries Risks', *Stratfor* (2001), https://worldview.stratfor.com/analysis/indias-help-carries-risks.

36. 'Musharraf Rallies Pakistan', *BBC News* (2001), http://news.bbc.co.uk/2/hi/world/monitoring/media_reports/1553542.stm.

37. Devirupa Mitra, 'How India Nearly Gave in to US Pressure to Enter the Iraqi Killing Zone', *The Wire* (2016), https://thewire.in/50028/india-nearly-gave-us-pressure-join-iraq-war.

38. Haqqani, *Magnificent Delusions*, p. 58.

39. Christopher Hitchens, *The Trial of Henry Kissinger* (Twelve, 2012), p. 45.

40. Husain Haqqani, *Magnificent Delusions: Pakistan, the United States and an Epic History of Misunderstanding* (New York: Public Affairs, 2013), p. 162.

41. C. Christine Fair, 'Beguiling Americans: A Guide for Indian Diplomats', *Gateway House*, http://www.gatewayhouse.in/wp-content/uploads/2015/06/How-to-Beguile-the-Americans_C.Christine-Fair_2015.pdf.

42. 'Global Indicators Database', *Pew Research Centre* (2017), https://www.pewresearch.org/global/database/indicator/1/country/PK.

43. Richard Wike, 'Few Americans Trust Pakistan', *Pew Research Centre* (2013), http://www.pewresearch.org/fact-tank/2013/10/23/few-americans-trust-pakistan.

44. Bruce Stokes, 'Which Countries Americans Like . . . And Don't', *Pew Research Centre* (2013), http://www.pewresearch.org/fact-tank/2013/12/30/which-countries-americans-like-and-dont/.

45. https://www.pewresearch.org/global/2017/11/15/india-and-the-world/.

46. Husain Haqqani, *Magnificent Delusions: Pakistan, the United States and an Epic History of Misunderstanding* (New York: Public Affairs, 2013), p. 333.

47. 'Remarks by President Trump and Prime Minister Khan of the Islamic Republic of Pakistan Before Bilateral Meeting', *Official Website of the White House* (2019), https://www.whitehouse. gov/briefings-statements/remarks-president-trump-prime-minister-khan-islamic-republic-pakistan-bilateral-meeting/.

48. David Brunnstrom, 'Pakistan says Cannot Kill Taliban While Inviting Them to Peace Talks', *Reuters* (2015), http://www. reuters.com/article/us-usa-pakistan-taliban/pakistan-says-cannot-kill-taliban-while-inviting-them-to-peace-talks-idUSKCN0SH2MA20151023.

49. Varghese K. George, 'Ties with India and Pakistan not Zero Sum: White House', *The Hindu* (2017), http://www.thehindu. com/news/international/ties-with-india-and-pakistan-not-zero-sum-white-house/article19142136.ece.

50. Briefing by a White House official ahead of the Modi–Trump meeting.

51. Helene Cooper and Eric Schmitt, 'White House Debate Led to Plan to Widen Afghan Effort', *The New York Times* (2009), http://www.nytimes.com/2009/03/28/us/politics/28prexy. html?mcubz=1.

52. 'Remarks by the President on a New Strategy for Afghanistan and Pakistan', *Official Website of the White House—President Barack Obama* (2009), https://obamawhitehouse.archives. gov/the-press-office/remarks-president-a-new-strategy-afghanistan-and-pakistan.

53. Varghese K. George, 'India Rejects U.S. Role in Mending Ties with Pakistan', *The Hindu* (2017), http://www.thehindu. com/news/international/cant-wait-until-something-happens-says-us-on-india-pakistan-tensions/article17813489.ece.

54. 'Remarks by President Trump on the Strategy in Afghanistan and South Asia', *Official Website of the White House* (2017), https://www.whitehouse.gov/briefings-statements/remarks-president-trump-strategy-afghanistan-south-asia/.

55. John Bolton, 'The Danger of a Jihadist Pakistan', *The Wall Street Journal* (2017), https://www.wsj.com/articles/the-danger-of-a-jihadist-pakistan-1503960880.

56. 'Remarks by the President on a New Strategy for Afghanistan and Pakistan', *Official Website of the White House—President Barack Obama* (2009), https://obamawhitehouse.archives. gov/the-press-office/remarks-president-a-new-strategy-afghanistan-and-pakistan.

57. 'Direct Overt U.S. Aid Appropriations for and Military Reimbursements to Pakistan, FY2002–FY2020' (2017), https://fas.org/sgp/crs/row/pakaid.pdf.

58. PTI, 'Trump to Leave NATO if Members Don't Perform Well', *The Hindu BusinessLine* (2017), https://www. thehindubusinessline.com/news/world/trump-to-leave-nato-if-members-dont-perform-well/article9706765.ece.

59. Varghese K. George, '"The U.S Has Leverage with Pakistan, but Not without Risks"', *The Hindu* (2017), http://www. thehindu.com/opinion/interview/joshua-t-white-interview/article19661508.ece.

60. Richard G. Olson, 'How Not to Engage with Pakistan', *The New York Times* (2018), https://www.nytimes. com/2018/01/09/opinion/pakistan-trump-aid-engage. html?login=email&auth=login-email; 'Afghanistan: The Reconciliation Option—Remarks by Ambassador Richard G. Olson', Stimson (2017), https://www.stimson.org/sites/ default/files/Remarks%20by%20Amb.%20Richard%20 Olson_0.pdf.

61. Pamela Constable, 'Trump Sends Letter to Pakistan Asking for Help with Afghan Peace Process', *The Washington Post* (2018), https://www.washingtonpost.com/world/asia_pacific/ trump-sends-later-to-pakistan-asking-for-help-with-afghan-peace-process/2018/12/03/9fd99e88-f6f1-11e8-8d64-4e79db33382f_story.html.

62. Madiha Afzal, 'Evaluating the Trump Administration's Pakistan Reset', *Brookings* (2020), https://www.brookings. edu/blog/order-from-chaos/2020/10/26/evaluating-the-trump-administrations-pakistan-reset/.

63. Varghese K. George, '"The U.S Has Leverage with Pakistan, but Not without Risks"', *The Hindu* (2017), http://

www.thehindu.com/opinion/interview/joshua-t-white-interview/article19661508.ece.

64. Hans M. Kristensen and Robert S. Norris, 'Pakistani Nuclear Forces, 2016', *Bulletin of the Atomic Scientists* (2016), Vol. 72, No. 6, 368–76, http://www.tandfonline.com/doi/pdf/10.1080/00963402.2016.1241520?needAccess=true.

65. Ibid.

66. Laura Rozen, 'White House White Paper on U.S. Policy to Afghanistan and Pakistan', *Foreign Policy* (2009), http://foreignpolicy.com/2009/03/27/white-house-white-paper-on-u-s-policy-to-afghanistan-and-pakistan.

67. Chidanand Rajghatta, 'Pakistan Stoking Terror, Hurting India Ties, Says Trump Administration', *The Times of India* (2017), https://timesofindia.indiatimes.com/world/us/trump-administration-has-no-doubts-about-pakistans-terror-credentials-imposes-more-sanctions/articleshow/58648227.cms.

68. Varghese K. George, 'India-Pakistan Ties may Slide Further: U.S. Intelligence,' *The Hindu* (2017), https://www.thehindu.com/news/international/india-pak-ties-may-slide-further-us-intelligence/article18440222.ece.

69. Varghese K. George, '"The U.S Has Leverage with Pakistan, but Not without Risks"', *The Hindu* (2017), http://www.thehindu.com/opinion/interview/joshua-t-white-interview/article19661508.ece.

70. Varghese K. George, 'The Final Frontier of Hindutva?', *The Hindu* (2014), http://www.thehindu.com/todays-paper/tp-opinion/the-final-frontier-of-hindutva/article6709933.ece.

71. Ibid.

72. Bashaarat Masood, 'Syed Salahuddin Designated Global Terrorist: How Much does he Matter in the Valley?', *The Indian Express* (2017), http://indianexpress.com/article/beyond-the-news/hizbul-mujahideen-syed-salahuddin-how-global-terrorist-much-does-he-matter-in-kashmir-valley-4724454.

73. Mukund Padmanabhan, 'How India Kept Kashmir out of U.S. Af–Pak Envoy's Brief', *The Hindu* (2016), http://

www.thehindu.com/news/the-india-cables/how-india-kept-kashmir-out-of-us-afpak-envoys-brief/article2035576.ece.

74. Ibid.

75. '"The Anti-Muslim, Hindutva Approach of the BJP in Kashmir Is Damaging"', *The Telegraph* (2017), https://www.telegraphindia.com/7-days/the-anti-muslim-hindutva-approach-of-the-bjp-in-kashmir-is-damaging/cid/1315530.

76. 'Remarks by President Trump to the People of Poland', *Official Website of the White House* (2017), https://www.whitehouse.gov/the-press-office/2017/07/06/remarks-president-trump-people-poland-july-6-2017.

77. 'President Trump's Speech to the Arab Islamic American Summit', *Official Website of the White House* (2017), https://www.whitehouse.gov/the-press-office/2017/05/21/president-trumps-speech-arab-islamic-american-summit.

78. Laura Rozen, 'White House White Paper on U.S. Policy to Afghanistan and Pakistan', *Foreign Policy* (2009), http://foreignpolicy.com/2009/03/27/white-house-white-paper-on-u-s-policy-to-afghanistan-and-pakistan.

79. Sultan Faizy and Shashank Bengali, 'U.S. Military Apologizes for "Highly Offensive" Leaflets it Distributed in Afghanistan', *Los Angeles Times* (2017), http://www.latimes.com/world/asia/la-fg-afghanistan-usmilitary-apology-20170906-story.html.

80. 'What's New in the Strategy for Afghanistan and Pakistan', *Official Website of the White House—Barack Obama* (2009), https://obamawhitehouse.archives.gov/the-press-office/whatrsquos-new-strategy-afghanistan-and-pakistan.

81. Anwar Iqbal, 'Biden Administration to Revive Military-to-military Ties with Pakistan', Dawn, 2021, https://www.dawn.com/news/1602541.

82. 'New US Strategy for Afghanistan Is "Dead-End"—Lavrov', *RT* (2017), https://www.rt.com/news/400756-us-afghanistan-dead-end-lavrov.

83. PTI, 'Russia Seeking to Undermine US Reputation in Afghanistan: US Official', *NDTV* (2017), http://www.ndtv.com/

world-news/russia-seeking-to-undermine-us-reputation-in-afghanistan-us-official-1742309.

84. Erin Cunningham, 'While the U.S. Wasn't Looking, Russian and Iran Began Carving out a Bigger Role in Afghanistan', *The Washington Post* (2017), https://www.washingtonpost.com/world/asia_pacific/with-us-policy-in-flux-russia-and-iran-challenge-american-power-in-afghanistan/2017/04/12/f8c768bc-1eb8-11e7-bb59-a74ccaf1d02f_story.html?utm_term=.849819010caa.

85. 'Enhancing Security and Stability in Afghanistan', *Official Website of the Department of Defense* (2017), https://www.defense.gov/Portals/1/Documents/pubs/June_2017_1225_Report_to_Congress.pdf.

86. Charlie Savage, Eric Schmitt and Michael Schwirtz, 'Russia Secretly Offered Afghan Militants Bounties to kill U.S. Troops, Intelligence says', *The New York Times* (2020), https://www.nytimes.com/2020/06/26/us/politics/russia-afghanistan-bounties.html.

87. Enhancing Security and Stability in Afghanistan', *Official Website of the Department of Defense* (2017), https://www.defense.gov/Portals/1/Documents/pubs/June_2017_1225_Report_to_Congress.pdf.

88. PTI, 'China Might Be Interested in Seeing Stability in Afghanistan, South Asia: Official', *The Indian Express* (2017), http://indianexpress.com/article/world/china-might-be-interested-in-seeing-stability-in-afghanistan-south-asia-official-4814536/.

89. Carlotta Gall, 'In Afghanistan, U.S. Exits, and Iran Comes In', *The New York Times* (2017), https://www.nytimes.com/2017/08/05/world/asia/iran-afghanistan-taliban.html.

90. Condoleezza Rice, *No Higher Honour: A Memoir of My Years in Washington* (New York: Broadway Paperbacks, 2012), p. 62.

91. Fareed Zakaria, 'The United States is Stumbling into Another Decade of War', *The Washington Post* (2017), https://www.washingtonpost.com/opinions/global-opinions/the-united-states-is-stumbling-into-another-decade-of-

war/2017/06/22/7cd589f2-5796-11e7-a204-ad706461fa4f_
story.html.

92. Greg Jaffe and Missy Ryan, 'A Dubai Shopping Trip
     and a Missed Chance to Capture the Head of the
     Taliban', *The Washington Post* (2018), https://www.
     washingtonpost.com/world/national-security/a-dubai-
     shopping-trip-and-a-missed-chance-to-capture-the-head-
     of-the-taliban/2018/03/24/0137dd66-2ba0-11e8-8ad6-
     fbc50284fce8_story.html?utm_term=.45d4a843fcf3.

93. 'Retired Army Gen. David Petraeus Describes Trump's
     Options in Afghanistan', Heard on 'All Things Considered',
     WAMU 88.5, National Public Radio (2017), http://wamu.org/
     story/17/08/21/retired-army-gen-david-petraeus-describes-
     trumps-options-in-afghanistan/.

94. PTI, 'Biden seeks Restoration of Peoples' Rights in Kashmir;
     Disappointed with CAA, NRC', *The Hindu* (2020), https://
     www.thehindu.com/news/international/biden-seeks-
     restoration-of-peoples-rights-in-kashmir-disappointed-with-
     caa-nrc/article31921284.ece.

95. C. Raja Mohan, 'Fresh Military Crisis in Kashmir Can Help
     Pakistan Test Biden's South Asia Policies', *The Indian Express*
     (2020), https://indianexpress.com/article/opinion/columns/
     joe-biden-us-president-kashmir-dispute-india-7053843/.

96. Madiha Afzal, 'Evaluating the Trump Administration's
     Pakistan Reset', *Brookings* (2020), https://www.brookings.
     edu/blog/order-from-chaos/2020/10/26/evaluating-the-
     trump-administrations-pakistan-reset/.

97. Katherine Zimmerman, 'Al Qaeda's Strengthening in the
     Shadows', *American Enterprise Institute* (2017), https://docs.
     house.gov/meetings/HM/HM05/20170713/106235/
     HHRG-115-HM05-Wstate-ZimmermanK-20170713.pdf.

98. Tim McGirk and Syed Talat Hussain, 'Interview with
     Pakistan's Abdul Qadeer Khan', *Time* (1998), http://content.
     time.com/time/world/article/0,8599,2054533,00.html.

99. Aparna Pande, *Explaining Pakistan's Foreign Policy: Escaping
     India* (London: Routledge, 2011), p. 44.